1

ILLINOIS CENTRAL COLLEGE

W9-BVY-742

Withdrawn

Withdrawn

4/08

I.C.C. LIBRARY

THE LAW OF VIOLENCE AGAINST WOMEN

Revised and Updated by

by
Margaret C. Jasper

2nd Edition

Oceana's Legal Almanac Series:
Law for the Layperson

I.C.C. LIBRARY

Oceana®
NEW YORK

KF
9322
.J37
2007

OXFORD
UNIVERSITY PRESS

*Oxford University Press, Inc., publishes works that further Oxford University's
objective of excellence in research, scholarship, and education.*

Copyright © 2007 by Oxford University Press, Inc.
Published by Oxford University Press, Inc.
198 Madison Avenue, New York, New York 10016

Oxford is a registered trademark of Oxford University Press
Oceana is a registered trademark of Oxford University Press, Inc.

All rights reserved. No part of this publication may be reproduced, stored in a
retrieval system, or transmitted, in any form or by any means, electronic,
mechanical, photocopying, recording, or otherwise, without the prior permission
of Oxford University Press, Inc.

Library of Congress Cataloging-in-Publication Data

Jasper, Margaret C.
  The law of violence against women / by Margaret C. Jasper. -- 2nd ed.
    p. cm. -- (Oceana's legal almanac series : law for the layperson)
  Includes bibliographical references.
  ISBN 978-0-19-533904-8 ((clothbound) : alk. paper) 1. Women--Crimes
against--United States. 2. Offenses against the person--United States 3. Abused
women--Legal status, laws, etc.--United States. 4. Family violence--Law and
legislation--United States. 5. Violent crimes--United States. I. Title.
  KF9304.J37 2007
  345.73'025--dc22

                                                              2007024343

Note to Readers:

This publication is designed to provide accurate and authoritative information in
regard to the subject matter covered. It is based upon sources believed to be accurate
and reliable and is intended to be current as of the time it was written. It is sold with
the understanding that the publisher is not engaged in rendering legal, accounting,
or other professional services. If legal advice or other expert assistance is required,
the services of a competent professional person should be sought. Also, to confirm
that the information has not been affected or changed by recent developments,
traditional legal research techniques should be used, including checking primary
sources where appropriate.

*(Based on the Declaration of Principles jointly adopted by a Committee of the
American Bar Association and a Committee of Publishers and Associations.)*

You may order this or any other Oxford University Press publication
by visiting the Oxford University Press website at www.oup.com

1/08 Oxford 29.75

To My Husband Chris

Your love and support
are my motivation and inspiration

To My Sons, Michael, Nick and Chris

-and-

In memory of my son, Jimmy

Table of Contents

CHAPTER 3:
SEXUAL ASSAULT

CHAPTER 4:
THE SEX OFFENDER REGISTRATION AND NOTIFICATION ACT (SORNA)

CHAPTER 5:
STALKING

CHAPTER 6:
TEENAGE DATING VIOLENCE

CHAPTER 7:
BATTERED IMMIGRANT WOMEN AND CHILDREN

CHAPTER 8:
HUMAN TRAFFICKING AND THE SEX TRADE

APPENDICES

ABOUT THE AUTHOR

MARGARET C. JASPER is an attorney engaged in the general practice of law in South Salem, New York, concentrating in the areas of personal injury and entertainment law. Ms. Jasper holds a Juris Doctor degree from Pace University School of Law, White Plains, New York, is a member of the New York and Connecticut bars, and is certified to practice before the United States District Courts for the Southern and Eastern Districts of New York, the United States Court of Appeals for the Second Circuit, and the United States Supreme Court.

Ms. Jasper has been appointed to the law guardian panel for the Family Court of the State of New York, is a member of a number of professional organizations and associations, and is a New York State licensed real estate broker operating as Jasper Real Estate, in South Salem, New York.

Margaret Jasper maintains a website at http://www.JasperLawOffice.com.

In 2004, Ms. Jasper successfully argued a case before the New York Court of Appeals, which gives mothers of babies who are stillborn due to medical negligence the right to bring a legal action and recover emotional distress damages. This successful appeal overturned a 26-year old New York case precedent, which previously prevented mothers of stillborn babies to sue their negligent medical providers.

Ms. Jasper is the author and general editor of the following legal almanacs:

AIDS Law
The Americans with Disabilities Act
Animal Rights Law
Auto Leasing
Bankruptcy Law for the Individual Debtor
Banks and their Customers

The Law of Violence Against Women

The Law of Capital Punishment
The Law of Child Custody
The Law of Contracts
The Law of Debt Collection
The Law of Dispute Resolution
The Law of Immigration
The Law of Libel and Slander
The Law of Medical Malpractice
The Law of No-Fault Insurance
The Law of Obscenity and Pornography
The Law of Personal Injury
The Law of Premises Liability
The Law of Product Liability
The Law of Speech and the First Amendment
Lemon Laws
Living Together: Practical Legal Issues
Marriage and Divorce
Missing and Exploited Children: How to Protect Your Child
Motor Vehicle Law
Nursing Home Negligence
Patent Law
Pet Law
Prescription Drugs
Privacy and the Internet: Your Rights and Expectations Under the
    Law
Probate Law
Protecting Your Business: Disaster Preparation and the Law
Real Estate Law for the Homeowner and Broker
Religion and the Law
Retirement Planning
The Right to Die
Rights of Single Parents
Small Claims Court
Social Security Law
Special Education Law
Teenagers and Substance Abuse
Trademark Law
Trouble Next Door: What to do With Your Neighbor
Victim's Rights Law
Violence Against Women
Welfare: Your Rights and the Law
What if It Happened to You: Violent Crimes and Victims' Rights
What if the Product Doesn't Work: Warranties & Guarantees
Workers' Compensation Law

Your Child's Legal Rights: An Overview
Your Rights in a Class Action Suit
Your Rights as a Tenant
Your Rights Under the Family and Medical Leave Act
You've Been Fired: Your Rights and Remedies

INTRODUCTION

This almanac addresses a serious problem facing American society: violence against women. Violence against women in America is a national crisis and nobody can afford to look the other way. Violence against women takes many forms, including domestic violence, rape and other sexual assaults.

Violent acts against women may be committed by strangers as well as friends, family members and those with whom the victim has had an intimate relationship. Violence against women does not discriminate based on race, ethnicity, age, education, income, marital status or residence.

This almanac examines the many aspects of violence against women, including domestic violence, dating violence, and sexual assault, and the legislative efforts to address these crimes. The various provisions of the Violence Against Women Act of 1994, 2000 and 2005 are set forth. This almanac also discusses the growing problem of human trafficking and the sex trade, and the sex offender registration requirements.

The Appendix provides resource directories, applicable statutes, and other pertinent information and data. The Glossary contains definitions of many of the terms used throughout the almanac.

CHAPTER 1:
AN OVERVIEW OF THE PROBLEM

IN GENERAL

According to the U.S. Department of Justice, Bureau of Justice Statistics (BJS), women are the victims of more than 4.5 million violent crimes each year. This alarming figure includes approximately 500,000 rapes or other sexual assaults. In addition, this figure may not accurately reflect the rate of violence against women because many women are reluctant to report a number of violent crimes to law enforcement authorities, including sexual assaults and offenses committed by intimates. There is a general belief that no purpose would be served by reporting these crimes. Sexual attacks, in particular, are perceived as too personal to reveal, and many women feel that the subsequent investigation subjects them to additional trauma.

Violence against women takes many forms, including domestic violence, rape and other sexual assaults. Violent acts against women may be committed by strangers as well as friends, family members, and those with whom the victim has had an intimate relationship. Violence against women does not discriminate based on race, ethnicity, age, education, income, marital status or residence.

The U.S. Department of Justice Violence Against Women Hotline Numbers are set forth at Appendix 1.

NATIONAL CRIME VICTIMIZATION SURVEY

In an effort to improve their data on those crimes committed against women which are particularly difficult to track, such as rape, sexual assault and domestic violence, the Bureau of Justice Statistics (BJS) redesigned its National Crime Victimization Survey. Approximately 50,000 households and more than 100,000 individuals participate in this nationwide survey annually. The BJS survey provides additional information on rapes, sexual assaults and domestic violence that was not previously available. The BJS survey attempts to measure crime from the victim's perspective.

THE VIOLENCE AGAINST WOMEN ACT OF 1994

The first comprehensive federal legislation responding to violence against women was the Violence Against Women Act (VAWA) which was initially introduced in 1990 and after much debate, finally signed into law in August of 1994 as a part of the Violent Crime Control and Law Enforcement Act of 1994 (PL-103-322) (the "Crime Bill"). The VAWA set forth firm law enforcement tactics and important safeguards for female victims of sexual assault and domestic violence, including:

1. Law enforcement and prosecution grants (STOP grants);

2. Grants to encourage arrest;

3. Rural domestic violence and child abuse enforcement grants;

4. The National Domestic Violence Hotline; and

5. Grants to battered women's shelters.

Following is an overview of the most important aspects of the VAWA:

Subtitle A: The Safe Streets for Women Act

The Safe Streets for Women Act provides for stiffer federal penalties for repeat sex crime offenders; authorizes mandatory restitution enforceable by victims of sex crimes; and provides funding to the U.S. Attorney Office for the purpose of hiring federal victim/witness counselors in connection with the prosecution of sex and domestic violence crimes. The Act also makes an important amendment to the Federal Rules of Evidence, limiting inquiries into a victim past sexual behavior or predisposition, and ensuring the confidentiality of communications between victims and their counselors.

Selected provisions of Subtitle A: The Safe Streets for Women Act is set forth at Appendix 2.

Subtitle B: The Safe Homes for Women Act

The Safe Homes For Women Act provides for interstate enforcement of domestic violence offenses, making it a crime to cross state lines to continue to abuse a spouse or partner; and authorizes mandatory restitution enforceable by victims of domestic violence. The Act also provides that protection orders are entitled to full faith and credit by the courts of another jurisdiction with the same enforceability as if that jurisdiction had issued the order, and provides for the confidentiality of domestic violence shelters and the addresses of abuse victims. The Act further implements programs designed to educate young people about domestic violence and provides funding for a National Domestic Violence Hotline.

Selected provisions of Subtitle B: The Safe Homes for Women Act is set forth at Appendix 3.

Subtitle C: The Civil Rights Remedies for Gender-Motivated Violence Act

The Civil Rights Remedies for Gender-Motivated Violence Act establishes a Federal civil rights cause of action for victims of crimes of violence motivated by gender, and authorizes legal fees for the victim. This civil rights remedy was designed to complement existing federal civil rights laws that do not protect women from gender-motivated violence. Under the Act, victims of gender-motivated violent crimes, such as rape and domestic violence, now have the right to sue their attackers for damages under federal law.

Selected provisions of Subtitle C: The Civil Rights Remedies for Gender-Motivated Violence Act is set forth at Appendix 4.

Subtitle D: The Equal Justice for Women in the Courts Act

The Equal Justice for Women in the Courts Act provides monetary grants for the purpose of developing programs for training judges and court personnel about sexual assault, domestic violence and other crimes of violence motivated by gender.

Selected provisions of Subtitle D: The Equal Justice for Women in the Courts Act is set forth at Appendix 5.

Subtitle E: The Violence Against Women Act Improvements

The Violence Against Women Act Improvements section strengthens the provisions of the Act by providing for pre-trial detention in sex offense cases; increasing penalties against victims below the age of 16; requiring payment for the cost of testing victims for sexually transmitted diseases in sex offense cases; requiring defendants in sex offense cases to be tested for HIV/AIDS disease; strengthening the restitution provisions by enforcing restitution orders through suspension of the defendants federal benefits; and providing for studies on campus sexual assault and battered women syndrome.

Selected provisions of Subtitle E: The Violence Against Women Act Improvements is set forth at Appendix 6.

Subtitle F: National Stalker and Domestic Violence Reduction

The National Stalker and Domestic Violence Reduction section authorizes access to federal criminal information databases for use in domestic violence or stalking cases; and provides monetary grants to States and local governmental units to improve methods of entering data regarding stalking and domestic violence incidents into local, State and national crime information databases.

Selected provisions of Subtitle F: National Stalker and Domestic Violence Reduction is set forth at Appendix 7.

Subtitle G: Protections for Battered Immigrant Women and Children

Subtitle G provides certain statutory protection to battered immigrant women and their children, thus permitting them to petition for classification and/or avoid deportation.

Selected provisions of Subtitle G: Protections for Battered Immigrant Women and Children is set forth at Appendix 8.

THE VIOLENCE AGAINST WOMEN ACT OF 2000

Authorization for the original VAWA expired in 2000, therefore, Congress acted to reauthorize this vital piece of legislation and passed the Violence Against Women Act of 2000 (PL-106-386) (VAWA 2000). VAWA 2000 was merged with the Victims of Trafficking and Violence Protection Act of 2000 and several smaller bills, and signed into law on October 28, 2000.

VAWA 2000 basically continued the existing programs under the original VAWA without any major changes. VAWA 2000 authorized $3.3 billion in funding for five years, and created several new programs, and strengthened the existing legislation, as follows:

1. The Civil Legal Assistance program was established to help women with protection orders, family court matters, housing, immigration and administrative matters.

2. The Transitional Housing program was established to provide grants to homeless individuals, however, it was never funded.

3. A pilot project was established authorizing grants to state and local law enforcement to provide supervised visitation exchange for the children of victims of domestic violence, child abuse and sexual assault.

4. The Full Faith and Credit provision authorized protection orders from one state to be recognized in another state and funded technology necessary to assist in the enforcement of interstate protection orders and those between state and tribal jurisdictions.

5. The provision addressing the needs of battered women was the most significant addition to the original VAWA. It removed the U.S. residency and extreme hardship requirements for immigrant women to receive VAWA protection; allows battered immigrant women to ob-

tain lawful permanent residence without leaving the country; restores access to VAWA protections for immigrants regardless of how they entered the country; and creates a new type of visa for victims of serious crimes that will allow some to attain lawful permanent residence.

6. A provision was included defining dating violence and authorizing funding for programs that address dating violence.

7. Funding was provided to train law enforcement and develop policies to address the needs of older and disabled victims of domestic and sexual violence.

THE VIOLENCE AGAINST WOMEN ACT OF 2005

In December 2005, the Violence Against Women Act of 2005 (VAWA 2005) (Public Law No: 109-162) was enacted as part of the Department of Justice Reauthorization Act and subsequently signed into law on January 5, 2006. VAWA 2005 consists of nine sections:

Title I: Crimes and Courts

The STOP Grants Program—Title I authorizes funding of $225 million for five years; provides greater support for emergency and long-term victim services; provides new definitions of key crimes and practices for all VAWA grant programs; strengthens definitions and distribution language to ensure better support for culturally-specific programs; and adds language to include racial and ethnic minorities in the state planning process.

The Grants to Encourage Arrest and Enforce Protection Orders Program—Title I authorizes funding of $75 million for 5 years; establishes the Family Justice Center program; improves language to deter dual arrests; adds sexual assault and stalking to the scope of work authorized; and encourages community policing protocols in addressing domestic violence, sexual assault, dating violence and stalking.

The Legal Assistance for Victims Program—Title I authorizes funding of $65 million per year for five years; permits use of funding for teen and campus dating violence victims; and allows grantees to help clients with related criminal justice system issues.

The Court Improvement Program—Title I improves court responses to domestic violence through training, improvement of court case management, and the development of best practices; focuses on improving internal court functions on both the civil and criminal divisions of courts; provides for victim services within the courthouse and court personnel education; includes discretionary grants for special projects;

and proposes the development of a national judicial training curriculum.

Title II: Services and Outreach

Services for Victims of Abuse Later in Life—According to the National Elder Abuse Incidence Study, in 90% of elder abuse cases, the perpetrator was a family member. Title II authorizes grants for providing services for domestic violence, dating violence, sexual assault and stalking victims over age 60, and increase accessibility to buildings where the services will be provided; and dedicates 10% of the authorized funds to Tribal organizations.

Enhanced Services for Women with Disabilities—Women with disabilities are more likely to be victims of abuse because of their increased physical, economic and social dependence on others. Title II adds construction and personnel costs for shelters to better serve victims with disabilities; focuses on the development of collaborative partnerships between victim services organizations and organizations serving individuals with disabilities; and allocates funding toward the development of model programs that place advocacy and intervention services within organizations serving individuals with disabilities.

Public Education Campaigns—Title II provides grants for public information campaigns targeting racial and ethnic minority and immigrant communities about domestic violence, dating violence, sexual assault and stalking.

The Sexual Assault Services Program—The Sexual Assault Services Program (SASP) was initiated to provide assistance to victims of sexual violence. Specifically, SASP will provide funds for services providers and make resources available to state, territorial and tribal sexual assault coalitions who work to increase the effectiveness and efficiency of local rape crisis centers.

Rural Services for Victims Program—Victims of domestic violence and sexual violence in rural communities face unique obstacles because of geographic isolation and lack of resources. Title II increases authorization within the Department of Justice to extend direct grants to state and local governments for services in rural areas; encourages stronger collaboration between victim services, law enforcement, prosecutors, courts, health care providers and other agencies; and expands program coverage to sexual assault, child sexual assault and stalking victims.

Title III: Children and Youth

The original VAWA and VAWA 2000 focused primarily on violence against adult women but did not address problems facing children and young adults who witness or experience domestic violence, dating violence, sexual assault or stalking. Title III provides for the treatment and education of youth and young adults.

Title IV: Prevention

The original VAWA and VAWA 2000 was instrumental in addressing the problem of violence against women, and created many programs to combat this problem. However, the law did not deal with prevention of violence. Title IV focuses on prevention and provides supportive services to children exposed to domestic violence to mitigate future harm and build up protective factors in children's lives; provide support for young and vulnerable parents to help them strengthen their parenting, promote healthy child development and address past violence so as to break the often intergenerational cycle of violence; and supports the development of public education campaigns working with men, teens, and boys to raise awareness that violence against women is unacceptable.

Title V: Health Care Response

Domestic violence is responsible for numerous health care problems including both the immediate injuries caused by the abuse as well as the chronic health problems experienced by victims of abuse. Title V includes provisions that would train health care providers and students in health professional schools to identify victims of domestic and sexual violence; promote public health programs that integrate domestic and sexual violence assessment and intervention into basic care; and support research and evaluation on effective interventions in the health care setting to improve abused women's health and safety and prevent initial victimization.

Title VI: Housing

Studies have demonstrated a strong link between homelessness and domestic violence. Title VI provides for improved safety for victims in housing and shelters; creates a $10 million program to fund collaborative efforts to create permanent housing options for victims; expands the existing transitional housing program for victims to include funds for creating and operating transitional housing projects and helping victims maintain safety and self-sufficiency; and authorizes a $10 million grant program to help public and Indian housing authorities and assisted housing providers respond to domestic violence, dating violence, sexual assault and stalking in a way that protects victims while holding perpetrators accountable.

Title VII: Economic Security

Abusers often retain control over survivors through economic dependence. Title VII ensures that victims have the economic security they need to escape violent relationships including confidentiality; unpaid emergency leave so that victims can go to court, get medical treatment, or do safety planning without losing their jobs.

Title VIII: Immigrant Issues

The original VAWA and VAWA 2000 included immigration provisions designed to remove obstacles that prevent immigrant victims from safely fleeing domestic violence and prosecuting their abusers. VAWA 2000 extended immigration relief to immigrant victims of sexual assault, human trafficking and other violent crimes who agree to cooperate in criminal investigations or prosecutions.

Title VIII implements the Act's original intent by stopping the deportation of immigrant victims of domestic violence, sexual assault, and human trafficking: stopping the Department of Homeland Security from seizing domestic violence, sexual assault and trafficking victims at domestic violence shelters, rape crisis centers, and protection order courts; bars the detention and deportation of victims who qualify for VAWA immigration relief; removes obstacles in immigration law that bar otherwise qualified victims from obtaining VAWA immigration relief; ensures the confidential treatment of immigrant victims' cases so that they can safely access urgently needed relief; extends immigration relief to all victims of family violence; prevents victims of incest and child abuse perpetrated by a U.S. citizen or permanent-resident parent from being cut off from VAWA's immigration protections when they turn 21; protects parents abused by their adult U.S. citizen sons or daughters; protects abused adopted children; and secures protection for children of immigrant victims of domestic violence, sexual assault and human trafficking.

Title VIII also guarantees economic security for immigrant victims and their children by granting employment authorization to adult victims who have filed valid VAWA immigration cases; allowing organizations funded by the Legal Services Corporation to represent all victims of domestic abuse, human trafficking, or sexual assault, regardless of immigration status; removing the bar that makes immigrant victims wait five years before they can access public benefits; and affording cooperating witness immigrant victims of domestic violence, sexual assault, child abuse and trafficking access to public benefits.

Title VIII stabilizes and secures the safety of trafficking victims by protecting their family members living abroad from retaliation by traffickers; allowing trafficking victims to immediately seek permanent residence; and removing barriers in immigration law that cut victims off from trafficking victim protections.

Title IX: Tribal Programs

American Indian and Alaska Native women are battered, raped and stalked at far greater rates than any other group of women in the United States. While many issues need to be addressed to confront this crisis, it is clear that jurisdictional limitations placed on Indian nations are key factors in creating this disproportionate violence.

Title IX decreases the incidents of violent crimes against Indian women; strengthens the capacity of Indian nations to exercise their sovereign authority to respond to violent crimes committed against Indian women; ensures that perpetrators of violent crimes committed against Indian women are held accountable for their criminal behavior; restores the authority of Indian tribes to appropriately respond to domestic violence and rape by sentencing perpetrators of such crimes beyond one year and $5,000 fine; increases the analysis and research on violence against Indian women; permits Indian law enforcement agencies to enter and obtain criminal information from Federal criminal information databases; establishes a national tribal sex offender and tribal protection order registry; increases support for essential tribal services for Indian women; ensures the proper government-to-government relationship between Indian nations and the Department of Justice by requiring an annual consultation with Indian nations, and creating a Tribal Division within the Office on Violence Against Women. c/o Legal Momentum, 1522 K Street, NW, Suite 550, Washington, DC 20005 Tel: (202) 326.0040 /Fax: (202) 589-0511.

THE OFFICE ON VIOLENCE AGAINST WOMEN

The Office on Violence Against Women (OVW) is a federal agency established in March 1995 under the jurisdiction of the U.S. Department of Justice to reduce violence against women through the implementation of the Violence Against Women Act (VAWA).

The OVW is responsible for the overall coordination and focus of Department of Justice efforts to combat violence against women, serving as the primary point of contact for other federal agencies, state and local governments, outside organizations, and Congress. The goal of the OVW is to promote greater awareness of the problem of violence against women, and to find effective solutions.

The OVW administers financial and technical assistance to communities across the country that are developing programs, policies, and practices aimed at ending domestic violence, dating violence, sexual assault, and stalking.

By coordinating state, local, and tribal partnerships among police, prosecutors, victim advocates, health care providers, faith leaders, and others, OVW grant programs help provide victims with the protection and services they need to pursue safe and healthy lives, while simultaneously enabling communities to hold offenders accountable for their violence.

In addition to overseeing 12 federal grant programs, the OVW often undertakes a number of special initiatives including the Judicial Oversight Demonstration Initiative, the President's Family Justice Center Initiative, the Safety for Indian Women from Sexual Assault Offenders Demonstration Initiative, and the National Protocol for Sexual Assault Forensic Exams. These special initiatives allow the OVW to explore different innovations in the violence against women field and share knowledge that can be replicated nationwide.

Further information may be obtained from the OVW by contacting their headquarters:

Office on Violence Against Women (OVW)
800 K Street, N.W., Suite 920
Washington, D.C. 20530
Phone: 202-307-6026
Fax: 202-307-3911
TTY: 202-307-2277
Website: http:// www.usdoj.gov/ovw/

CHAPTER 2:
DOMESTIC VIOLENCE

IN GENERAL

Domestic violence generally refers to felony or misdemeanor crimes of violence committed by a current or former spouse of the victim, by a person with whom the victim shares a child in common, by a person who is cohabitating or has cohabitated with the victim as a spouse, or by a person similarly situated to a spouse.

A table depicting the rate of intimate partner violence against females, by age and victim/offender relationship (1993-1999) is set forth at Appendix 9.

Domestic violence is also referred to as "violence between intimates."

Domestic violence can be defined as a pattern of abusive behavior in any relationship that is used by one partner to gain or maintain power and control over another intimate partner.

In addition to the victim, domestic violence negatively impacts any children of the relationship. Studies show that children who witness frequent domestic violence suffer psychological and social problems, and are at risk for becoming abusers later in life.

According to the U.S. Bureau of Justice Statistics, slightly more than half of female victims of intimate violence live in households with children under age 12, and studies suggest that between 3.3-10 million children witness some form of domestic violence annually. A survey of more than 6,000 American families by the National Institute of Justice and Centers for Disease Control and Prevention reports that fifty percent of men who frequently assaulted their wives also frequently abused their children.

TYPES OF VIOLENCE

According to the National Center for Victims of Crime, domestic violence can be physical, sexual, emotional, economic, or psychological actions or threats of actions that influence another person. This includes any behaviors that intimidate, manipulate, humiliate, isolate, frighten, terrorize, coerce, threaten, blame, hurt, injure, or wound someone.

Physical Abuse

Physical abuse includes hitting, slapping, shoving, grabbing, pinching, biting, hair pulling, etc. Physical abuse also includes denying a partner medical care or forcing alcohol and/or drug use.

Sexual Abuse

Sexual abuse includes coercing or attempting to coerce any sexual contact or behavior without consent. Sexual abuse includes, but is not limited to marital rape, attacks on sexual parts of the body, forcing sex after physical violence has occurred, or treating one in a sexually demeaning manner.

Emotional Abuse

Emotional abuse includes undermining an individual's sense of self-worth and/or self-esteem. This may include, but is not limited to constant criticism, diminishing one's abilities, name-calling, or damaging one's relationship with his or her children.

Economic Abuse

Economic abuse includes making or attempting to make an individual financially dependent by maintaining total control over financial resources, withholding one's access to money, or forbidding one's attendance at school or employment.

Psychological Abuse

Psychological abuse includes causing fear by intimidation; threatening physical harm to self, partner, children, or partner's family or friends; destruction of pets and property; and forcing isolation from family, friends, or school and/or work.

UNDERREPORTING

Historically, domestic violence was often viewed as a private family matter, and that it was nobody's right to interfere. Law enforcement often took the position that domestic violence was not a criminal offense. The victim was all too often blamed for causing the abusive behavior, e.g., by "button pushing." As a result, the victim frequently remained silent about the abuse, rather than suffer criticism and shame, and possible retaliation by the abuser for involving the police.

A table depicting intimate partner violence against females and rate of reporting to police, by age (1993-1999) is set forth at Appendix 10.

According to the National Center for Women and Policing, only about half of domestic violence incidents are reported to police, and African-American women are more likely than others to report their victimization to police.

By enacting the Violence Against Women Act (VAWA), the federal government has demonstrated its commitment, along with states, local governmental units, and tribal governments, to put an end to the silence, to create tougher legislation, and to require greater police protection for domestic violence victims.

SCOPE OF THE PROBLEM

The following facts and statistics demonstrate the scope of the domestic violence national and worldwide crisis:

1. It is estimated that 6 million women are assaulted by their husband or male companion every year, a significant number of which are considered to involve severe injuries and, on average, more than three women are murdered by their husbands or boyfriends in this country every day.

2. According to a survey conducted by the National Violence Against Women, nearly 25% of American women report being raped and/or physically assaulted by a current or former spouse, cohabiting partner or date at sometime in their lifetime.

3. One out of every four American women will experience violence by an intimate partner sometime during her lifetime (The National Center for Women and Policing).

4. According to the U.S. Department of Justice, while women are less likely than men to be victims of violent crimes overall, women are five to eight times more likely than men to be victimized by an intimate partner (U.S. Department of Justice).

5. According to the U.S. Bureau of Justice Statistics, in 2001, intimate partner violence made up 20 percent of violent crime against women (588,490), and three percent of all violent crime against men.

6. Studies show that, worldwide, at least one in every three women has been beaten, coerced into sex or otherwise abused during her lifetime. According to a UNICEF study, approximately 20-50% of the

female population of the world will become the victims of domestic violence.

7. According to the U.S. Department of Justice, as many as 324,000 women each year experience intimate partner violence during their pregnancy, and pregnant and recently pregnant women are more likely to be victims of homicide than to die of any other cause.

8. According to the National Center for Women and Policing, approximately 40-50% of female victims are physically injured when assaulted by their intimate partner, accounting for over 200,000 visits to the hospital emergency room each year, although only 1 in 5 domestic violence victims with physical injuries seek professional medical treatment. The Centers for Disease Control reports that the health-related costs of rape, physical assault, stalking, and homicide by intimate partners exceed $5.8 billion dollars each year.

PROFILE OF THE VICTIM

According to the U.S. Department of Justice, intimate partner violence is primarily a crime against women. Their study indicates that women are 7 to 14 times more likely than men to report suffering severe physical assaults from an intimate partner. In 2001, women accounted for 85 percent of the victims of intimate partner violence (588,490 total) and men accounted for approximately 15 percent of the victims (103,220 total).

According to the National Center for the State Courts, male violence against women does much more damage than female violence against men, and women are much more likely to be injured than men. In addition, studies show that women are much more likely than men to be killed by an intimate partner. According to the National Center for Women and Policing, approximately 3 out of 4 of the murders committed by intimate partners have a female victim. In 2000, the Bureau of Justice Statistics reported that intimate partner homicides accounted for 33.5 percent of the murders of women (1,247) and less than four percent of the murders of men (440).

Demographics

As the following facts demonstrate, domestic violence can happen to anyone regardless of race, age, sexual orientation, religion, or gender. Domestic violence affects people of all socioeconomic backgrounds and education levels. Domestic violence occurs in both opposite-sex and same-sex relationships and can happen to intimate partners who are married, living together, or dating.

Age

According to the National Center for Women and Policing, women age 16 to 24 are most likely to be victimized by an intimate partner.

A table setting forth rate of intimate partner violence against females, by age (1993-1999) is set forth at Appendix 11.

Education

College graduates had the lower rates of violence committed by intimates compared to women with less than a high school education.

Geographic Location

Women living in central cities, suburban areas and rural locations experience similar rates of violence committed by intimates.

Income

Studies show that women in families with incomes below $10,000 per year were more likely than other women to be violently attacked by an intimate.

Marital Status

Divorced or separated women had higher rates of violence by intimates than married women or women who never married. According to the National Center for Women and Policing, women are most vulnerable to violence when separated from their intimate partner, and the second most vulnerable group are those who are divorced.

Race/Nationality

According to the Bureau of Justice Statistics, women of all races were about equally vulnerable to attacks by intimates. According to the National Center for Women and Policing, Black women experience more domestic violence than White women in the age group of 20-24, however, Black and White women experience the same level of victimization in all other age categories. In comparison, Hispanic women are less likely to be victimized than non-Hispanic women in every age group.

PROFILE OF THE OFFENDER

Research has indicated a number of identifying factors which place a man at risk as a potential batterer, including: (i) unemployment; (ii) poverty; (iii) drug or alcohol use; (iv) witnessing spousal abuse among parents as a child; (v) lack of education; and (vi) age 18 to 30 years old.

A recent study suggests that possessiveness is the most prevalent reason given by male offenders for killing their partners, and spousal homicide occurs more frequently during a period when the couple are separated, particularly if the separation was initiated by the wife.

Over half of the defendants convicted of killing their spouse had prior criminal records, although they were less likely to have a criminal history than defendants who had killed nonfamily members. In addition, as compared to nonfamily murder defendants, intimates were less likely to be unemployed, but more likely to have a history of mental illness.

Statistics gathered from a 1988 study of murder cases in large urban counties determined that the majority of defendants who killed their spouses were male (60%) and over the age of 30 (77%), as compared to the majority of defendants who killed nonfamily members, who were overwhelmingly male (93%) and under the age of 30 (65%). Approximately 80% of the defendants in the 1988 study of spousal murder cases were convicted or pleaded guilty.

While friends and acquaintances of women victims committed more than half of the rapes and sexual assaults, intimates committed 26 percent, and strangers were responsible for about one in five. In fact, women were attacked about six times more often by offenders with whom they had an intimate relationship than were male violence victims. Men, however, were more likely than women to experience violent crimes committed by both acquaintances and strangers. In fact, men were about twice as likely as women to experience acts of violence by strangers.

CHARACTERISTICS OF A SPOUSAL MURDER CASE

According to the Bureau of Justice Statistics, over one third of spousal murders took place during the day, the majority of which took place at home (86%). Most defendants murdered only their spouse. Over half of the defendants had been drinking alcohol at the time of the murder, and almost half of the victims had also been drinking at the time the offense took place.

In approximately 23% of the incidents, the murdered spouses allegedly precipitated the incident by provoking the defendant, e.g. with a deadly weapon, nonlethal weapon or other physical contact.

In addition, over 62% of the defendants accused of murdering their spouses were arrested on the day the crime took place as compared to 32% of defendants accused of killing nonfamily members.

DOMESTIC VIOLENCE ENFORCEMENT

Protection Orders

A domestic violence victim is often advised to obtain a protection order. A protection order is basically an injunction issued by the court for the purpose of preventing violent or threatening acts of domestic violence. A protection order in a domestic relationship is usually obtained by filing a petition with the Family Court of the jurisdiction where the victim lives. An order of protection is issued on either a temporary or permanent basis.

The court will likely issue a temporary order of protection, upon the filing of the petition, based on the victim's allegations that she is in imminent danger of physical harm. The abuser is entitled to respond to the allegations contained in the petition for a protection order. If it is determined that the allegations are true, a permanent protection order will be issued. The maximum length of time a protection order may last varies according to state law.

A typical protection order may (i) prohibit the abuser from contacting the victim; (ii) prohibit the abuser from further abusing or harassing the victim; (iii) require the abuser to provide support to the victim and children; and/or (iv) require counseling.

After a victim has obtained a protection order, she can call the police if the abuser violates it. As discussed below, in some states, police are required to arrest the abuser if there appears to be a violation, e.g. the abuser is found outside the victim's home.

Full Faith and Credit Provision

The VAWA's "full faith and credit" provision requires states to honor protection orders issued by other jurisdictions to protect battered women who hold protection orders and move to another state, only to have their abusers follow them there. The following case history demonstrates the importance of giving full faith and credit to out-of-state protection orders, and the need for public awareness of this important VAWA provision.

In February 1993, a woman living in Metropolis, Illinois went to court to obtain a protection order against her abusive live-in boyfriend. The police escorted the woman home and searched the house to make sure her boyfriend was not on the premises. Unknown to police, the boyfriend was hiding in the house.

After the police left, the boyfriend left his hiding place in the ceiling of the woman's home and threatened her. The police were summoned, however, the boyfriend was not arrested because the police had not witnessed the protection order violation. A few months later, the woman was severely beaten by her boyfriend.

Officials at the Metropolis Domestic Violence Center immediately and covertly relocated the woman to Paducah, Kentucky, a larger town just across the Ohio River from Metropolis. Shortly thereafter, the woman was again beaten and her Paducah apartment was destroyed by arson. The woman's boyfriend was convicted and sent to jail for the beating.

After spending a few months in jail, the boyfriend was released. He followed the woman to a Paducah gas station. He kidnapped, beat and sexually assaulted her. When the woman was found in Kentucky, local police declined to arrest the boyfriend because they deemed the Illinois protection order to be invalid within the Kentucky borders. This man was never arrested for the assault, and the victim was told her only relief would be to seek an emergency protection order in a Kentucky court.

When the Metropolis Domestic Violence Center questioned the Paducah Police as to why the woman's Illinois protection order had not been upheld under the Full Faith and Credit provision of the Violence Against Women Act, they responded that they had never heard of such a provision. As a result, the Illinois Attorney General issued a two-page fact sheet describing the major provisions of the Violence Against Women Act, including the Full Faith and Credit provision. This information sheet has since been posted on the bulletin boards of local police stations.

The VAWA provides that a civil protection order issued by the court of one State or Indian Tribe (the "issuing state or tribe") shall be accorded full faith and credit by the court of another State or Indian Tribe (the "enforcing state or tribe"), and shall be enforced as if it were the order of the court of the second state or tribe.

Nevertheless, failure by the issuing state to satisfy due process requirements will not entitle a protection order to full faith and credit. The issuing court must have had both personal and subject matter jurisdiction and the respondent must have received reasonable notice and an opportunity to be heard for the provision to be in effect.

Prior to the enactment of the VAWA, a victim with a protection order often could not use that order as the basis for protection if the victim went to work, traveled or moved to another state. Under the "full faith and credit" provision, the second state must enforce the order issued by another jurisdiction, even if the victim otherwise would be ineligible for protection in the second state. A victim does not have to wait for abuse to occur in the second state nor does a victim need to be concerned if he or she cannot meet its jurisdictional requirements.

Furthermore, a victim does not have to register a protection order in the second state for it to be effective. The protection order of the issuing state provides continuous protection to the victim.

In addition, as set forth above, the FBI maintains a national database concerning persons subject to protection orders, which will be available for criminal justice purposes, and to civil courts in domestic violence cases. This database will increase the ability of states to verify the existence of restraining orders throughout the United States.

Federal Interstate Domestic Violence Enforcement

Victims of domestic violence often seek safety and shelter with friends and relatives living in other states, where they are often followed by their abusers. The VAWA addressed this problem by establishing new federal offenses in cases where an abuser crosses state lines to violate a protection order or injure, harass or intimidate a spouse or intimate partner.

These provisions are crucial to prosecuting cases where the abuser's travel across state lines makes state prosecution difficult, and/or where state penalties may not be tough enough to deter the abusive behavior. They also provide additional important benefits for domestic violence victims, including strengthened restitution provisions and the right to address the court prior to a pre-trial release of the defendant regarding the victim's concerns about danger posed by the defendant's release.

The VAWA authorizes severe federal sentences for abusers who travel interstate with the intent to injure, harass or intimidate a domestic partner or violate a protection order. The VAWA ensures that the law follows an abuser who crosses state lines, and provides victims with protection throughout the United States.

As set forth below, the DOJ's first successful conviction under the VAWA's interstate domestic violence enforcement provision occurred in the Southern District of West Virginia.

> In November 1994, Christopher Bailey of St. Albans, West Virginia beat his wife Sonya until she collapsed. He then placed her in the trunk of their car and drove for five days through West Virginia and Kentucky before taking her to a hospital emergency room. Sonya Bailey suffered irreversible brain damage and remains in a permanent vegetative state.

Under the VAWA's prohibition against interstate domestic violence, federal prosecutors in West Virginia were able to secure a conviction against Christopher Bailey, who was sentenced to life in prison for the kidnapping and interstate domestic violence perpetrated against his wife.

This case illustrates the value of federal action against interstate domestic violence. Although Mr. Bailey was arrested in Kentucky, local police dropped the charges because they were unable to document what had occurred in their jurisdiction. Under West Virginia law, Mr. Bailey might have received less than a two-year sentence for his brutal assault. In contrast, under the federal law, Mr. Bailey received a life sentence.

As set forth below, the nation's second conviction under the VAWA's interstate domestic violence prohibition occurred in the Eastern District of California.

Ricky Steele abused and beat his domestic partner in Oregon, and then forced her to drive with him to California. Mr. Steele was subsequently arrested, convicted under federal law, required to make restitution to his victim, and sentenced to 87 months in prison.

Federal prosecutors have initiated other cases under the VAWA interstate domestic violence prohibition against traveling across state lines with the intent of violating court issued protection orders.

Wayne Hayes was indicted in the Eastern District of New York on charges of traveling interstate with the intention of violating a court order that prohibited him from harassing his ex-wife, and mailing threatening communications to her.

This indictment marks the first use of the VAWA provision that prohibits traveling across a state line in order to violate certain protection orders. The DOJ continues to work with state and local law enforcement to combat interstate domestic violence and identify those cases where use of these new federal remedies is appropriate.

Firearms Disability Provision

The Violent Crime Control and Law Enforcement Act of 1994 (the "Crime Bill") includes a provision that makes it unlawful for persons subject to certain restraining orders to possess firearms. This provision is designed to protect victims of domestic violence. As set forth below, the first successful prosecution under the Act's firearms disability provision occurred in South Dakota.

On October 18, 1994, a South Dakota court issued the estranged wife of Robert M. Goben a restraining order against her husband which prohibited him from harassing or threatening her. Under the firearms disability provision of the newly enacted Crime Bill, Mr. Goben was also prohibited from possessing a firearm while the restraining order remained in effect.

Approximately five months later, while the restraining order was still in effect, local police discovered that Mr. Goben possessed a loaded .22-caliber magnum revolver. As a result, Mr. Goben was arrested and pled guilty to illegally possessing a firearm in violation of federal law. Mr. Goben was sentenced to twelve months in prison followed by two years of supervised release, during which time he was prohibited from contacting his former spouse.

Following the Goben case, federal prosecutors in the Northern District of Iowa brought another case under the newly-enacted law.

On October 24, 1995, Shawn A. Hungate, 25, of Fort Dodge, Iowa, was charged with illegally possessing a firearm while subject to a restraining order. According to the complaint, when purchasing the firearm, Hungate allegedly answered "No" to a question on a government form regarding whether he was subject to a restraining order. If convicted on the firearms charge, Mr. Hungate faces up to ten years in prison and a $250,000 fine or both.

The firearms disability provision provides some measure of security to victims in that their abusers can be arrested if they attempt to purchase or possess firearms during the period of the restraining order. The DOJ is working with state and local law enforcement groups to implement this provision.

Mandatory Arrest Policies

Police officers have historically been reluctant to become involved in domestic violence disputes, largely because such calls for police assistance are among the most complex, emotionally charged and potentially dangerous calls to which police respond.

Many jurisdictions have implemented mandatory arrest policies. A mandatory arrest policy requires police to arrest a domestic assault offender whenever the officer determines that a crime has been committed and probable cause for arrest exists. These policies convey a message to the victim, the family, and the community that domestic violence is a serious crime that will not be tolerated.

The primary goal of these policies and the immediate and primary responsibility of the arresting officer must be to ensure the safety of the victim because the arrest of the abuser does not guarantee their safety. It has been recognized that a strong mandatory arrest policy must be supported by a community and criminal justice system which also takes a strong stand against domestic violence and makes every attempt to provide safety for the victim once an arrest is made.

Rural Domestic Violence and Child Abuse Enforcement

If a domestic violence victim in a rural area of this country needs assistance, she may be faced with many difficulties. Very few police officers patrol in small rural communities, therefore, it may be too late once a call for assistance is answered. In addition, there is understandable fear that any report of abuse will not remain a secret in small communities.

Geographic isolation, culturally close communities, and lack of domestic violence information and services are among the problems unique to rural areas. Victims in rural areas also may not trust systems outsider their communities to protect them from their abusers. Therefore, they may elect to continue living in emotional isolation rather than seek help. Because rural areas in the United States are also experiencing growth in their immigrant populations, victims may be further isolated as a result of language and cultural barriers.

The VAWA has established monetary grant programs which address the issues of domestic violence and child abuse in rural states. These grants are designed to (i) create training programs for those most likely to be in contact with domestic violence victims, such as law enforcement, shelter workers, health care providers, and clergy; (ii) increase public awareness and implement community education campaigns; and (iii) expand direct services for rural and Native American victims and their children.

A variety of entities, including states, tribal and local governments, and public and private organizations in rural states, are eligible to receive funding under the grant programs.

Community Oriented Policing Services ("COPS")

As part of the VAWA, the "COPS" (Community Oriented Policing Services) Office was established. The COPS' Community Policing to Combat Domestic Violence Program provides law enforcement agencies with an opportunity to implement innovative strategies utilizing community policing to deal with domestic violence.

To be eligible for funding under this program, police departments and sheriffs' offices are required to collaborate with non-profit, non-governmental victim service programs, domestic violence shelters, or community service groups to coordinate efforts to fight domestic abuse. As a few jurisdictions have already found, community policing—a strategy which emphasizes problem solving and community partnership—can be an effective weapon in decreasing the incidence of domestic violence.

For example, efforts have been made to educate and involve the public on ways they can help to diminish domestic violence. Individuals who come in contact with suspected domestic abuse are advised not to ignore the situation. If a violent incident is witnessed or overheard, one should contact the police immediately. Medical providers and clergy members should make further inquiries when evidence of domestic violence are present, and teachers must watch for signs that children have witnessed violence in the home, such as violent tendencies exhibited by the child.

As the case below demonstrates, a successful victory over domestic violence can only be accomplished if a coordinated effort is made by all individuals who come in contact with domestic abuse.

> In 1992, a 39 year old Alexandria, Virginia woman went to the hospital with a black eye and cuts which required stitches. She told the nurse that her husband had caused her injuries, but asked the nurse not to call the police because she feared retaliation from her husband.

> The nurse did not comply with the woman's wishes and called the police to report the abuse. Once the police came, they enabled the victim to get help. The husband was charged with abuse, and the woman was given lodging and counseling at a shelter for battered women.

> Armed with advice concerning her legal rights, the woman was able to obtain a protective order from the court which allowed her to return to her apartment and prohibited her husband from returning. The court ordered the husband into an anger management program.

> This woman credits that nurse's intervention, although against her wishes, with freeing her from the violent relationship when she did not have the courage to leave on her own.

STRATEGIES FOR THE DOMESTIC VIOLENCE VICTIM

It is important for women who are in abusive relationships to recognize the risk factors, and to prepare themselves for the possibility of flight in case the situation becomes dangerous. The following advice and information has been gathered from nationwide domestic violence organizations, such as the National Victim Center, in order to give the domestic violence victim some coping strategies at various stages of a domestic violence relationship.

Risk Factors for Abusive Behavior

Research has indicated a number of identifying factors which place a man at risk as a potential batterer, including: (i) unemployment; (ii) poverty; (iii) drug or alcohol use; (iv) witnessing spousal abuse between parents as a child; (v) lack of education; and (vi) age 18 to 30 years old.

Studies suggest that possessiveness is the most prevalent reason given by male offenders for killing their partners, and spousal homicide occurs more frequently during a period when the couple are separated, particularly if the separation was initiated by the wife.

Strategies While Still in the Abusive Relationship

Of course, a victim of domestic violence is advised to immediately leave the abusive relationship to avoid serious personal injury to herself or the children. Nevertheless, it is recognized that many women, for whatever reason, try to endure the violent behavior for as long as possible. In those cases, the following advice should be heeded:

1. If it appears that abuse is about to occur, don't be combative. Try to diffuse the situation by backing down or leaving the situation to allow your partner to cool off.

2. Prepare safety areas in your home where you can go if you must escape abuse. Keep all types of weapons, if any, locked up in a remote location. If an abusive situation appears imminent, go to the safety area. Maintain a phone in that area in case you need to call for help. Try to remember a list of important phone numbers, such as the police, ambulance, shelter, and hotline numbers, including the national domestic violence hotline number, which is further, discussed below.

3. If you have children, try to stay away from them during an abusive episode so that they do not also become targets of the abuser.

4. If you are unable to avoid the violent attack, protect vulnerable areas of your body—e.g. your head and face—by blocking with your arms.

5. Don't hide your situation from family and close friends. You may have to rely on them for help if the situation gets really out of hand.

6. Teach your children how to get help if the need arises. Caution them not to involve themselves in the altercation. Explain to them that violence is wrong, and they are not at fault.

Making Plans to Leave the Abusive Relationship

If the relationship becomes too turbulent and unpredictable to endure, the domestic violence victim must make plans to leave the situation. In that case, the following advice should be heeded:

1. Maintain a journal of all of the violent incidents, and keep it and any evidence of physical abuse, such as photographs, in a safe place where you will have access to them after you leave.

2. If you are injured, seek medical care at the emergency room of a hospital or your physician. Make sure your account of the injuries is documented.

3. Contact your local battered women's shelter for information about your legal rights, sources of financial assistance, counseling and other available resources. Again, the national domestic violence hotline is also equipped to provide resource information to victims.

4. If you are unemployed, seek out job training and educational programs to help prepare you for entering the workforce.

5. Practice an escape plan in case the need arises. Plan for all possible contingencies. For example, get into the habit of having your car ready for emergency departures and a spare set of keys in case yours are confiscated. Hide some emergency money, and keep a suitcase packed with some essential clothing and supplies for yourself and your children.

Leaving the Abusive Relationship

1. Ask the police to accompany you while you remove your personal belongings from the home and to escort you from the home.

2. Make sure you take with you important items that you will need and may not want to risk reentering the home to retrieve, such as your drivers license; legal documents, such as your marriage license, birth certificates, citizenship documents and social security cards; banking information and checkbook; property ownership documents, such as titles and deeds; credit cards; medical records and prescription medication; school records; insurance information; personal valuables and effects; and your personal telephone book with important phone numbers.

3. Try to create a false trail so that the abuser cannot easily track you down. Don't use calling card numbers that can be traced back to your whereabouts. Don't use credit cards in areas that you intend to relocate.

After you successfully leave the violent relationship, seek advice from domestic violence organizations on how to proceed to protect yourself and your children from further abuse. Court intervention may be necessary. In extreme cases, relocation may be the only alternative.

CHANGING YOUR NAME

An abusive relationship may be so dangerous that you must relocate and do everything possible so that the abuser cannot locate you. You may even need to change your name. Generally, you can pick any name you choose, for yourself or your minor child, with some exceptions:

1. You cannot change your name for fraudulent purposes, e.g., as part of an illegal scheme to defraud others, to avoid prosecution for a criminal act, to avoid paying debts, shield yourself from a lawsuit, or elude law enforcement or immigration officials.

2. In most states, you cannot change your name if you are a convicted sex offender.

3. If you are a male between the ages of 18 and 26, you must be registered with the Selective Service System. If you change your name, you must notify Selective Service so that they can amend their records.

4. You cannot choose a name that would interfere with the rights of others, e.g., you cannot use a famous name if you are doing so for fraudulent purposes or financial benefit, and you cannot use a copyrighted fictional name.

5. You cannot use a name that would be intentionally confusing, such as a number or a punctuation mark.

6. You cannot use a name that would be considered a "fighting word," such as an obscenity or racial slur.

Procedure for Changing Your Name

Although changing your name does not involve a difficult or complicated procedure, it used to be much easier. For example, before identity theft and terrorism raised concerns, you could simply pick a new name, openly and consistently start using it in your business and social affairs, and eventually the new name would stick, and become your legal name. It was not necessary to file any papers in court. This name change procedure is known as "common usage." Now it is preferable to obtain a court order as many institutions, e.g. banks, will not recognize your new name without a court order. If you are adamant about avoiding a formal court procedure, you can try to enforce the law by providing a copy of the state law that supports your position.

In order to obtain a court order, a name change petition must be filed with the court, along with a filing fee and any additional documentation required by your state, e.g., proof of identity, such as a birth certificate.

Most states will require you to publish an announcement in the local newspaper in order to give the public notice of your proposed name change. However, in the case of a woman who is escaping an abusive situation, he or she may request an exemption from the publication requirement in order to protect her identity and safety. This makes sense since requiring publication in such a case would defeat the purpose for the name change in the first place.

Section (2) of the Colorado name change statute addresses this situation, as follows:

Colorado Code §13-15-102 - Publication of change.

(2) Public notice of such name change through publication as required in subsection (1) of this section shall not be required if the petitioner has been:

(a) The victim of a crime, the underlying factual basis of which has been found by the court on the record to include an act of domestic violence, as defined in section 18-6-800.3 (1), C.R.S.;

(b) The victim of child abuse, as defined in section 18-6-401, C.R.S.; or

(c) The victim of domestic abuse as that term is defined in section 14-4-101 (2), C.R.S.

Once your name change petition is filed, some states require a court appearance before a judge, who will review your petition and supporting documentation, and ask any relevant questions. After reviewing your petition, the judge will decide whether or not to grant your name change request. If the petition is approved, the judge will sign a court order permitting you to use the new name, and return a signed copy to you. In some states, the judge signs the name change order based solely on the documents submitted without the necessity of a court appearance.

If you don't feel comfortable filing your own name change petition and appearing in court before a judge, you can hire a lawyer to handle the process on your behalf. Some states allow paralegals, who are less expensive, to file name change petitions.

Additional information regarding changing your name is set forth in this author's legal almanac entitled "How to Change Your Name."

A directory of state name change laws is set forth at Appendix 12.

THE NATIONAL DOMESTIC VIOLENCE HOTLINE

Pursuant to the VAWA, a nationwide, 24-hour toll-free domestic violence hotline was implemented. The hotline is the first federally funded national domestic violence hotline in this country. The hotline provides help for domestic violence victims across the country-24-hours a day, 365 days a year. The service is toll-free, operating throughout the United States, Puerto Rico, and the Virgin Islands.

The hotline is designed to help create a more seamless system among local, state, and national service providers. Although there are already a number of local domestic violence hotlines in place, many areas in this country still lack a comprehensive response system. The national hotline is especially important for victims who live in rural or isolated areas that may lack their own local hotlines or other comprehensive domestic violence services.

When someone calls the hotline, they speak to a trained domestic violence advocate, who offers them crisis intervention, support, and referrals to local services in their community. The advocate has access to a national database that contains the most current information on emergency shelters, legal advocacy, social services, and other programs in communities across the country. In an emergency, the hotline is also equipped to connect callers to their local police. Services are also available to the hearing impaired, and translators are available for non-English speaking victims of domestic violence.

The National Domestic Violence Hotline can be reached at 1-800-799-SAFE. The TDD number for the hearing impaired is 1-800-787-3224. It is important to note that callers who need help in an emergency should always call "911" directly for immediate assistance.

A directory of national domestic violence organizations, and state and tribal domestic violence coalitions is set forth at Appendix 13, 14 and 15, respectively.

CHAPTER 3:
SEXUAL ASSAULT

IN GENERAL

Sexual assault is a general term which refers to a number of sex-related offenses, including rape, sexual contact, and indecent exposure. The crime of sexual assault almost always involves sexual intercourse, including oral or anal intercourse, or some other type of penetration of the genitals by another's body or by an object.

Sexual assault involves the commission of those acts against another who is either unwilling to consent, or who lacks the physical, mental or legal capacity to consent, e.g., if the victim is forced, threatened, unconscious, drugged, developmentally or mentally disabled, or a minor. Use of force may include physical violence, with or without a weapon, or psychological coercion.

The offender may be a stranger, family member or acquaintance of the victim. Most offenders are male, whether the victim is male or female.

PROFILE OF THE VICTIM

Victims can be males or females of any age, race, social class, appearance, or sexual orientation.

Age

Approximately 44% of rape victims are under age 18 and 80% are under age 30.

Gender

One out of every six women will be raped during her lifetime, and one in six American women are victims of sexual assault. Although the majority of sexual assault victims are female, studies show that one in 33 American men are also victims of sexual assault, thus, many states have recently amended their laws to make such crimes gender-neutral.

Income

According to the Bureau of Justice Statistics, approximately half of all rape victims are in the lowest third of income distribution, and about half are in the upper two-thirds.

Race/Nationality

Although approximately 80% of all sexual assault victims are white, minorities are somewhat more likely to be attacked. Following is the lifetime rate of rape/attempted rape for women, according to the Prevalence, Incidence and Consequences of Violence Against Women Survey:

All: 17.6%

White: 17.7%

Black: 18.8%

Asian/Pacific Islander: 6.8%

American Indian/Alaskan: 34.1%

Mixed Race: 24.4%

SCOPE OF THE PROBLEM

According to the US Department of Justice (DOJ), every two and a half minutes, somewhere in America, someone is sexually assaulted. This figure is calculated as follows:

> There are 525,600 minutes in a non-leap year (365 days x 24 hours x 60 minutes = 525,600). That makes 31,536,000 seconds per year (525,600 minutes x 60 seconds = 31,536,000).
>
> According to the most recent data available from the U.S. Department of Justice National Crime Victimization Survey (NCVS)—the nation's largest and most reliable crime study—there was an average of 200,780 sexual assaults each year in 2004-2005.
>
> 31,536,000 divided by 200,780 comes out to one sexual assault every 157 seconds, or about one every two and a half minutes.

A table depicting U.S. forcible rape statistics, by volume and rate (1990-2005) is set forth at Appendix 16.

According to the 2005 DOJ National Crime Victimization Survey:

> 1. In 2005, there were 191,670 victims of rape, attempted rape or sexual assaults.
>
> 2. Of the average annual 200,780 victims in 2004-2005, about 64,080 were victims of completed rape, 51,500 were victims of attempted rape, and 85,210 were victims of sexual assault.

3. In 2005, law enforcement received 69,370 reports of rapes.

4. In 2005, more than 170,000 women were victims of attempted or completed rapes.

5. In 2005, more than 15,000 men were victims of attempted or completed rapes.

6. In 2005, almost two-thirds of all rapes were committed by someone who is known to the victim: 73% of sexual assaults were perpetrated by a non-stranger; 38% of perpetrators were a friend or acquaintance of the victim; 28% were an intimate; and 7% were another relative.

OBTAINING MEDICAL TREATMENT

A victim of rape or sexual assault must seek immediate medical attention. It is advisable to go to the local hospital emergency room for treatment. Medical personnel in the emergency room are trained to perform the necessary examination, known as a "rape kit," which obtains the evidence necessary for law enforcement to find and prosecute the offender. In order to preserve this evidence, the victim should not shower or remove the clothing he or she was wearing during the attack before going to the hospital.

Another important reason for going to the hospital is so medical personnel can test whether the victim had been drugged before the assault. Medical personnel may also perform a pregnancy test and an HIV test, and provide medication to reduce the victim's chances of being infected by a sexually transmitted disease.

In addition to medical assistance, victims of rape or sexual assault may be offered counseling and referrals to organizations that can provide them with assistance and support.

A directory of state sexual assault coalitions is set forth at Appendix 17.

RAPE-RELATED POST-TRAUMATIC STRESS DISORDER (RR-PTSD)

According to the National Victim Center, nearly one-third of all rape victims develop what is known as Rape-Related Post-Traumatic Stress Disorder (RR-PTSD) at some point in their life following the attack.

The first symptom of RR-PTSD is the feeling of reliving the traumatic experience. This occurs when the victim is unable to block out remembrances—e.g. flashbacks—about the rape incident. There are often accompanying nightmares in which the victim relives the whole experience. In addition, the victim often feels overwhelming distress when confronted with stimuli that symbolize the trauma.

Another major symptom of RR-PTSD is social withdrawal, also referred to as "psychogenic numbing," which leaves the victim feeling emotionally dead. The victim no longer experiences normal feelings such as those felt prior to the traumatic incident. For example, victims may no longer feel the normal range of human emotions, such as happiness and sorrow. Survivors of crime victims may also experience a decreased interest in living. The victim is also likely to develop a form of amnesia concerning the details of the experience. This is a defense mechanism that takes over to protect the victim from experiencing further psychic trauma.

A third major symptom of RR-PTSD involves avoidance behavior. Avoidance behavior occurs when the victim attempts to avoid any thoughts, feelings or contacts that might stimulate a remembrance of the trauma. For example, a rape victim may refuse to drive in the area close to where the sexual assault occurred.

The fourth set of symptoms include an exaggerated startle response, inability to sleep, memory impairment, and difficulty concentrating. Victims may also exhibit episodes of anger and irritability that have no identifiable cause. Rape victims are three times more likely to suffer major depressive episodes as compared to those who have not been victimized. In addition, rape victims are 4.1 times more likely to contemplate suicide, and thirteen percent actually follow through with a suicide attempt. Some also develop drug and alcohol problems following the traumatic experience.

SEXUALLY TRANSMITTED DISEASE

An additional factor in the psychological trauma associated with sexual assault is the fear that the victim has been exposed to a sexually transmitted disease and, in particular, to the potentially deadly and widespread HIV infection. The fear is real and greatly exacerbates the stress a victim of sexual assault is already caused to endure.

Following the assault, the victim must make the decision on whether to be tested. It is recommended that the victim receive counseling both before and after being tested for HIV infection. If they wish to be tested, it is important that the test be taken as soon after the assault as possible for a baseline reading. If the test results are negative, it is suggested that additional testing take place every six months for the following eighteen months. Of course, if the test results are positive, the impact will be devastating and intensive counseling will be required.

Nevertheless, the victim should be aware that a positive HIV test does not mean he or she has, or will develop, full-blown AIDS. Further, medical treatment has advanced to the point where death is not imminent, and some HIV infected individuals experience little, if any, symptoms.

SEXUAL ASSAULT AND DATE RAPE

Alcohol and drugs are known to be a significant factor in the sexual assault of young women by young men with whom they are acquainted. This is generally referred to as "date rape" or "acquaintance rape," and has become a problem on college campuses. According to the National College Women Sexual Victimization (NCWSV) study, 20–25 percent of college women are victims of an attempted or completed rape, and in 9 out of 10 cases, the offenders are known to the victims.

In fact, 12.8 percent of completed rapes, 35.0 percent of attempted rapes, and 22.9 percent of threatened rapes take place during a date. Although a woman's behavior does not cause acquaintance rape, it appears that frequent or excessive drinking is a contributing factor.

Sexual assault and acquaintance rape results from multiple factors, including the offender's misperception of verbal and nonverbal cues, particularly when alcohol and drugs are involved. In fact, most men who commit acquaintance rape or sexual assault are not even aware that their behavior is offensive or unreasonable. Because alcohol slows motor functions, reducing the likelihood that a woman can verbally or physically resist an attack, the perpetrator often misinterprets this lack of resistance as consent.

Date Rape Drugs

There are also a variety of drugs that are used to overpower a woman's will, or even cause her to suffer blackouts during which time a sexual assault takes place. These drugs have become known as "date rape drugs." Although alcohol is the most commonly used date rape "drug," other nonalcoholic date rape drugs include marijuana, cocaine, rohypnol, gamma hydroxybutyrate (GHB), benzodiazepines, ketamine, barbiturates, chloral hydrate, methaqualone, heroin, morphine, LSD, and other hallucinogens. Because of the serious side effects of these drugs, and their impact on memory, victims who are given the drugs oftentimes cannot recall whether they were actually sexually assaulted.

UNDERREPORTING

According to the National Crime Victimization Survey, which includes statistics on reported and unreported crimes in America, sexual assault is one of the most underreported crimes. The FBI estimates that only 37% of all rapes are reported to the police. U.S. Justice Department statistics are even lower, estimating that only 26% of all rapes or attempted rapes are reported to law enforcement officials. Males are the least likely to report a sexual assault, though it is estimated they make up 10% of all victims.

PROSECUTION ISSUES

Burden of Proof

In prosecuting a sexual assault case, the issue of consent is of primary importance. If the victim was acquainted with the offender—e.g. date rape—it often becomes a matter of credibility unless there is further corroborating evidence, such as witnesses. However, some states have passed laws prohibiting law enforcement officers from requiring the victim of a sexual assault to submit to a polygraph test as a condition of beginning the criminal investigation. In addition, most states no longer require evidence that the victim attempted to physically resist the attacker, and in all 50 states, it is now a crime to sexually assault one's spouse.

Rape Shield Laws

The defense usually attempts to undermine the sex crime victim's credibility by exploring the victim's sexual history and reputation. It is because of this embarrassment that the majority of sexual assaults go unreported to police. Over the last two decades, many states have passed laws to reform the procedures for prosecuting sexual assault so that permissible evidence focuses on the specific facts of the alleged assault, rather than the victim's past sexual conduct. In fact, most states have passed legislation—known as "rape shield" laws—prohibiting the introduction of the victim's past sexual history into evidence.

In addition to these state laws, the Safe Streets for Women Act, as set forth in Chapter 1, amended the Federal Rules of Evidence to prohibit the admission of evidence offered to prove: (1) that a victim engaged in other sexual behavior; or (2) a victim's alleged sexual predisposition. The only exceptions to the federal rules apply in criminal cases where: (1) evidence of specific instances of sexual behavior by the victim is offered to prove that a person other than the accused was the actual perpetrator; (2) evidence of specific instances of sexual behavior by the victim with respect to the accused is offered to prove consent; and (3) the evidence, if excluded, would violate the defendant's constitutional rights.

In addition, in a civil case, evidence offered to prove the sexual behavior or sexual predisposition of a victim is admissible if its probative value substantially outweighs the danger of harm to any victim and unfair prejudice to any party. Nevertheless, evidence of a victim's reputation is admissible only if it has been placed in controversy by the victim.

Similar Crimes Evidence

The Violent Crime Control and Law Enforcement Act sets forth general rules of admissibility in federal sexual assault cases for evidence that the defendant has committed other similar offenses, facilitating the effective prosecution of habitual sex offenders. The new evidence rules provide the basis for informed decisions by juries regarding questions of propensity to commit future crimes in light of the defendant's past conduct.

This amendment to the Federal Rules of Evidence serves as a model for the states, which prosecute the majority of sex offense crimes. As the facts of the following case demonstrate, reforming state evidentiary rules to admit evidence of prior sexual offenses is crucial to ensuring the safety of women against sexual predators.

> Joey Sanza raped and murdered Theresa Cha when she came to meet her husband in the building where Mr. Sanza worked. There was extensive physical and circumstantial evidence that Mr. Sanza committed the crime. In addition, the jury was informed about three other rapes that Mr. Sanza had committed in another state.

> Mr. Sanza's other sexual offenses were relevant to help confirm his identity as Theresa Cha's attacker by showing his propensity and capacity to commit sexually violent crimes. Nevertheless, Sanza's conviction for raping and murdering Theresa Cha was reversed on appeal because the jury was told of his other crimes. People v. Sanza, 509 N.Y.S.2d 311 (App. Div. 1986).

Under the amended Federal Rules of Evidence, Mr. Sanza's conviction for rape and murder would have been upheld on appeal.

Confidential Communications for Rape Victims

Unfortunately, when a woman who has been victimized by sexual assault reports the crime and seeks help through counseling, she all too often finds herself victimized again when the attorney defending the sex offender issues subpoenas for her counseling records. Because many sexual assault and domestic violence counselors are not psychologists or psychotherapists, they cannot claim that such communications are privileged under many state statutes.

In order to encourage victims of sexual assault to report the crimes, the victims must be able to communicate freely and confidentially with their counselors. Without this guarantee of confidentiality, sexual assault and domestic violence victims will continue to be reluctant to report these serious crimes, and will avoid seeking necessary crisis intervention and counseling.

Establishing statutory testimonial privileges for sexual assault and domestic violence counselors helps to ensure that these important communications will remain confidential and that victims will not be reluctant to report the crimes and seek help. To address this important concern, the majority of states and the District of Columbia have enacted statutes that protect these confidential communications.

TREATMENT FOR SEX OFFENDERS

The Violence Against Women Act (VAWA) requires the Attorney General to ensure that relevant sex offender treatment information is provided to sex offenders prior to their release from prison. The Bureau of Prisons ("BOP") has coordinated these efforts with two offender treatment program information clearinghouses in the United States. The BOP, together with the U.S. Probation Office, is also ensuring that released sex offenders follow-up with community-based treatment.

SEX OFFENDER REGISTRATION AND COMMUNITY NOTIFICATION

In general, sex offender registration and community notification systems assist the investigation of sex crimes by informing law enforcement authorities of the identities and whereabouts of convicted sex offenders. These systems may also inhibit offenders—who know that the authorities know who they are and where they are—from committing additional crimes. Community notification enables communities to take common sense measures to protect themselves and their families, such as ensuring that their children do not associate or visit with known child molesters.

The Department of Justice ("DOJ") has implemented a number of provisions designed to stop sex offenders before they strike, as set forth in The Jacob Wetterling Crimes Against Children and Sexually Violent Offender Registration Act, which was strengthened by the subsequent "Megan's Law" amendment.

In addition, the DOJ has participated in state and federal litigation defending the validity of sex offender registration and notification systems in a number of jurisdictions. Most recently, it assisted in the successful defense of the validity of the New Jersey sex offender registration and notification system.

In 2006, Congress passed The Sex Offender Registration and Notification Act (SORNA) in order to strengthen the existing nationwide network of sex offender registration and notification programs, and to provide a comprehensive set of minimum standards for sex offender registration and notification in the United States. All jurisdictions must comply with the SORNA provisions by 2009.

SORNA is discussed more fully in Chapter 4 of this almanac.

CHAPTER 4:
THE SEX OFFENDER REGISTRATION AND NOTIFICATION ACT (SORNA)

IN GENERAL

The Sex Offender Registration and Notification Act (SORNA) is set forth in Title I of the Adam Walsh Child Protection and Safety Act of 2006 (Public Law 248-109). SORNA was enacted in order to strengthen the existing nationwide network of sex offender registration and notification programs, and to provide a comprehensive set of minimum standards for sex offender registration and notification in the United States.

Selected provisions of the Sex Offender Registration and Notification Act are set forth at Appendix 18.

Under SORNA, the registration requirement is expanded to include all 50 states, the District of Columbia, U.S. territories, and federally recognized Indian tribes. Jurisdictions must register incarcerated sex offenders before their release from imprisonment for the registration offense or, in case of a non-imprisonment sentence, within three business days of sentencing for the registration offense. Jurisdictions are also required to promptly share sex offender information among registration jurisdictions, and disclose much of the information to the general public and certain entities.

Jurisdictions that fail to substantially implement SORNA by July 27, 2009 are subject to a mandatory 10% reduction in funding under the Byrne Justice Assistance Grant (42 U.S.C. 3750 et seq.).

REGISTRATION REQUIREMENTS

Under SORNA, a sex offender must initially register in the jurisdiction in which convicted if it is different from the jurisdiction of residence. In addition, sex offenders are required to register and maintain current registration in each jurisdiction in which the sex offender resides, is an employee, or is a student. For example, if a sex offender resides in one jurisdiction but commutes to work in another jurisdiction, both jurisdictions must require the sex offender to register.

A sex offender who enters a jurisdiction to commence residency, employment or school attendance, must appear in person to register or update the registration within three business days. A sex offender who changes his or her place of residence, employment or school attendance within the same jurisdiction—e.g., from one county to another county in the same state—must appear in person to register or update the registration within three business days. The physical location of this in-person appearance requirement is controlled by the state of residency, employment or school attendance.

The provisions of SORNA are retroactive and thus they apply to all sex offenders, including those sex offenders convicted prior to the enactment of SORNA on July 27, 2006, or prior to a particular jurisdictions' implementation of the SORNA requirements. Jurisdictions are required to register pre-SORNA convicted sex offenders.

Failure to Register

Under SORNA, jurisdictions are required to assess a criminal penalty for the failure of a sex offender to comply with the law. The required criminal penalty must include a maximum term of imprisonment greater than one year. Indian tribes are not included in this requirement because tribal court jurisdiction does not extend to imposing terms of imprisonment exceeding one year.

Under the federal failure-to-register offense (18 U.S.C. 2250), a federal criminal penalty of up to 10 years of imprisonment may be assessed for sex offenders required to register under SORNA, who knowingly fail to register or update a registration as required, where circumstances supporting federal jurisdiction exist, e.g., a conviction of a federal sex offense for which registration is required.

A state convicted sex offender may also be prosecuted in the federal system for failure to register if the sex offender who was convicted or adjudicated delinquent in state court knowingly fails to register or update a registration as required, and the sex offender engages in interstate or international travel, or enters, leaves or resides in a tribal jurisdiction.

Maintaining a Current Registration

In order to maintain a current registration, a sex offender must appear in person, no later than three business days after each change of name, residence, employment, or student status, in at least one jurisdiction in which the sex offender is required to register and inform that jurisdiction of all changes in the required information for the sex offender registry. This information must be immediately provided to all other jurisdictions in which the sex offender is required to register.

Prior to relocating, jurisdictions must also require a sex offender to provide notice of their intent to move, including information about the jurisdiction to which he or she is going.

Personal Appearance Requirement

Under SORNA, sex offenders are required to appear in person from time to time to verify and update their registration information, and allow the jurisdiction to take a current photograph. A sex offender is required to appear according to the following timetable:

1. Tier I Sex Offender—Annually.

2. Tier II Sex Offender—Every six months.

3. Tier III Sex Offender—Every three months.

Sex offenders must carry out this schedule of personal appearances in all jurisdictions where they reside, are employed or attend school. Any jurisdiction may require personal appearances by sex offenders with greater frequency than the minimum required by SORNA.

Covered Sex Offense Convictions

SORNA requires registration for a more comprehensive group of sex offenses, including sex offense convictions in any U.S. jurisdiction whether under federal, military, state, territorial, tribal or local law. Foreign convictions are also covered if certain conditions are satisfied.

The following acts are considered sex offenses under SORNA:

1. Sexual Acts and Sexual Contact Offenses - This includes criminal offenses that have an element involving a sexual act or sexual contact with another, including all sexual offenses whose elements involve: (i) any type or degree of genital, oral, or anal penetration, or (ii) any sexual touching of or contact with a person's body, either directly or through the clothing.

2. Specified Offenses Against Minors—This includes a criminal offense that is a specified offense against a minor as defined in the Act.

3. Specified Federal Offenses—This includes most sexual offenses under federal law.

4. Specified Military Offenses—This includes sex offenses under the Uniform Code of Military Justice, as specified by the Secretary of Defense.

5. Attempts and Conspiracies—This includes attempts and conspiracies to commit offenses that are otherwise covered by the definition of sex offenses.

Required Sex Offender Registration Information

Sex offenders are required to provide the following information for the sex offender registry:

1. Names, including all aliases used by the sex offender.

2. Date of birth, including both actual date of birth and any false date(s) of birth used by the sex offender.

3. All Internet identifiers and addresses, such as e-mail and instant messaging addresses.

4. All telephone numbers, including both land lines and cell phone numbers.

5. Social Security Numbers, including both valid governmentally assigned social security numbers and any other social security numbers used by the sex offender.

6. Residence address.

7. Other residence information for sex offenders who do not have a residence address for whatever reason, e.g., due to homelessness or living in a rural or tribal area that does not have a street address.

8. Temporary lodging information, including any place in which the sex offender is staying for 7 or more days.

9. Passport and immigration document information.

10. Employer's name and address.

11. Other employment information, e.g., if the sex offender has no fixed place of employment, such as travel routes.

12. Professional licenses.

13. School name and address.

14. Vehicle information, including a description of the vehicle and the license plate and/or registration number.

15. A physical description of the sex offender.

16. Text of the registration offense or offenses.

17. Criminal history and other criminal justice information.

18. A current photograph.

19. Fingerprints.

20. Palm prints.

21. DNA information.

22. Driver's license or identification card.

PUBLIC ACCESS SEX OFFENDER WEBSITES

In order to comply with SORNA, certain registry information about each sex offender that lives, works, or goes to school in a particular jurisdiction must be included on that jurisdiction's public access sex offender website.

Required Disclosure

The following registry information must be included:

1. The name of the sex offender, including all aliases.

2. The address of each residence at which the sex offender resides or will reside and, if the sex offender does not have a present or expected residence address, any other information about where the sex offender has his or her home or habitually lives. If the sex offender is in violation of this registration requirement, or unable to be located, the sex offender website must note this fact.

3. The address of any place where the sex offender is an employee or will be an employee and, if the sex offender is employed but does not have a definite employment address, any other information about where the sex offender works.

4. The address of any place where the sex offender is a student or will be a student.

5. The license plate number and a description of any vehicle owned or operated by the sex offender.

6. A physical description of the sex offender.

7. The text of the sex offense for which the sex offender is registered and any other sex offense for which the sex offender has been convicted.

8. A current photograph of the sex offender.

Information Exempt from Public Access

Jurisdictions must exempt four types of information from disclosure on their public access sex offender websites, however, this information may be disclosed to other entities, such as to law enforcement agencies. The four types of exempt information include:

1. The victim's identity.

2. The social security number of the sex offender.

3. Any reference to arrests of the sex offender that did not result in conviction.

4. Passport and immigration document numbers.

Optional Exemptions

Under the law, at the discretion of the jurisdiction, the following information may also be exempt from public access:

1. Any information about a Tier I sex offender convicted of an offense other than a specified offense against a minor.

2. The name of an employer of the sex offender.

3. The name of an educational institution where the sex offender is a student.

4. Any other information that the Attorney General allows to be exempted.

Nevertheless, jurisdictions are permitted to include this information on their public access sex offender websites if they wish to do so.

INFORMATION-SHARING REQUIREMENTS

Under SORNA, after a sex offender registers or updates a registration, all registry information not exempt from disclosure by the Attorney General must be provided to the following entities and individuals:

1. National databases.

2. Law enforcement and supervision agencies.

3. Any jurisdiction where the sex offender resides, is an employee, or is a student, and each jurisdiction from or to which a change of residence, employment, or student status occurs.

4. Any agency responsible for conducting employment-related background checks under Section 3 of the National Child Protection Act of 1993.

5. Each school and public housing agency in each area in which the sex offender resides, is an employee, or is a student.

6. Social service entities responsible for protecting minors in the child welfare system.

7. Volunteer organizations in which contact with minors or other vulnerable individuals might occur.

8. Any organization, company, or individual who requests such notification pursuant to procedures established by the jurisdiction.

REGISTRATION DURATION REQUIREMENTS

SORNA specifies the minimum required duration of sex offender registration as follows:

1. Tier I Sex Offender—15 years

2. Tier II Sex Offender—25 years

3. Their III Sex Offender—Life

The registration period begins to run upon release from custody for a sex offender sentenced to incarceration for the registration offense, or in the case of a non-incarcerated sex offender, at the time of sentencing for the sex offense.

Under SORNA, jurisdictions are allowed to reduce the registration period for a Tier I sex offender by 5 years after the sex offender maintains a clean record for 10 years. In addition, the jurisdiction may terminate registration for a sex offender who is required to register under SORNA based on juvenile delinquency adjudication, after the sex offender maintains a clean record for 25 years.

Achieving a clean record means:

1. The sex offender must not be convicted of any offense for which imprisonment for more than one year may be imposed.

2. The sex offender must not be convicted of any sex offense regardless of the penalty.

3. The sex offender must successfully complete any periods of supervised release, probation, and parole.

4. The sex offender must successfully complete an appropriate sex offender treatment program certified by a jurisdiction or by the Attorney General.

PROVISIONS FOR JUVENILE SEX OFFENDERS

Under SORNA, a juvenile who is prosecuted and convicted of a sex offense as an adult is treated identical to an adult sex offender. Juvenile offenders not prosecuted as adults are not required to register unless: (i) the offender is 14 years of age or older at the time of the offense; and (ii) has been adjudicated delinquent for an offense comparable to, or more severe than, the crime of aggravated sexual abuse as set forth in 18 U.S.C. 2241, or an attempt or conspiracy to commit such an offense.

State offenses that are comparable to the federal offense include:

1. Engaging in a sexual act with another by force or the threat of serious violence (see 18 U.S.C. 2241(a));

2. Engaging in a sexual act with another by rendering the victim unconscious or drugging the victim involuntarily (see 18 U.S.C. 2241(b)); or

3. Engaging in a sexual act with a child under the age of 12 (see 18 U.S.C. 2241(c)).

THE SMART OFFICE

SORNA established the Office of Sex Offender Sentencing, Monitoring, Apprehending, Registering, and Tracking (the "SMART Office"). The SMART Office is a component of the Office of Justice Programs within the U.S. Department of Justice, authorized by law to administer the SORNA standards for sex offender registration and notification. The SMART Office is further authorized to cooperate with and provide assistance to states, local governments, tribal governments, and other public and private entities regarding sex offender registration and notification, and other measures designed to protect the public from sexual abuse or exploitation.

THE DRU SJODIN NATIONAL SEX OFFENDER PUBLIC REGISTRY

On November 22, 2003, Dru Kathrina Sjodin, a student at the University of North Dakota, left the mall where she worked in Grand Forks, North Dakota. On December 1st, a 50-year-old registered level III sex offender named Alfonso Rodriguez was arrested in connection with Dru's disappearance. Rodriguez had been released from jail in May of 2003 after completing a 23-year prison term for stabbing and trying to kidnap a woman. Rodriguez had also previously pleaded guilty to raping another woman.

On April 17, 2004, Dru's body was recovered after the large snowdrifts began to melt. Her body was found partially nude and face down in a ravine. Her hands were tied behind her back and she had been beaten, stabbed, sexually assaulted, and had several lacerations including a five and a half inch cut on her neck. A rope was also tied around her neck and remnants of a shopping bag were found under the rope suggesting that a bag had been placed on her head. On August 30, 2006, Rodriguez was found guilty and on September 22, 2006, he was sentenced to death.

In 2006, legislation dubbed "Dru's Law," which set up the Dru Sjodin National Sex Offender Public Registry was passed in Dru's memory, and signed into law by President George W. Bush. The Dru Sjodin National Sex Offender Public Registry, coordinated by the Department of Justice, is a cooperative effort between the state agencies hosting public sexual offender registries and the federal government. This website (http://www.nsopr.gov/) is a search tool that allows a user to submit a single national query to obtain information about sex offenders through a number of search options, e.g., by name, zip code, county, city, town and/or state.

The criteria for searching the website are limited to what each individual state may provide. Also, because information is hosted by each state and not by the federal government, search results should be verified by the user in the state where the information is posted. Users are advised to log on to pertinent state websites for further information and/or guidance, as appropriate.

CHAPTER 5:
STALKING

IN GENERAL

The term "stalking" describes any unwanted contact by an individual—referred to as a "stalker"—and his or her victim, which places the victim in fear for his or her safety. However, the legal definition of stalking varies according to state law, which may specifically define prohibited stalking behavior.

The act of stalking is not new. It is essentially conduct which was previously described as a form of harassment. The act of stalking is now categorized as a separate offense, in large part due to the number of celebrity victims who have been subjected to stalking.

Stalking behaviors may include:

1. Following the victim;

2. Repeated, unwanted, intrusive, and frightening communications from the perpetrator by phone, mail, and/or email;

3. Repeatedly leaving or sending victim unwanted notes, items, presents, or flowers;

4. Showing up at the victim's place of business, home, school or recreation place;

5. Vandalizing or threatening to damage the victim's property;

6. Making direct or indirect threats to harm the victim, the victim's children, relatives, friends, or pets;

7. Harassing victim through the Internet—a practice known as "cyberstalking;"

8. Posting information or spreading rumors about the victim on the Internet, in a public place, or by word of mouth;

9. Gathering personal information about the victim by accessing public records, using internet search services, hiring private investigators, going through the victim's garbage; and

10. Contacting the victim's friends, family, work, or neighbors, and making inquiries about the victim.

The stalker's actions may or may not culminate in violent behavior. As set forth below, the legal definition of stalking varies according to state law, which may specifically define prohibited stalking behavior.

STALKING STATISTICS

According to recent studies by the U.S. Department of Justice and the National Center for Victims of Crime (NCVC):

1. 1,006,970 women and 370, 990 men are stalked annually in the United States.

2. 78% of stalking victims are women.

3. Women are significantly more likely than men (60 percent and 30 percent, respectively) to be stalked by intimate partners.

4. 503,485 women are stalked annually by an intimate partner.

5. 80% of women who are stalked by former husbands are physically assaulted by that partner.

6. 30% of women who are stalked by former husbands are sexually assaulted by that partner.

7. 77% of female and 64 percent of male victims know their stalker.

8. 82% of stalkers who pursued female victims followed them, spied on them, stood outside their home, place of work, or recreation.

9. 61% of stalkers made unwanted phone calls.

10. 33% of stalkers sent or left unwanted letters or items.

11. 29% of stalkers vandalized property.

12. 9 % of stalkers killed or threatened to kill a family pet.

13. Most victims are stalked for 1.8 years

PROFILE OF A STALKING VICTIM

A stalking victim can be either male or female, however, most victims are female. Most stalking victims are acquainted with their stalker, who is generally alone. This is particularly so in the case of women, who are most often stalked by a current or former spouse, or a boyfriend. Studies indicate that the stalking behavior in such cases often ceases when the stalker begins a relationship with a new partner.

Men are more likely to be stalked by a stranger, and half of the time, the stalkers have an accomplice. Young adults are most often the victims of stalking. In fact, more than one-half of all stalking victims are age 18 to 29.

PROFILE OF A STALKER

Although most stalkers are male, a stalker can be any gender. Stalkers come from all types of backgrounds. Forensic psychologists generally place stalkers in one of three broad categories: (i) Love Obsession Stalkers; (ii) Simple Obsession Stalkers; (iii) Erotomanic Stalkers.

Love Obsession Stalkers

A love obsession stalker is one who becomes fixated on an individual with whom they have no relationship, e.g. a total stranger or someone who they barely know. Love obsession stalkers accounts for approximately one-fourth of all stalking behavior.

Psychologists believe that most love obsession stalkers suffer from schizophrenia or paranoia which is manifested in delusional thoughts and behavior. Their inability to function normally in relationships causes them to create a fantasy life in which their victim plays an important role as their love interest. They then proceed to try and live out this fantasy life.

Of course, the victims are unaware of their role in this obsession, and are unwilling to participate. In turn, this causes the stalker concern as he or she tries to make the victim conform to his or her role. The stalker may resort to threats, intimidation, and even violence, so that their fantasy can be brought to fruition.

Simple Obsession Stalkers

A simple obsession stalker is one who is obsessed with an individual with whom they had a previous personal relationship. This category makes up the majority of stalking behavior. The simple obsession stalker is commonly an ex-husband or partner who desires to control his former partner. "Fatal attraction" stalkers—individuals who become obsessed during a casual short-term relationship—also fall under this category.

Simple obsession stalkers generally do not have a mental disorder as do love obsession stalkers, however, psychologists do believe these individuals suffer serious personality disorders, similar to those exhibited by physical abusers in domestic violence situations.

The characteristics which appear to be common to all simple obsession stalkers, include:

1. The inability to maintain relationships;

2. Extreme jealousy and possessiveness;

3. Emotional immaturity and insecurity;

4. Low self-esteem; and

5. The need to control their partners through intimidation and/or violence.

Thus, once their partner leaves, this rejection causes their self-esteem to plummet as they become paranoid about their loss of control over that person. They become obsessed with regaining possession and total control over their former partner. If they are unable to do so, they often resort to violence—e.g., "if I can't have him/her, nobody else will." In fact, there is a very high incidence of spousal murder associated with domestic violence victims who decide to leave their partners.

Nevertheless, the behavior of stalkers is often unpredictable. That is what makes the crime so dangerous. The perpetrator may be sending love letters and roses one day, and the following day, may physically assault the object of their obsession. Conversely, the stalker may engage in non-threatening stalking behavior for many, many months without ever escalating to a more aggressive stage.

Erotomanic Stalkers

Similar to love obsession stalkers, the erotomanic stalker suffers from a delusional belief that they are passionately loved by another. They go to great lengths to contact the person of their delusion, usually a person of higher socio-economic class and status, or an unattainable public figure. These stalkers are often described as celebrity stalkers or obsessed fans.

ANTI-STALKING LEGISLATION

California Anti-Stalking Law

In 1990, California became the first state to pass a law which specifically defined stalking as a crime. This action was taken in response to several cases in which stalking victims were eventually murdered. These victims had previously tried to make complaints to the police about the stalking behavior, however, the existing law required that the offender take some affirmative action before they could make an arrest. This requirement was changed with the new stalking law, permitting police to intervene at an earlier stage. A 1999 amendment to the law added prohibitions on the use of the internet and other electronic means for stalking.

State Anti-Stalking Laws

After California enacted its anti-stalking statute, all states followed by enacting some type of anti-stalking legislation. Although the specific provisions may vary state by state, they all generally prohibit stalking behaviors that are intimidating and place the victim in fear for his or her safety. Most states statutes define stalking as the willful, malicious, and repeated following and harassing of another person. Some of the statutes identify specific acts of stalking, such as surveillance, telephone harassment, vandalism, and specify how many acts of stalking must occur in order to qualify as stalking. Many statutes also require that the alleged stalker must make a credible threat of violence against the victim to be actionable whereas some statutes deem the stalking conduct itself as the credible threat.

The reader is advised to check the law of his or her own jurisdiction for specific provisions of their state anti-stalking law.

The Violence Against Women Act of 1994

As set forth in Chapter 1, Subtitle F of the Violence Against Women Act (VAWA), entitled National Stalker and Domestic Violence Reduction, addresses the problem of stalking. The law prohibits an individual from crossing state lines for the purposes of stalking his or her victim. The law also authorizes federal and state criminal justice agents to enter data into—and access information from—local, state and national crime information databases. These databases contain identification records, criminal history records, protection orders and wanted person records concerning individuals who have been arrested or convicted on stalking charges, or for whom arrest warrants or protection orders for stalking are pending.

The Interstate Anti-Stalking Punishment and Prevention Act

The Interstate Anti-Stalking Punishment and Prevention Act was enacted by Congress in 1996 in order to improve existing anti-stalking provisions and create a uniform federal law to protect stalking victims when they travel across state lines. Anyone who travels across state lines with the intent to injure or harass another person, and in the course of such travel, places that person in reasonable fear of death or serious bodily injury to that person or a member of his or her immediate family, would be in violation of federal law. The Act also applies to stalking behavior which take place on all federal property, including military installations, and when entering or exiting Indian territory. A violation of the statute is a felony.

The Violence Against Women Act of 2005

As set forth in Chapter 1, the Violence Against Women Act of 2005 (VAWA-2005) was enacted to strengthen the existing provisions and provide additional safeguards.

Title I: Crimes and Courts—The Grants to Encourage Arrest and Enforce Protection Orders Program—This section established the Family Justice Center program, added stalking to the scope of work authorized; and encourages community policing protocols in addressing stalking.

Title II: Services and Outreach—Services for Victims of Abuse Later in Life—This section authorizes grants for providing services for stalking victims over age 60.

Title II: Services and Outreach—Public Education Campaigns—This section provides grants for public information campaigns targeting stalking.

Title II: Services and Outreach—Rural Services for Victims Program—This section expands program coverage to stalking victims.

Title III: Children and Youth—The original VAWA and VAWA 2000 focused primarily on violence against adult women. This section provides treatment and education of youth and young adults who witness or experience domestic violence, dating violence, sexual assault or stalking.

Title VI: Housing—This section authorizes a grant program to help public and Indian housing authorities and assisted housing providers respond to domestic violence, dating violence, sexual assault and stalking in a way that protects victims while holding perpetrators accountable.

SAFETY STRATEGIES AND TIPS

Under no circumstances should the victim contact the stalker. However, when dealing with a former partner who is engaged in stalking conduct, one must advise the stalker, in a firm and direct manner, that they do not wish to be contacted. Avoid any language that sounds unsure that the stalker may misinterpret as the possibility of another chance.

A stalking victim who is being subjected to particularly threatening behavior should go to the nearest police station and immediately report the crime. If it is not possible to find a nearby police station at the time, safety may be sought at a church, shelter or other public place where a stalker is less likely to make a scene. Until the situation is brought under control, the stalking victim may consider relocating to a location where he or she will not be found.

If the danger is not imminent, but the potential for violence is there, a stalking victim should consider petitioning the court for an order of protection, as discussed in Chapter 2 of this almanac. Again, however, the reader is cautioned that an order of protection is merely a piece of paper, and will not stop a perpetrator who is intent on harming his or her victim.

In the meantime, one must make sure that their personal information is kept private, including their address, telephone number, and social security number. The stalking victim should have an unpublished and unlisted telephone number, and should change their e-mail address if they are being harassed on the internet.

INTERNET STALKING

As the worldwide web developed and became more accessible to the average citizen, stalkers found a new medium through which to harass their victims. Law enforcement agencies estimate that electronic communications are a factor in a large percentage of all stalking cases.

Internet stalking, also known as "cyberstalking," is popular with stalkers because of the relative anonymity of the system. Many stalkers who have been deterred from physically stalking their victim due to a restraining order or threatened criminal prosecution, turn to the internet to carry on their behaviors. Threatening and harassing e-mails can be sent to victims from virtually any computer with internet access.

The majority of state laws now explicitly include electronic forms of communication within stalking or harassment laws. Statutes that do not include specific references to electronic communication may still apply to those who threaten or harass others through the internet.

ESTABLISHING PROBABLE CAUSE

Although stalking laws no longer require the victim to wait until the stalker takes some affirmative action, the victim is still required to provide sufficient evidence to establish probable cause that the perpetrator engaged in illegal conduct. The victim is advised to keep a journal documenting each stalking incident. Photographs and videotapes, voice mail messages, correspondence and witness affidavits are types of evidence that may be used to establish probable cause.

The victim should also obtain a copy of their state anti-stalking statute to find out what behavior constitutes a stalking offense so that the proof obtained will convince law enforcement that a violation has taken place. The evidence should be taken to the appropriate law enforcement official. If they refuse to investigate the conduct, the victim should take their case to the local district attorney's office and speak with a prosecutor.

CHAPTER 6:
TEENAGE DATING VIOLENCE

IN GENERAL

Teenage dating violence is characterized by controlling, abusive, and aggressive behavior in a romantic relationship. Dating violence occurs regardless of the gender, race, or socioeconomic background of the victim and offender, and takes place in both heterosexual and homosexual relationships. Some teen victims experience occasional violence while others are abused on a daily basis. As an abusive dating relationship becomes more serious, the potential for violence increases.

Boys and girls are both potential victims of dating violence, however, the abusive behaviors involved are different. For example, girls may scream, scratch, kick, pinch, bite, and try to manipulate their partner by threatening self-mutilation or suicide. Boys will likely inflict greater injury to a girl, and the violent behavior often involves forcing a partner to engage in unwanted sexual activity.

RECOGNIZING ABUSIVE DATING BEHAVIOR

Abusive dating behavior can include physical, sexual, verbal and emotional abuse. The offender usually tries to exercise control over the victim. Among teenagers, this may include isolating their partner from friends and family; controlling how their partner acts and dresses; accompanying the victim at all times or maintaining frequent contact to monitor their partner's activities. Extreme possessiveness and jealousy are indicators of potential violence. Name-calling, threatening violence, engaging in physical violence, and forcing the victim to engage in unwanted sexual acts are all examples of abuse.

Victims of dating violence often remain in these abusive relationships. This may be because they believe they love their partner and feel disloyal if they leave the relationship. Some victims blame themselves for the violence. Other victims are afraid of their perpetrators and fear the consequences if they leave. In addition, due to immaturity, many teenage girls misinterpret indicators of potentially abusive behavior, such as jealousy, as a sign of love.

STATISTICS

According to the U.S. Department of Justice:

1. One of five teens in a serious relationship reports having been hit, slapped, or pushed by a partner.

2. Approximately one in five female high school students reports being physically and/or sexually abused by a dating partner (U.S. Department of Justice).

3. 40% of girls age 14 to 17 report knowing someone their age who has been hit or beaten by a boyfriend (U.S. Department of Justice).

4. Young women, ages 16-24, experience the highest rates of relationship violence.

5. Approximately one in 10 teens has been verbally or physically abused by a boyfriend or girlfriend who was drunk or high on drugs.

6. 14% of teens report having been threatened with physical harm to avoid a breakup.

7. Homosexual teenagers are as likely to experience violence in their dating relationships as those involved in heterosexual relationships.

8. Among older teens, the percentage of violent crime involving an intimate partner was 10 times higher for females than males.

9. Many studies indicate that as a dating relationship becomes more serious, the potential for and nature of violent behavior also escalates.

10. In 2001, more than 97,000 students between the ages of 18 and 24 were victims of alcohol-related sexual assault or date rape.

11. 12% of respondents in a study on violence against women reported having been stalked before the age of 18.

12. 20% of teenage girls and young women have experienced some type of dating violence.

13. 32% of college students report dating violence by a previous partner, and 21% report violence by a current partner.

14. 39% - 54% of dating violence victims remain in physically abusive relationships.

15. 12% of completed rapes, 35% of attempted rapes, and 22% of threatened rapes occur on a date.

16. 60% of acquaintance rapes on college campuses occur in casual or steady dating relationships.

17. An estimated 5% of college women experience a completed or attempted rape in a given year.

18. In one year, more than 13% of college women indicated they had been stalked, 42% by a boyfriend or ex-boyfriend.

19. 51% of college males admit perpetrating one or more sexual assault incidents during college.

20. 75% of men and 55% of women involved in acquaintance rape had been drinking or taking drugs prior to the incident.

REPORTING VIOLENCE

Many teenagers believe that dating violence is a private matter, or it is not important enough to report. Many fear reprisal from their perpetrators and helpless to stop the abuse. Many feel threatened and humiliated. Many dating violence victims blame themselves for what happened to them and try to protect their partner.

Unfortunately, statistics demonstrate that only half of all dating violence victims report the violence to someone else. The majority (80%) of victims reported the violence to a friend while only 20% reported the violence to criminal justice authorities. In addition, only 44% of victims who are raped by a steady boyfriend or spouse report the assault whereas 77% of victims raped by strangers contact law enforcement authorities.

All 50 states and the District of Columbia have laws against crimes associated with dating violence, including sexual assault, domestic violence, and stalking, although the specific term "dating violence" is rarely used in these laws.

PROTECTION ORDERS

The teenager who escapes an abusive relationship may need a court order to protect the teen from the abuser, regardless of whether he or she has sought criminal prosecution of the offender. Although adult victims of domestic violence often obtain an order of protection against their offender, such orders are not available to teenage victims in many states.

According to the Dating Violence Resource Center, all state protection order laws cover dating partners who have a child in common, who are currently or formerly living together, or those who have been involved in an intimate relationship. However, only 19 states and the District of Columbia permit teenage victims to obtain a protection order without being represented by a parent or legal guardian. In 10 of those states, it is up to the judge to decide whether the teenager can petition the court on their own.

Insofar as studies have shown that most teenagers do not tell their parents about the abuse they have suffered in a relationship, it is unlikely that they will seek help if parental representation is required. Thus, they often remain in the violent relationship.

If the teenage victim is able to secure a protection order, she must renew the order periodically for it to remain in effect. The average duration of a protection order is one year, although some states have no time limit while others are very short-lived. Nevertheless, all states will renew or extend a protection order at the victim's request.

A table of state protection order provisions is set forth at Appendix 19 of this almanac.

GETTING HELP

Studies demonstrate that dating violence victims experience more anxiety, depression, and thoughts of suicide than non-victims. Their initial reactions to rape and sexual assault include anger, sadness, loneliness, confusion, depression, embarrassment, and guilt. Thus, they should be encouraged to seek help.

Crisis hotlines can provide immediate assistance to victims, and referrals to sexual assault or domestic violence programs that provide advocacy, counseling, safety planning, legal assistance, emergency shelter, and support groups. School-based student assistance programs, guidance offices, and school resource officers can provide referrals for help. In addition, campus police or school judicial programs can provide guidance on school policies and assess sanctions for violent behavior by students on campus.

It should be noted that certain adults are mandatory reporters, which means that they are legally obligated to report suspected neglect or abuse to a child protective service or the police. If you do not want law enforcement or social services involvement, you should ask the people you plan to confide in whether they are mandated reporters. Some examples of mandated reporters include but are not limited to teachers, counselors, doctors, and social workers.

ROLE OF THE OFFICE ON VIOLENCE AGAINST WOMEN

Preventing teenage dating violence is a priority of the Office on Violence Against Women (OVW). In 2002, the OVW funded the national Teen Dating Violence Resource Center at the National Center for Victims of Crime. This Center provides training, resources and information to communities and programs throughout the country.

The OVW, along with the Centers for Disease Control and Prevention (CDC), has also collaborated on a 2006 initiative developed by the CDC called "Choose Respect," which is aimed at preventing teenage dating violence through education and early detection. The program is designed to teach adolescents how to form healthy relationships.

CHAPTER 7:
BATTERED IMMIGRANT
WOMEN AND CHILDREN

IN GENERAL

Women and children make up two-thirds of all legal immigrants in the United States and, like all women, immigrant women are at risk for domestic violence. However, immigrant women often face unique obstacles in escaping their abusers, in large part due to their immigration status. Many immigrant women feel trapped in their relationship with the abuser, due to language barriers, lack of financial resources, and unfamiliarity with the law and their rights.

The following facts and statistics compiled by the Family Violence Prevention Fund demonstrate the extent of the problem:

A recent study in New York City found that 51 percent of intimate partner homicide victims were foreign-born, while 45 percent were born in the United States.

Forty-eight percent of Latin women in one study reported that their partner's violence against them had increased since they immigrated to the United States.

A survey of immigrant Korean women found that 60 percent had been battered by their husbands.

Married immigrant women experience higher levels of physical and sexual abuse (59.5%) than unmarried immigrant women (49.8%).

Immigrant women often suffer higher rates of battering than U.S. citizens because they may come from cultures that accept domestic violence or because they have less access to legal and social services than U.S. citizens.

Immigrant batterers and victims may believe that the penalties and protections of the U.S. legal system do not apply to them.

Battered immigrant women may not be able to obtain social services assistance or report complaints to the law enforcement or court personnel due to the language barrier and lack of available interpreters.

PROTECTION UNDER THE VIOLENCE AGAINST WOMEN ACT (VAWA)

Generally, U.S. citizens and Lawful Permanent Residents (LPRs) can file an immigrant visa petition with the U.S. Citizenship and Immigration Services (USCIS) on behalf of their spouse or child, so that these family members may emigrate to or remain in the United States. In order to do so, the U.S. citizen or LPR petitioner files a Petition for Alien Relative (USCIS Form I-130) on behalf of the family member. The petitioner chooses when and whether to file a visa petition, and can revoke the petition at any time prior to the issuance of permanent residency to their spouse.

Unfortunately, some U.S. citizens and LPRs misuse their control of this process to abuse their family members. They use the threat of withdrawing the petition and having the spouse deported as a means of controlling the abused spouse and keeping them in the violent relationship. These threats also prevent the abused spouse from reporting the offender to law enforcement authorities.

To address this problem, Subtitle G of the Violence Against Women Act of 1994 (VAWA), entitled Protections for Battered Immigrant Women and Children, was enacted. Subtitle G provides statutory protection to certain battered immigrant spouses and children of U.S. citizens or LPRs, allowing them to "self-petition" for immigration classification and/or avoid deportation without the consent or knowledge of the abuser. The VAWA provisions relating to immigration are codified in Section 204(a) of the Immigration and Nationality Act (INA), as more fully discussed below.

ELIGIBILITY FOR SELF-PETITIONING

Under the law, a qualified spouse or child is entitled to self-petition for immigrant classification based on their relationship to the abusive citizen or lawful permanent resident of the United States, and further allows certain abused spouses and children who have been continuously physically present in the United States for the past 3 years to apply for suspension of deportation.

A spouse who is self-petitioning for immigrant classification must show that:

1. The self-petitioner is the spouse of a citizen or lawful permanent resident of the United States;

2. The self-petitioner is eligible for immigrant classification under section 201(b)(2)(A)(i) or 203(a)(2)(A) of the INA based on that relationship;

3. The self-petitioner resides in the United States;

4. The self-petitioner has resided in the United States with the citizen or lawful permanent resident spouse;

5. The self-petitioner has been battered by, or has been the subject of extreme cruelty perpetrated by, the citizen or lawful permanent resident during the marriage; or is the parent of a child who has been battered by, or has been the subject of extreme cruelty perpetrated by, the citizen or lawful permanent resident during the marriage;

6. The self-petitioner is a person of good moral character;

7. The self-petitioner is a person whose deportation would result in extreme hardship to the petitioner or the petitioner's child; and

8. The self-petitioner entered into the marriage to the citizen or lawful permanent resident in good faith.

Changes in the abuser's citizenship or lawful permanent resident status will not affect the validity of an approved self-petition. This regulatory provision eliminates the possibility that an abuser could recapture control over the abused spouse's immigration classification by changing his or her own immigration status.

In addition, an approved self-petition will not be revoked solely because the abuser subsequently abandons lawful permanent resident status, renounces United States citizenship, is deported, or otherwise changes immigration status.

REQUIREMENT OF PRESENT MARRIAGE

The law provides that the battered spouse must be presently married to a citizen or lawful permanent resident of the United States. There are no provisions for filing a self-petition based on a former spousal relationship. Therefore, the self-petitioning spouse must be legally married to the abuser when the petition is filed or the petition will be denied. This is so whether the marriage ended by annulment, death, or divorce before the petition was filed.

Although the law does not allow the petitioner to file a self-petition based on a former spousal relationship, it directs the U.S. Citizenship and Immigration Services (USCIS) not to revoke approval of a self-petition solely because the marriage has legally ended. This statutory provision protects the self-petitioner against an abuser's attempt to regain control over the petitioning process through legal termination of the marriage.

Although the law requires the marriage to be legally valid at the time of filing, and specifies that its termination after approval will not be the sole basis for revocation, it does not address the effect of a legal termination occurring between the filing and the approval of the self-petition. In the absence of explicit legislative guidelines, the USCIS has determined that protection for spouses whose self-petitions have been approved should be extended to cover the entire period after the self-petition is filed.

EFFECT OF REMARRIAGE

If the self-petitioner chooses to remarry while the petition is pending, the self-petitioner has established a new spousal relationship and has shown that he or she no longer needs the protection of the law to equalize the balance of power in the relationship with the abuser. Thus, the petition will be denied.

However, if the new husband or wife is a citizen or lawful permanent resident of the United States, he or she may file for the former self-petitioner's classification as an immigrant. The self-petitioner also would not be precluded from filing a self-petition based on the new family relationship if the new spouse is an abusive citizen or lawful permanent resident of the United States.

EVIDENCE OF MARRIAGE

Primary evidence of a marital relationship is a marriage certificate issued by civil authorities and proof of the termination of all prior marriages, if any, of both the self-petitioner and the abuser.

Primary evidence of the abuser's U.S. citizenship or lawful permanent residence is:

1. A birth certificate issued by a civil authority establishing the abuser's birth in the United States;

2. The abuser's unexpired full-validity United States passport;

3. A statement issued by a U.S. consular officer certifying the abuser to be a U.S. citizen and the bearer of a currently valid U.S. passport;

4. The abuser's Certificate of Naturalization or Certificate of Citizenship;

5. A Department of State Form FS-240, Report of Birth Abroad of a Citizen of the United States, relating to the abuser; or

6. Any proof given by the USCIS as evidence of lawful permanent residence.

If primary or secondary evidence of an abuser's immigration or citizenship status is not available, the law provides that the USCIS will attempt to electronically verify the abuser's status from information contained in USCIS computerized records. Other USCIS records may also be reviewed at the discretion of the adjudicating officer.

MARRIAGE FRAUD

Self-petitioners are subject to certain provisions of the Immigration Marriage Fraud Amendments of 1986 (IMFA), which were enacted by Congress to detect and deter immigration-related marriage fraud. Thus, a petition must be denied under the provisions of section 204(c) of the INA if there is substantial and probative evidence that the self-petitioner has ever attempted or conspired to enter into a marriage for the purpose of evading the immigration laws.

The self-petitioner need not have been convicted of, or even prosecuted for, the attempt or conspiracy, nor is it necessary for the self-petitioner to have received a benefit thereby. The mere evidence of the attempt or conspiracy must be contained in the self-petitioner's immigration file.

In addition, Section 204(g) of the INA prohibits the approval of a self-petition if the marriage creating the relationship to the citizen or permanent resident took place while the self-petitioner was in deportation, exclusion, or related proceedings, unless the self-petitioner provides clear and convincing evidence that the marriage was not entered into for the purpose of obtaining immigration benefits.

RESIDENCE IN THE UNITED STATES WITH THE ABUSER

The law requires that the self-petitioner lived with the abuser in the United States. A self-petition will not be approved if the self-petitioner is not living in the United States or has never lived with the abuser in the United States. Under the provisions of this rule, however, the self-petitioner is not required to be residing with the abuser when the petition is filed.

"Residence" is defined in Section 101(a)(33) of the INA as a person's general place of abode. It is also described as a person's principal, actual dwelling place in fact, without regard to intent. A self-petitioner cannot meet the residency requirements by merely visiting the United States or visiting the abuser's home in the United States while continuing to maintain a general place of abode or principal dwelling place elsewhere.

However, the self-petitioner is not required to have lived in the United States or with the abuser in the United States for any specific length of time. A qualified self-petitioner may have moved to the United States only recently, made any number of trips abroad, or resided with the abuser in the United States for only a short time.

Evidence of residency with the abuser in the United States may take many forms, including:

1. Employment records;

2. Utility receipts;

3. School records;

4. Hospital or medical records;

5. Birth certificates of children born to the spouses in the United States;

6. Deeds, mortgages, and leases; or

7. Insurance policies.

A self-petitioner may also submit affidavits to establish residency with the abuser. Self-petitioners who file affidavits are encouraged to provide the affidavits of more than one person. Other types of evidence may also be submitted as the USCIS will consider any relevant credible evidence.

EVIDENCE OF BATTERY OR EXTREME CRUELTY

The law requires a self-petitioning spouse to have been battered, or the subject of extreme cruelty, by the citizen or lawful permanent resident spouse; or to be the parent of a child who was battered, or the subject of extreme cruelty, by the citizen or lawful permanent resident during the marriage.

This law further specifies that only certain types of abuse will qualify a spouse to self-petition. The qualifying abuse must have taken place during the marriage to the abuser. Battery or extreme cruelty that happened at other times is not qualifying abuse. However, there is no limit on the time that may have elapsed since the last incident of qualifying abuse occurred.

The qualifying abuse also must have been committed by the abusive citizen or lawful permanent resident spouse or parent. Battery or extreme cruelty committed by any other person is not qualifying abuse, unless it can be shown that the citizen or lawful permanent resident willfully condoned or participated in the abuse.

The law provides that evidence of abuse may include, but is not limited to reports and affidavits from police, judges and other court officials, medical personnel, school officials, clergy, social workers, and other social service agency personnel.

Persons who have obtained an order of protection against the abuser or taken other legal steps to end the abuse are strongly encouraged to submit documentation. Evidence that the abuse victim sought refuge in a battered women's shelter may also be relevant. In addition, photographs of the injuries sustained by the self-petitioner, supported by affidavits, would be credible evidence.

REQUIREMENT OF GOOD MORAL CHARACTER

The law requires all self-petitioners to be of good moral character, and requires self-petitioning spouses to provide evidence showing that they have been persons of good moral character for the 3 years immediately preceding the date the self-petition is filed. However, the law does not preclude the USCIS from choosing to examine the self-petitioner's conduct and acts prior to that period if there is reason to believe that the self-petitioner may not have been a person of good moral character in the past. The law provides that a self-petition may be denied or revoked if there is evidence establishing that the person lacks good moral character contained in the USCIS file.

DERIVATIVE CHILD INCLUDED IN THE SELF-PETITION

The law allows any child of a self-petitioning spouse to be derivatively included in the self-petition, if the child has not been classified as an immigrant based on his or her own self-petition. No separate petition is necessary for derivative classification, and the child is not required to have been the victim of abuse.

The derivative child does not need to have lived in the United States or to otherwise satisfy the criteria for filing a self-petition. The child must, however, meet the requirements for immigrant visa issuance abroad or adjustment of status in the United States. In addition, the derivative child need not be the child of the abuser, but must qualify as the self-petitioning spouse's child under the definition of "child" as defined in Section 101(b)(1) of the INA. The statutory definition includes an unmarried person under twenty-one years of age who is:

(A) a child born in wedlock;

(B) a stepchild, whether or not born out of wedlock, provided the child had not reached the age of eighteen years at the time the marriage creating the status of stepchild occurred;

(C) a child legitimated under the law of the child's residence or domicile, or under the law of the father's residence or domicile, whether in or outside the United States, if such legitimation takes place before the child reaches the age of eighteen years and the child is in the legal custody of the legitimating parent or parents at the time of such legitimation;

(D) a child born out of wedlock, by, through whom, or on whose behalf a status, privilege, or benefit is sought by virtue of the relationship of the child to its natural mother or to its natural father if the father has or had a bona fide parent-child relationship with the person;

(E) certain adopted or orphaned children subject to the provisions of the INA.

Any relevant credible evidence that can prove the parent/child relationship will be considered by the USCIS.

THE BATTERED IMMIGRANT WOMEN PROTECTION ACT

The Battered Immigrant Women Protection Act (BIWPA) was enacted under Title V of the Violence Against Women Act of 2000 (VAWA-2000). The BIWPA made significant amendments to INA Section 204(a), and the manner in which self-petitions may be filed, as set forth below.

As set forth below, the VAWA-2000 addressed certain residual immigration law obstacles standing in the path of battered immigrant spouses and children that either had not come to the attention of the drafters of the original VAWA, or that arose as a result of 1996 changes to immigration law.

Section 1503

Section 1503 allows abused spouses and children who have already demonstrated to the USCIS that they have been the victims of battery or extreme cruelty by their spouse or parent to file their own petition for a lawful permanent resident visa without also having to show they will suffer "extreme hardship" if forced to leave the United States.

Section 1503 eliminates U.S. residency as a prerequisite for a battered spouse or child of a citizen or LPR to file for his or her own visa.

Section 1503 maintains the current requirement that abused spouses and children demonstrate good moral character, but modifies it to give the Attorney General authority to find good moral character despite certain otherwise disqualifying acts if those acts were connected to the abuse.

Section 1503 allows a battered spouse to file a visa petition if they believed they were the spouse of a U.S. citizen or LPR and went through a marriage ceremony, even though the marriage was invalid because the U.S. citizen or LPR committed bigamy.

Section 1503 allows a battered spouse to file a visa petition even if (i) their U.S. citizen spouse died or lost citizenship; or (ii) heir LPR lost lawful permanent residency,; or the battered spouse was divorced from the U.S. citizen or LPR, provided that the petition is filed within two years of the death, loss of citizenship or lawful permanent residency, or divorce, as long as the loss of citizenship, status or divorce was connected to the abuse suffered by the spouse.

Section 1503 allows a battered spouse to naturalize after three years residency as other spouses may do, but without requiring the battered spouse to live in marital union with the abusive spouse during that period.

Section 1503 allows abused children or children of abused spouses whose petitions were filed when they were minors to maintain their petitions after they attain age 21.

Section 1504

Section 1504 clarifies a provision dealing with the continuous physical presence requirement by stating that it does not apply to any absence by the battered spouse if the absence is connected to the abuse.

Section 1505

Section 1505 grants the Attorney General the authority to waive certain bars to admissibility or grounds of deportability with respect to battered spouses and children, including (i) domestic violence crimes where there was a connection between the crime and the abuse suffered; (ii) misrepresentation connected with immigration benefits in cases of extreme hardship to the alien; (iii) crimes of moral turpitude where the crime was connected to the abuse; (iv) health-related grounds of inadmissibility; (v) unlawful presence after a prior immigration violation if there is a connection between the abuse and the alien's removal, departure, reentry, or attempted reentry.

Section 1506

Section 1506 establishes a mechanism available to spouses, and children petitioned for by their spouse or parent, to enable VAWA-qualified battered spouse or child to obtain status as lawful permanent resident in the United States rather than having to go abroad to get a visa.

Section 1507

Section 1507 provides that negative changes of immigration status of abuser, or divorce after the abused spouse or child files a petition under VAWA, have no effect on the status of the abused spouse or child. This Section also clarifies that remarriage has no effect on pending VAWA immigration petition.

Section 1512

Section 1512 provides that Stop grants, Grants to Encourage Arrest, Rural VAWA grants, Civil Legal Assistance grants, and Campus grants can all be used to provide assistance to battered immigrants.

Section 1513

Section 1513 creates a new nonimmigrant visa for victims of certain serious crimes that tend to target vulnerable foreign individuals without immigration status if (i) the victim has suffered substantial physical or mental abuse as a result of the crime, (ii) the victim has information about the crime, and (iii) a law enforcement official or a judge certifies that the victim has been helpful, is being helpful, or is likely to be helpful in investigating or prosecuting the crime.

The crime must involve rape, torture, trafficking, incest, sexual assault, domestic violence, abusive sexual contact, prostitution, sexual exploitation, female genital mutilation, hostage-holding, peonage, involuntary servitude, slave trade, kidnapping, abduction, unlawful criminal restraint, false imprisonment, blackmail, extortion, manslaughter, murder, felonious assault, witness tampering, obstruction of justice, perjury, attempt or conspiracy to commit any of the above, or other similar conduct in violation of Federal, State, or local criminal law.

Section 1513 also allows the Attorney General to adjust these individuals to lawful permanent resident status if the alien has been present for 3 years and the Attorney General determines this is justified on humanitarian grounds, to promote family unity, or is otherwise in the public interest.

THE SELF-PETITION PROCESS AND APPLICATION FOR BENEFITS

To begin the self-petition process and qualify for benefits, the self-petitioner must complete and file USCIS Form I-360, including all supporting documentation. Self-petitions are filed with the USCIS Vermont Service Center and should be sent by certified return receipt mail or any other method that will provide proof of receipt. The self-petitioner should keep the proof of mailing and a copy of everything they submit, including the application and supporting documentation. The USCIS will send an acknowledgement or Notice of Receipt within a few weeks after the application and fee are mailed.

Prima Facie Determination

Battered immigrants filing self-petitions who can establish a "prima facie" case are considered "qualified aliens" for the purpose of eligibility for public benefits (Section 501 of the Illegal Immigrant Responsibility and Immigration Reform Act (IIRIRA)). The USCIS reviews each petition initially to determine whether the self-petitioner has addressed each of the requirements and has provided some supporting evidence. This may be in the form of a statement that addresses each requirement. This is called a prima facie determination.

If the USCIS makes a prima facie determination, the self-petitioner will receive a Notice of Prima Facie Determination valid for 150 days. The notice may be presented to state and federal agencies that provide public benefits.

If the I-360 self-petition is approved, the USCIS may exercise the administrative option of placing the self-petitioner in deferred action, if the self-petitioner does not have legal immigration status in the United States. Deferred action means that the USCIS will not initiate removal—i.e., deportation—proceedings against the self-petitioner. Deferred action decisions are made by the Vermont Service Center (VSC) and are granted in most cases.

Deferred action validity is 27 months for those for whom a visa was available on the date that the self-petition was approved. All others have a validity of 24 months beyond the date a visa number becomes available. The VSC has the authority to grant appropriate extensions of deferred action beyond those time periods upon receipt of a request for extension from the self-petitioner.

Employment Authorization

Self-petitioners and their derivative children who have an approved Form I-360 and are placed in deferred action are also eligible for an Employment Authorization Card. To apply, an Application for Employment Authorization (USCIS Form I-765) should be filed with the Vermont Service Center. Applicants should indicate that they are seeking employment authorization pursuant to 8 CFR 274a.12(c) (14). Form I-765 must be filed with a copy of the self-petitioner's USCIS Form I-360 approval notice.

Adjustment to Permanent Resident Status

Self-petitioners who qualify as immediate relatives of U.S. citizens—i.e., spouses and unmarried children under the age of 21—do not have to wait for an immigrant visa number to become available. They may file an Application To Register Permanent Residence or Adjust Status (USCIS Form I-485) with their local USCIS office.

Self-petitioners who require a visa number to adjust must wait for a visa number to be available before filing Form I-485. Currently, the wait for visa numbers can be anywhere from 2-10 years.

Filing an Appeal

If the application is denied, the denial letter will tell the self-petitioner how to appeal. Generally, a Notice of Appeal may be filed along with the required fee at the Vermont Service Center within 33 days of receiving the denial. Once the fee is collected and the form is processed at the Service Center, the appeal will be referred to the Administrative Appeals Unit in Washington, D.C.

GETTING HELP

Battered Immigrant Women may contact the USCIS District Office near their home for a list of community-based, non-profit organizations that may be able to assist them in applying for immigration benefits. Help is also available to victims of domestic violence through the National Domestic Violence Hotline. The Domestic Violence Hotline can be reached by calling 1-800-799-7233 or 1-800-787-3224 [TDD]. Information about shelters, mental health care, legal advice and other types of assistance, including information about self-petitioning for immigration status, is available.

CHAPTER 8:
HUMAN TRAFFICKING
AND THE SEX TRADE

WHAT IS HUMAN TRAFFICKING?

The Trafficking Victims Protection Act was enacted as part of The Victims of Trafficking and Violence Protection Act of 2000. The Trafficking Victims Protection Act defines human trafficking as: (A) The recruitment, harboring, transportation, provision, or obtaining of a person for the purpose of a commercial sex act where such an act is induced by force, fraud, or coercion, or in which the person induced to perform such act has not attained 18 years of age, or (B) The recruitment, harboring, transportation, provision, or obtaining of a person for labor or services, through the use of force, fraud, or coercion for the purpose of subjection to involuntary servitude, peonage, debt bondage, or slavery.

Human trafficking is a form of modern-day slavery. Human trafficking is one of the largest and fastest growing illegal enterprises in the world. At least 700,000 persons annually, primarily women and children, are trafficked within or across international borders, and approximately 50,000 women and children are trafficked into the United States each year.

Many victims of trafficking—predominantly women and girls—are placed in the international sex trade, often by force, fraud, or coercion. They are exploited for purposes of prostitution, pornography, sex tourism, and other commercial sexual services. The low status of women in many parts of the world has contributed to this growing industry.

Trafficking in persons is not limited to the international sex trade. It also involves labor exploitation, including domestic servitude, sweatshop factories, and migrant agricultural work, in violation of labor, public health, and human rights standards.

Victims are often taken from their home communities to unfamiliar destinations, including foreign countries away from family and friends, religious institutions, and other sources of protection and support, leaving them defenseless and vulnerable. They are then forced through physical violence to engage in sex acts or perform slavery-like labor. Force includes rape and other forms of sexual abuse, torture, starvation, imprisonment, threats, psychological abuse, and coercion. Traffickers often threaten their victims with physical harm if they try to escape.

CAUSATION

The serious problem of human trafficking may be attributed to poverty, lack of employment opportunities, organized crime, violence against women and children, discrimination against women, government corruption, political instability, armed conflict, and the lure of a higher standard of living.

Modern day slave traders prey primarily upon vulnerable women and children, gaining their trust through coercion and trickery. Traffickers lure their victims by making false promises of marriage, educational and employment opportunities, good pay and working conditions, and a better life. Traffickers also buy children from poor families and sell them into prostitution or into various types of forced or bonded labor.

Trafficking in persons is increasingly perpetrated by organized, sophisticated criminal enterprises. Profits from the trafficking industry contribute to the expansion of organized crime in the United States and worldwide. Trafficking in persons is often perpetuated by official corruption in the countries of origin, transit, and destination.

STATISTICS

According to the 2004 U.S. Department of Justice report:

1. Approximately 14,500 to 17,500 people are trafficked annually into the United States, and 600,000 to 800,000 are trafficked globally.

2. Approximately 80 percent of the victims are female.

3. 70 percent of the female victims are trafficked for the commercial sex industry.

4. Approximately two-thirds of the global victims are trafficked intra-regionally.

5. Approximately 260,000 to 280,000 people are trafficked within East Asia and the Pacific.

6. Approximately 170,000 to 210,000 people are trafficked within East Europe and Eurasia.

7. Approximately 5,000 to 7,000 people are trafficked into the United States from East Asia and the Pacific.

8. Approximately 3,500 people are trafficked into the United States from Latin America.

9. Approximately 5,500 people are trafficked into the United States from Europe and Eurasia.

VICTIM ASSISTANCE

Victims of human trafficking may be eligible for services that are generally available to Federal crime victims. The FBI, U.S. Attorney's Offices and U.S. Citizenship and Immigration Services employs victim specialists who can assist victims with the following:

1. Protection and remedies against threats and intimidation.

2. Emergency medical and social services.

3. Shelter.

4. Referrals to public and private programs available to provide counseling, treatment, and other services.

5. Support services, such as domestic violence and rape crisis centers.

6. Understanding of their rights and their role in the criminal justice process.

7. Information on the investigation status and notice of important case events.

8. Crime victim compensation through State compensation programs and how to apply.

9. Restitution.

10. Privacy and confidentiality issues.

For more information on human trafficking, visit the U.S. Department of Health and Human Services website at http://www.acf.hhs.gov/trafficking/. Additional information may be obtained by contacting the Trafficking Information and Referral Hotline at (888) 373-7888.

HUMAN TRAFFICKING LEGISLATION

The Trafficking Victims Protection Act of 2000

Congress recognized that legislation and law enforcement in the United States and other countries was inadequate to deter trafficking and bring traffickers to justice, and failed to reflect the gravity of the offenses involved. In addition, there was no comprehensive law in the United States that penalized the range of offenses involved in the trafficking scheme. The most brutal instances of trafficking in the sex industry were often punished under laws that also applied to lesser offenses, so that traffickers typically escaped just punishment. The sentencing guidelines did not take into account the serious nature of the crime, resulting in weak penalties for convicted traffickers.

In addition, there were no provisions to assist the victims of trafficking in rebuilding their lives. Instead, victims of severe forms of trafficking were inappropriately incarcerated, fined, or otherwise penalized solely for unlawful acts committed as a direct result of being trafficked. Such acts included using false documents, entering the country without documentation, or working without documentation.

To address these serious issues, Congress enacted The Trafficking Victims Protection Act of 2000 (TVPA). The TVPA provides a means for non-citizen victims in the United States to apply for a special visa and other benefits and services so that they can safely and securely rebuild their lives. Under the Act, adult victims of human trafficking age 18 and over who are certified by the U.S. Department of Health and Human Services (HHS) can receive Federally-funded services and benefits to the same extent as refugees.

Certification

To receive certification, an individual must:

1. Be a victim of human trafficking as defined by the TVPA;

2. Be willing to assist with the investigation and prosecution of traffickers; and

3. Have completed a bona fide application for a T visa; or have received Continued Presence status from the U.S. Department of Homeland Security (DHS).

The T visa was established to give victims of human trafficking temporary status in the United States. It recognizes that deporting victims to their country of origin is not in their best interests and that it is preferable to provide victims with the opportunity to rebuild their lives. After three years, a T visa recipient can apply for permanent residence status. In certain situations, it also enables victims of human trafficking to get T visas for family members.

Child victims of human trafficking under age 18 are immediately eligible for benefits and do not need to apply for a T visa or obtain Continued Presence status from the DHS. Once the U.S. Department of Health and Human Services (HHS) has received proof that the child is a victim of trafficking—known as a "letter of eligibility—the victim or the victim's advocate may then present the letter to social service providers as proof of eligibility for available benefits and services.

Benefits and Services

Certified and eligible victims of human trafficking are eligible to receive the following benefits and services:

1. Housing or shelter assistance;

2. English language training;

3. Food assistance;

4. Health care assistance;

5. Income assistance;

6. Mental health services;

7. Employment assistance; and

8. Assistance for victims of torture.

The Interagency Task Force to Monitor and Combat Trafficking

In an effort to eliminate trafficking and protect trafficking victims throughout the world, the TVPA created the Interagency Task Force to Monitor and Combat Trafficking. The responsibilities of the Task Force are to:

1. Coordinate the implementation of the Trafficking Victims Protection Act of 2000.

2. Measure and evaluate the progress of the United States and other countries in the areas of trafficking prevention, protection and assistance to victims of trafficking, and prosecution and enforcement against traffickers.

3. Expand interagency procedures to collect and organize data, including significant research and resource information on domestic and international trafficking.

4. Engage in efforts to facilitate cooperation among countries of origin, transit, and destination.

5. Evaluate the role of public corruption in facilitating trafficking.

6. Examine the role of the international "sex tourism" industry in the trafficking of persons and in the sexual exploitation of women and children around the world.

7. Engage in consultation and advocacy with governmental and nongovernmental organizations, among other entities, to advance the purposes of the TVPA.

Selected provisions of The Trafficking Victims Protection Act are set forth at Appendix 20.

The Trafficking Victims Protection Reauthorization Act of 2003

In 2003, the Trafficking Victims Protection Reauthorization Act was passed to authorize appropriations for fiscal years 2004 and 2005 for the Trafficking Victims Protection Act of 2000. The Act also amended three of the four minimum standards for the elimination of trafficking. In particular, the fourth minimum standard, which stated, "The government of the country should make serious and sustained efforts to eliminate severe forms of trafficking in persons," was strengthened. In addition, a "Special Watch List" of countries to receive special scrutiny during 2004 was created.

The Trafficking in Persons Reauthorization Act of 2005

In 2005, the Trafficking in Persons Reauthorization Act was passed to authorize appropriations for fiscal years 2006 and 2007 for the Trafficking Victims Protection Act of 2000.

The 13th Amendment to the United States Constitution

Human trafficking violates the 13th Amendment to the United States Constitution, which outlaws slavery and involuntary servitude, as follows:

Neither slavery nor involuntary servitude, except as a punishment for crime whereof the party shall have been duly convicted, shall exist within the United States, or any place subject to their jurisdiction.

Involuntary Servitude and Peonage (Title 18, U.S.C. §§ 1581, 1584)

Section 1581 prohibits using force, the threat of force, or the threat of legal coercion to compel a person to work against his or her will. In addition, the victim's involuntary servitude must be tied to the payment of a debt.

Section 1584 makes it unlawful to hold a person in a condition of slavery, that is, a condition of compulsory service or labor against his or her will. Section 1584 also prohibits compelling a person to work against his or her will by creating a "climate of fear" through the use of force, the threat of force, or the threat of legal coercion which is sufficient to compel service against a person's will.

APPENDIX 1:
U.S. DEPARTMENT OF JUSTICE—
VIOLENCE AGAINST
WOMEN HOTLINE NUMBERS

HOTLINE	TELEPHONE NUMBER	WEBSITE
National Domestic Violence Hotline	1-800-799-SAFE (7233)	http://www.ndvh.org/
Rape Abuse and Incest National Network (RAINN)	1-800-656-HOPE (4673)	http://www.rainn.org/
National Sexual Violence Resource Center (NSVRC)	1-877-739-3895	http://www.nsvrc.org/
National Center for Victims of Crime Stalking Resource Center	1-800-394-2255	http://www.ncvc.org/

SOURCE: U.S. Department of Justice, Office on Violence Against Women

APPENDIX 2:
SUBTITLE A—THE SAFE STREETS FOR WOMEN ACT—SELECTED PROVISIONS

CHAPTER 1—FEDERAL PENALTIES FOR SEX CRIMES

SECTION 40111. REPEAT OFFENDERS.

(a) IN GENERAL—Chapter 109A of title 18, United States Code, is amended by adding at the end the following new section:

'**Section 2247. Repeat offenders.**

'Any person who violates a provision of this chapter, after one or more prior convictions for an offense punishable under this chapter, or after one or more prior convictions under the laws of any State relating to aggravated sexual abuse, sexual abuse, or abusive sexual contact have become final, is punishable by a term of imprisonment up to twice that otherwise authorized.'.

SECTION 40113. MANDATORY RESTITUTION FOR SEX CRIMES.

(a) SEXUAL ABUSE—

(1) IN GENERAL—Chapter 109A of title 18, United States Code, is amended by adding at the end the following new section:

'**Section 2248. Mandatory restitution**

'(a) IN GENERAL—Notwithstanding section 3663, and in addition to any other civil or criminal penalty authorized by law, the court shall order restitution for any offense under this chapter.

'(b) SCOPE AND NATURE OF ORDER—

'(1) DIRECTIONS—The order of restitution under this section shall direct that—

'(A) the defendant pay to the victim (through the appropriate court mechanism) the full amount of the victim's losses as determined by the court, pursuant to paragraph (3); and

'(B) the United States Attorney enforce the restitution order by all available and reasonable means.

'(2) ENFORCEMENT BY VICTIM—An order of restitution also may be enforced by a victim named in the order to receive the restitution in the same manner as a judgment in a civil action.

'(3) DEFINITION—For purposes of this subsection, the term 'full amount of the victim's losses' includes any costs incurred by the victim for—

'(A) medical services relating to physical, psychiatric, or psychological care;

'(B) physical and occupational therapy or rehabilitation;

'(C) necessary transportation, temporary housing, and child care expenses;

'(D) lost income;

'(E) attorneys' fees, plus any costs incurred in obtaining a civil protection order; and

'(F) any other losses suffered by the victim as a proximate result of the offense.

'(4) ORDER MANDATORY—

(A) The issuance of a restitution order under this section is mandatory.

'(B) A court may not decline to issue an order under this section because of—

'(i) the economic circumstances of the defendant; or

'(ii) the fact that a victim has, or is entitled to, receive compensation for his or her injuries from the proceeds of insurance or any other source.

'(C)(i) Notwithstanding subparagraph (A), the court may take into account the economic circumstances of the defendant in determining the manner in which and the schedule according to which the restitution is to be paid.

'(ii) For purposes of this subparagraph, the term 'economic circumstances' includes—

'(I) the financial resources and other assets of the defendant;

'(II) projected earnings, earning capacity, and other income of the defendant; and

'(III) any financial obligations of the defendant, including obligations to dependents.

'(D) Subparagraph (A) does not apply if—

'(i) the court finds on the record that the economic circumstances of the defendant do not allow for the payment of any amount of a restitution order, and do not allow for the payment of any or some portion of the amount of a restitution order in the foreseeable future (under any reasonable schedule of payments); and '(ii) the court enters in its order the amount of the victim's losses, and provides a nominal restitution award.

'(5) MORE THAN 1 OFFENDER—When the court finds that more than 1 offender has contributed to the loss of a victim, the court may make each offender liable for payment of the full amount of restitution or may apportion liability among the offenders to reflect the level of contribution and economic circumstances of each offender.

'(6) MORE THAN 1 VICTIM—When the court finds that more than 1 victim has sustained a loss requiring restitution by an offender, the court shall order full restitution of each victim but may provide for different payment schedules to reflect the economic circumstances of each victim.

'(7) PAYMENT SCHEDULE—An order under this section may direct the defendant to make a single lump-sum payment or partial payments at specified intervals.

'(8) SETOFF—Any amount paid to a victim under this section shall be set off against any amount later recovered as compensatory damages by the victim from the defendant in—

'(A) any Federal civil proceeding; and

'(B) any State civil proceeding, to the extent provided by the law of the State.

'(9) EFFECT ON OTHER SOURCES OF COMPENSATION—The issuance of a restitution order shall not affect the entitlement of a victim to receive compensation with respect to a loss from insurance or any other source until the payments actually received by the victim under the restitution order fully compensate the victim for the loss.

'(10) CONDITION OF PROBATION OR SUPERVISED RELEASE—Compliance with a restitution order issued under this section shall be a condition of any probation or supervised release of a defendant. If an offender fails to comply with a restitution order, the court may, after a hearing, revoke probation or a term of supervised release, modify the terms or conditions of probation or a term of supervised release, or hold the defendant in contempt pursuant to section 3583(e). In determining whether to revoke probation or a term of supervised release, modify the terms or conditions of probation or supervised release or hold a defendant serving a term of supervised release in contempt, the court shall consider the defendant's employment status, earning ability and financial resources, the willfulness of the defendant's failure to comply, and any other circumstances that may have a bearing on the defendant's ability to comply.

'(c) PROOF OF CLAIM—

'(1) AFFIDAVIT—Within 60 days after conviction and, in any event, not later than 10 days prior to sentencing, the United States Attorney (or the United States Attorney's delegee), after consulting with the victim, shall prepare and file an affidavit with the court listing the amounts subject to restitution under this section. The affidavit shall be signed by the United States Attorney (or the United States Attorney's delegee) and the victim. Should the victim object to any of the information included in the affidavit, the United States Attorney (or the United States Attorney's delegee) shall advise the victim that the victim may file a separate affidavit and shall provide the victim with an affidavit form which may be used to do so.

'(2) OBJECTION—If, after the defendant has been notified of the affidavit, no objection is raised by the defendant, the amounts attested to in the affidavit filed pursuant to paragraph (1) shall be entered in the court's restitution order. If objection is raised, the court may require the victim or the United States Attorney (or the United States Attorney's delegee) to submit further affidavits or other supporting documents, demonstrating the victim's losses.

'(3) ADDITIONAL DOCUMENTATION AND TESTIMONY—If the court concludes, after reviewing the supporting documentation and considering the defendant's objections, that there is a substantial reason for doubting the authenticity or veracity of the records submitted, the court may require additional documentation or hear testimony on those questions. The privacy of any records filed, or testimony heard, pursuant to this section shall be maintained to the greatest extent possible, and such records may be filed or testimony heard in camera.

'(4) FINAL DETERMINATION OF LOSSES—If the victim's losses are not ascertainable by the date that is 10 days prior to sentencing as provided in paragraph (1), the United States Attorney (or the United States Attorney's delegee) shall so inform the court, and the court shall set a date for the final determination of the victim's losses, not to exceed 90 days after sentencing. If the victim subsequently discovers further losses, the victim shall have 60 days after discovery of those losses in which to petition the court for an amended restitution order. Such order may be granted only upon a showing of good cause for the failure to include such losses in the initial claim for restitutionary relief.

'(d) MODIFICATION OF ORDER—A victim or the offender may petition the court at any time to modify a restitution order as appropriate in view of a change in the economic circumstances of the offender.

'(e) REFERENCE TO MAGISTRATE OR SPECIAL MASTER—The court may refer any issue arising in connection with a proposed order of restitution to a magistrate or special master for proposed findings of fact and recommendations as to disposition, subject to a de novo determination of the issue by the court.

'(f) DEFINITION—For purposes of this section, the term 'victim' means the individual harmed as a result of a commission of a crime under this chapter, including, in the case of a victim who is under 18 years of age, incompetent, incapacitated, or deceased, the legal guardian of the victim or representative of the victim's estate, another family member, or any other person appointed as suitable by the court, but in no event shall the defendant be named as such representative or guardian.'.

CHAPTER 2—LAW ENFORCEMENT AND PROSECUTION GRANTS TO REDUCE VIOLENT CRIMES AGAINST WOMEN

SECTION 40121. GRANTS TO COMBAT VIOLENT CRIMES AGAINST WOMEN.

'PART T—GRANTS TO COMBAT VIOLENT CRIMES AGAINST WOMEN

'SECTION 2001. PURPOSE OF THE PROGRAM AND GRANTS.

'(a) GENERAL PROGRAM PURPOSE—The purpose of this part is to assist States, Indian tribal governments, and units of local government to develop and strengthen effective law enforcement and prosecution strategies to combat violent crimes against women, and to develop and strengthen victim services in cases involving violent crimes against women.

'(b) PURPOSES FOR WHICH GRANTS MAY BE USED—Grants under this part shall provide personnel, training, technical assistance, data collection and other equipment for the more widespread apprehension, prosecution, and adjudication of persons committing violent crimes against women, and specifically, for the purposes of—

'(1) training law enforcement officers and prosecutors to more effectively identify and respond to violent crimes against women, including the crimes of sexual assault and domestic violence;

'(2) developing, training, or expanding units of law enforcement officers and prosecutors specifically targeting violent crimes against women, including the crimes of sexual assault and domestic violence;

'(3) developing and implementing more effective police and prosecution policies, protocols, orders, and services specifically devoted to preventing, identifying, and responding to violent crimes against women, including the crimes of sexual assault and domestic violence;

'(4) developing, installing, or expanding data collection and communication systems, including computerized systems, linking police, prosecutors, and courts or for the purpose of identifying and tracking arrests, protection orders, violations of protection orders, prosecutions, and convictions for violent crimes against women, including the crimes of sexual assault and domestic violence;

'(5) developing, enlarging, or strengthening victim services programs, including sexual assault and domestic violence programs, developing or improving delivery of victim services to racial, cultural, ethnic, and language minorities, providing specialized domestic violence court advocates in courts where a significant number of protection orders are granted, and increasing reporting and reducing attrition rates for cases involving violent crimes against women, including crimes of sexual assault and domestic violence;

'(6) developing, enlarging, or strengthening programs addressing stalking; and

'(7) developing, enlarging, or strengthening programs addressing the needs and circumstances of Indian tribes in dealing with violent crimes against women, including the crimes of sexual assault and domestic violence.

'SECTION 2003. DEFINITIONS.

'In this part—

'(1) the term 'Domestic Violence' includes felony or misdemeanor crimes of violence committed by a current or former spouse of the victim, by a person with whom the victim shares a child in common, by a person who is cohabitating with or has cohabitated with the victim as a spouse, by a person similarly situated to a spouse of the victim under the domestic or family violence laws of the jurisdiction receiving grant monies, or by any other adult person against a victim who is protected from that person's acts under the domestic or family violence laws of the jurisdiction receiving grant monies;

'(2) the term 'Indian Country' has the meaning stated in section 1151 of title 18, United States Code;

'(3) the term 'Indian Tribe' means a tribe, band, pueblo, nation, or other organized group or community of Indians, including any Alaska Native village or regional or village corporation (as defined in, or established pursuant to, the Alaska Native Claims Settlement Act (43 U.S.C. 1601 et seq.)), that is recognized as eligible for the special programs and services provided by the United States to Indians because of their status as Indians;

'(4) the term 'Law Enforcement' means a public agency charged with policing functions, including any of its component bureaus (such as governmental victim services programs);

'(5) the term 'Prosecution' means any public agency charged with direct responsibility for prosecuting criminal offenders, including such agency's component bureaus (such as governmental victim services programs);

'(6) the term 'Sexual Assault' means any conduct proscribed by chapter 109A of title 18, United States Code, whether or not the conduct occurs in the special maritime and territorial jurisdiction of the United States or in a Federal prison and includes both assaults committed by offenders who are strangers to the victim and assaults committed by offenders who are known or related by blood or marriage to the victim;

'(7) the term 'Underserved Populations' includes populations underserved because of geographic location (such as rural isolation), underserved racial or ethnic populations, and populations underserved because of special needs, such as language barriers or physical disabilities; and

'(8) the term 'Victim Services' means a nonprofit, nongovernmental organization that assists domestic violence or sexual assault victims, including rape crisis centers, battered women's shelters, and other sexual assault or domestic violence programs, including nonprofit, nongovernmental organizations assisting domestic violence or sexual assault victims through the legal process.

'SECTION 2004. GENERAL TERMS AND CONDITIONS.

'(a) NONMONETARY ASSISTANCE—In addition to the assistance provided under this part, the Attorney General may request any Federal agency to use its authorities and the resources granted to it under Federal law (including personnel, equipment, supplies, facilities, and managerial, technical, and advisory services) in support of State, tribal, and local assistance efforts.

'**SECTION 2005. RAPE EXAM PAYMENTS.**

'(a) RESTRICTION OF FUNDS—

'(1) IN GENERAL—A State, Indian tribal government, or unit of local government, shall not be entitled to funds under this part unless the State, Indian tribal government, unit of local government, or another governmental entity incurs the full out-of-pocket cost of forensic medical exams described in subsection (b) for victims of sexual assault.

'(b) MEDICAL COSTS—A State, Indian tribal government, or unit of local government shall be deemed to incur the full out-of-pocket cost of forensic medical exams for victims of sexual assault if any government entity—

'(1) provides such exams to victims free of charge to the victim;

'(2) arranges for victims to obtain such exams free of charge to the victims; or

'(3) reimburses victims for the cost of such exams if—

'(A) the reimbursement covers the full cost of such exams, without any deductible requirement or limit on the amount of a reimbursement;

'(B) the reimbursing governmental entity permits victims to apply for reimbursement for not less than one year from the date of the exam;

'(C) the reimbursing governmental entity provides reimbursement not later than 90 days after written notification of the victim's expense; and

'(D) the State, Indian tribal government, unit of local government, or reimbursing governmental entity provides information at the time of the exam to all victims, including victims with limited or no English proficiency, regarding how to obtain reimbursement.

'**SECTION 2006. FILING COSTS FOR CRIMINAL CHARGES.**

'(a) IN GENERAL—A State, Indian tribal government, or unit of local government, shall not be entitled to funds under this part unless the State, Indian tribal government, or unit of local government—

'(1) certifies that its laws, policies, and practices do not require, in connection with the prosecution of any misdemeanor or felony domestic violence offense, that the abused bear the costs associated with the filing of criminal charges against the domestic violence offender, or the costs associated with the issuance or service of a warrant, protection order, or witness subpoena; or

'(2) gives the Attorney General assurances that its laws, policies and practices will be in compliance with the requirements of paragraph (1) within the later of—

'(A) the period ending on the date on which the next session of the State legislature ends; or

'(B) 2 years.

CHAPTER 3—SAFETY FOR WOMEN IN PUBLIC TRANSIT AND PUBLIC PARKS

SECTION 40131. GRANTS FOR CAPITAL IMPROVEMENTS TO PREVENT CRIME IN PUBLIC TRANSPORTATION.

(b) GRANTS FOR LIGHTING, CAMERA SURVEILLANCE, AND SECURITY PHONES—

(1) From the sums authorized for expenditure under this section for crime prevention, the Secretary is authorized to make grants and loans to States and local public bodies or agencies for the purpose of increasing the safety of public transportation by—

(A) increasing lighting within or adjacent to public transportation systems, including bus stops, subway stations, parking lots, or garages;

(B) increasing camera surveillance of areas within and adjacent to public transportation systems, including bus stops, subway stations, parking lots, or garages;

(C) providing emergency phone lines to contact law enforcement or security personnel in areas within or adjacent to public transportation systems, including bus stops, subway stations, parking lots, or garages; or

(D) any other project intended to increase the security and safety of existing or planned public transportation systems.

(e) SPECIAL GRANTS FOR PROJECTS TO STUDY INCREASING SECURITY FOR WOMEN—From the sums authorized under this section, the Secretary shall provide grants and loans for the purpose of studying ways to reduce violent crimes against women in public transit through better design or operation of public transit systems.

SECTION 40132. GRANTS FOR CAPITAL IMPROVEMENTS TO PREVENT CRIME IN NATIONAL PARKS.

Public Law 91-383 (16 U.S.C. 1a-1 et seq.) is amended by adding at the end the following new section:

'SECTION 13. NATIONAL PARK SYSTEM CRIME PREVENTION ASSISTANCE.

'(d) USE OF FUNDS—Funds provided under this section may be used—

'(1) to increase lighting within or adjacent to National Park System units;

'(2) to provide emergency phone lines to contact law enforcement or security personnel in areas within or adjacent to National Park System units;

'(3) to increase security or law enforcement personnel within or adjacent to National Park System units; or

---

'(4) for any other project intended to increase the security and safety of National Park System units.'.

SECTION 40133. GRANTS FOR CAPITAL IMPROVEMENTS TO PREVENT CRIME IN PUBLIC PARKS.

Section 6 of the Land and Water Conservation Fund Act of 1965 (16 U.S.C. 460 1-8) is amended by adding at the end the following new subsection:

'(h) CAPITAL IMPROVEMENT AND OTHER PROJECTS TO REDUCE CRIME—

'(1) AVAILABILITY OF FUNDS—In addition to assistance for planning projects, and in addition to the projects identified in subsection (e), and from amounts appropriated out of the Violent Crime Reduction Trust Fund, the Secretary may provide financial assistance to the States, not to exceed $15,000,000, for projects or combinations thereof for the purpose of making capital improvements and other measures to increase safety in urban parks and recreation areas, including funds to—

'(A) increase lighting within or adjacent to public parks and recreation areas;

'(B) provide emergency phone lines to contact law enforcement or security personnel in areas within or adjacent to public parks and recreation areas;

'(C) increase security personnel within or adjacent to public parks and recreation areas; and

'(D) fund any other project intended to increase the security and safety of public parks and recreation areas.

CHAPTER 4—NEW EVIDENTIARY RULES

SECTION 40141. SEXUAL HISTORY IN CRIMINAL AND CIVIL CASES.

(b) RULE—Rule 412 of the Federal Rules of Evidence is amended to read as follows:

'Rule 412. Sex Offense Cases; Relevance of Alleged Victim's Past Sexual Behavior or Alleged Sexual Predisposition

'(a) EVIDENCE GENERALLY INADMISSIBLE—The following evidence is not admissible in any civil or criminal proceeding involving alleged sexual misconduct except as provided in subdivisions (b) and (c):

'(1) Evidence offered to prove that any alleged victim engaged in other sexual behavior.

'(2) Evidence offered to prove any alleged victim's sexual predisposition.

'(b) EXCEPTIONS—

'(1) In a criminal case, the following evidence is admissible, if otherwise admissible under these rules:

'(A) evidence of specific instances of sexual behavior by the alleged victim offered to prove that a person other than the accused was the source of semen, injury or other physical evidence;

'(B) evidence of specific instances of sexual behavior by the alleged victim with respect to the person accused of the sexual misconduct offered by the accused to prove consent or by the prosecution; and

'(C) evidence the exclusion of which would violate the constitutional rights of the defendant.

'(2) In a civil case, evidence offered to prove the sexual behavior or sexual predisposition of any alleged victim is admissible if it is otherwise admissible under these rules and its probative value substantially outweighs the danger of harm to any victim and of unfair prejudice to any party. Evidence of an alleged victim's reputation is admissible only if it has been placed in controversy by the alleged victim.

'(c) PROCEDURE TO DETERMINE ADMISSIBILITY—

'(1) A party intending to offer evidence under subdivision (b) must—

'(A) file a written motion at least 14 days before trial specifically describing the evidence and stating the purpose for which it is offered unless the court, for good cause requires a different time for filing or permits filing during trial; and

'(B) serve the motion on all parties and notify the alleged victim or, when appropriate, the alleged victim's guardian or representative.

'(2) Before admitting evidence under this rule the court must conduct a hearing in camera and afford the victim and parties a right to attend and be heard. The motion, related papers, and the record of the hearing must be sealed and remain under seal unless the court orders otherwise.'.

CHAPTER 5—ASSISTANCE TO VICTIMS OF SEXUAL ASSAULT

SECTION 40151. EDUCATION AND PREVENTION GRANTS TO REDUCE SEXUAL ASSAULTS AGAINST WOMEN.

Part A of title XIX of the Public Health and Human Services Act (42 U.S.C. 300w et seq.) is amended by adding at the end the following new section:

'SECTION 1910A. USE OF ALLOTMENTS FOR RAPE PREVENTION EDUCATION.

'(a) PERMITTED USE—Notwithstanding section 1904(a)(1), amounts transferred by the State for use under this part may be used for rape prevention and education programs conducted by rape crisis centers or similar nongovernmental nonprofit entities for—

'(1) educational seminars;

'(2) the operation of hotlines;

'(3) training programs for professionals;

'(4) the preparation of informational materials; and

'(5) other efforts to increase awareness of the facts about, or to help prevent, sexual assault, including efforts to increase awareness in underserved racial, ethnic, and language minority communities.

'(b) TARGETING OF EDUCATION PROGRAMS—States providing grant monies must ensure that at least 25 percent of the monies are devoted to education programs targeted for middle school, junior high school, and high school students.

'(e) DEFINITION—For purposes of this section, the term 'rape prevention and education' includes education and prevention efforts directed at offenses committed by offenders who are not known to the victim as well as offenders who are known to the victim.

SECTION 40152. TRAINING PROGRAMS.

(a) IN GENERAL—The Attorney General, after consultation with victim advocates and individuals who have expertise in treating sex offenders, shall establish criteria and develop training programs to assist probation and parole officers and other personnel who work with released sex offenders in the areas of—

(1) case management;

(2) supervision; and

(3) relapse prevention.

(b) TRAINING PROGRAMS—The Attorney General shall ensure, to the extent practicable, that training programs developed under subsection (a) are available in geographically diverse locations throughout the country.

SECTION 40153. CONFIDENTIALITY OF COMMUNICATIONS BETWEEN SEXUAL ASSAULT OR DOMESTIC VIOLENCE VICTIMS AND THEIR COUNSELORS.

(a) STUDY AND DEVELOPMENT OF MODEL LEGISLATION—The Attorney General shall—

(1) study and evaluate the manner in which the States have taken measures to protect the confidentiality of communications between sexual assault or domestic violence victims and their therapists or trained counselors;

(2) develop model legislation that will provide the maximum protection possible for the confidentiality of such communications, within any applicable constitutional limits, taking into account the following factors:

(A) the danger that counseling programs for victims of sexual assault and domestic violence will be unable to achieve their goal of helping victims recover from the trauma associated with these crimes if there is no assurance that the records of the counseling sessions will be kept confidential;

(B) consideration of the appropriateness of an absolute privilege for communications between victims of sexual assault or domestic violence and their therapists or trained counselors, in light of the likelihood that such an absolute privilege will provide the maximum guarantee of confidentiality but also in light of the possibility that such an absolute privilege may be held to violate the rights of criminal defendants under the Federal or State constitutions by denying them the opportunity to obtain exculpatory evidence and present it at trial; and

(C) consideration of what limitations on the disclosure of confidential communications between victims of these crimes and their counselors, short of an absolute privilege, are most likely to ensure that the counseling programs will not be undermined, and specifically whether no such disclosure should be allowed unless, at a minimum, there has been a particularized showing by a criminal defendant of a compelling need for records of such communications, and adequate procedural safeguards are in place to prevent unnecessary or damaging disclosures; and

(3) prepare and disseminate to State authorities the findings made and model legislation developed as a result of the study and evaluation.

(c) REVIEW OF FEDERAL EVIDENTIARY RULES—The Judicial Conference of the United States shall evaluate and report to Congress its views on whether the Federal Rules of Evidence should be amended, and if so, how they should be amended, to guarantee that the confidentiality of communications between sexual assault victims and their therapists or trained counselors will be adequately protected in Federal court proceedings.

SECTION 40154. INFORMATION PROGRAMS.

The Attorney General shall compile information regarding sex offender treatment programs and ensure that information regarding community treatment programs in the community into which a convicted sex offender is released is made available to each person serving a sentence of imprisonment in a Federal penal or correctional institution for a commission of an offense under chapter 109A of title 18, United States Code, or for the commission of a similar offense, including halfway houses and psychiatric institutions.

APPENDIX 3:
SUBTITLE B—SAFE HOMES FOR WOMEN ACT—SELECTED PROVISIONS

SEC. 40211. GRANT FOR A NATIONAL DOMESTIC VIOLENCE HOTLINE

The Family Violence Prevention and Services Act (42 U.S.C. 10401 et seq.) is amended by adding at the end the following new section:

'SEC. 316. NATIONAL DOMESTIC VIOLENCE HOTLINE GRANT.

'(a) IN GENERAL—The Secretary may award a grant to a private, nonprofit entity to provide for the operation of a national, toll-free telephone hotline to provide information and assistance to victims of domestic violence.

'(d) ACTIVITIES—Funds received by an entity under this section shall be used to establish and operate a national, toll-free telephone hotline to provide information and assistance to victims of domestic violence. In establishing and operating the hotline, a private, nonprofit entity shall—

'(1) contract with a carrier for the use of a toll-free telephone line;

'(2) employ, train, and supervise personnel to answer incoming calls and provide counseling and referral services to callers on a 24-hour-a-day basis;

'(3) assemble and maintain a current database of information relating to services for victims of domestic violence to which callers may be referred throughout the United States, including information on the availability of shelters that serve battered women; and

'(4) publicize the hotline to potential users throughout the United States.

SEC. 40221. INTERSTATE ENFORCEMENT

(a) IN GENERAL—Part 1 of title 18, United States Code, is amended by inserting after chapter 110 the following new chapter:

'CHAPTER 110A—DOMESTIC VIOLENCE

'Sec. 2261. Interstate domestic violence.

'(a) OFFENSES-

'(1) CROSSING A STATE LINE—A person who travels across a State line or enters or leaves Indian country with the intent to injure, harass, or intimidate that person's spouse or intimate partner, and who, in the course of or as a result of such travel, intentionally commits a crime of violence and thereby causes bodily injury to such spouse or intimate partner, shall be punished as provided in subsection (b).

'(2) CAUSING THE CROSSING OF A STATE LINE—A person who causes a spouse or intimate partner to cross a State line or to enter or leave Indian country by force, coercion, duress, or fraud and, in the course or as a result of that conduct, intentionally commits a crime of violence and thereby causes bodily injury to the person's spouse or intimate partner, shall be punished as provided in subsection (b).

'(b) PENALTIES—A person who violates this section shall be fined under this title, imprisoned—

'(1) for life or any term of years, if death of the offender's spouse or intimate partner results;

'(2) for not more than 20 years if permanent disfigurement or life threatening bodily injury to the offender's spouse or intimate partner results;

'(3) for not more than 10 years, if serious bodily injury to the offender's spouse or intimate partner results or if the offender uses a dangerous weapon during the offense;

'(4) as provided for the applicable conduct under chapter 109A if the offense would constitute an offense under chapter 109A (without regard to whether the offense was committed in the special maritime and territorial jurisdiction of the United States or in a Federal prison); and

'(5) for not more than 5 years, in any other case, or both fined and imprisoned.

'Sec. 2262. Interstate violation of protection order.

'(a) OFFENSES-

'(1) CROSSING A STATE LINE—A person who travels across a State line or enters or leaves Indian country with the intent to engage in conduct that—

'(A)(i) violates the portion of a protection order that involves protection against credible threats of violence, repeated harassment, or bodily injury to the person or persons for whom the protection order was issued; or `(ii) would violate subparagraph (A) if the conduct occurred in the jurisdiction in which the order was issued; and

'(B) subsequently engages in such conduct, shall be punished as provided in subsection (b).

'(2) CAUSING THE CROSSING OF A STATE LINE—A person who causes a spouse or intimate partner to cross a State line or to enter or leave Indian country by force, coercion, duress, or fraud, and, in the course or as a result of that conduct, intentionally commits an act that injures the person's spouse or intimate partner in violation of a valid protection order issued by a State shall be punished as provided in subsection (b).

'(b) PENALTIES—A person who violates this section shall be fined under this title, imprisoned—

'(1) for life or any term of years, if death of the offender's spouse or intimate partner results;

'(2) for not more than 20 years if permanent disfigurement or life threatening bodily injury to the offender's spouse or intimate partner results;

'(3) for not more than 10 years, if serious bodily injury to the offender's spouse or intimate partner results or if the offender uses a dangerous weapon during the offense;

'(4) as provided for the applicable conduct under chapter 109A if the offense would constitute an offense under chapter 109A (without regard to whether the offense was committed in the special maritime and territorial jurisdiction of the United States or in a Federal prison); and

'(5) for not more than 5 years, in any other case, or both fined and imprisoned.

'Sec. 2263. Pretrial release of defendant.

'In any proceeding pursuant to section 3142 for the purpose of determining whether a defendant charged under this chapter shall be released pending trial, or for the purpose of determining conditions of such release, the alleged victim shall be given an opportunity to be heard regarding the danger posed by the defendant.

'Sec. 2264. Restitution.

'(a) IN GENERAL—Notwithstanding section 3663, and in addition to any other civil or criminal penalty authorized by law, the court shall order restitution for any offense under this chapter.

'(b) SCOPE AND NATURE OF ORDER-

'(1) DIRECTIONS—The order of restitution under this section shall direct that—

'(A) the defendant pay to the victim (through the appropriate court mechanism) the full amount of the victim's losses as determined by the court, pursuant to paragraph (3); and

'(B) the United States Attorney enforce the restitution order by all available and reasonable means.

'(2) ENFORCEMENT BY VICTIM—An order of restitution also may be enforced by a victim named in the order to receive the restitution in the same manner as a judgment in a civil action.

'(3) DEFINITION—For purposes of this subsection, the term 'full amount of the victim's losses' includes any costs incurred by the victim for—

'(A) medical services relating to physical, psychiatric, or psychological care;

'(B) physical and occupational therapy or rehabilitation;

'(C) necessary transportation, temporary housing, and child care expenses;

'(D) lost income;

'(E) attorneys' fees, plus any costs incurred in obtaining a civil protection order; and

'(F) any other losses suffered by the victim as a proximate result of the offense.

'(4) ORDER MANDATORY-

'(A) The issuance of a restitution order under this section is mandatory.

'(B) A court may not decline to issue an order under this section because of—

'(i) the economic circumstances of the defendant; or

'(ii) the fact that a victim has, or is entitled to, receive compensation for his or her injuries from the proceeds of insurance or any other source.

'(C)(i) Notwithstanding subparagraph (A), the court may take into account the economic circumstances of the defendant in determining the manner in which and the schedule according to which the restitution is to be paid.

'(ii) For purposes of this subparagraph, the term 'economic circumstances' includes—

'(I) the financial resources and other assets of the defendant;

'(II) projected earnings, earning capacity, and other income of the defendant; and

'(III) any financial obligations of the defendant, including obligations to dependents.

'(D) Subparagraph (A) does not apply if—

'(i) the court finds on the record that the economic circumstances of the defendant do not allow for the payment of any amount of a restitution order, and do not allow for the payment of any or some portion of the amount of a restitution order in the foreseeable future (under any reasonable schedule of payments); and

'(ii) the court enters in its order the amount of the victim's losses, and provides a nominal restitution award.

'(5) MORE THAN 1 OFFENDER—When the court finds that more than 1 offender has contributed to the loss of a victim, the court may make each offender liable for payment of the full amount of restitution or may apportion liability among the offenders to reflect the level of contribution and economic circumstances of each offender.

'(6) MORE THAN 1 VICTIM—When the court finds that more than 1 victim has sustained a loss requiring restitution by an offender, the court shall order full restitution of each victim but may provide for different payment schedules to reflect the economic circumstances of each victim.

'(7) PAYMENT SCHEDULE—An order under this section may direct the defendant to make a single lump-sum payment or partial payments at specified intervals.

'(8) SETOFF—Any amount paid to a victim under this section shall be set off against any amount later recovered as compensatory damages by the victim from the defendant in—

'(A) any Federal civil proceeding; and

'(B) any State civil proceeding, to the extent provided by the law of the State.

'(9) EFFECT ON OTHER SOURCES OF COMPENSATION—The issuance of a restitution order shall not affect the entitlement of a victim to receive compensation with respect to a loss from insurance or any other source until the payments actually received by the victim under the restitution order fully compensate the victim for the loss.

'(10) CONDITION OF PROBATION OR SUPERVISED RELEASE—Compliance with a restitution order issued under this section shall be a condition of any probation or supervised release of a defendant. If an offender fails to comply with a restitution order, the court may, after a hearing, revoke probation or a term of supervised release, modify the terms or conditions of probation or a term of supervised release, or hold the defendant in contempt pursuant to section 3583(e). In determining whether to revoke probation or a term of supervised release, modify the terms or conditions of probation or supervised release or hold a defendant serving a term of supervised release in contempt, the court shall consider the defendant's employment status, earning ability and financial resources, the willfulness of the defendant's failure to comply, and any other circumstances that may have a bearing on the defendant's ability to comply.

'(c) AFFIDAVIT—Within 60 days after conviction and, in any event, not later than 10 days before sentencing, the United States Attorney (or such Attorney's delegate), after consulting with the victim, shall prepare and file an affidavit with the court listing the amounts subject to restitution under this section. The affidavit shall be signed by the United States Attorney (or the delegate) and the victim. Should the victim object to any of the information included in the affidavit, the United States Attorney (or the delegate) shall advise the victim that the victim may file a separate affidavit and assist the victim in the preparation of the affidavit.

'(d) OBJECTION—If, after the defendant has been notified of the affidavit, no objection is raised by the defendant, the amounts attested to in the affidavit filed pursuant to subsection (a) shall be entered in the court's restitution order. If objection is raised, the court may require the victim or the United States Attorney (or the United States Attorney's delegate) to submit further affidavits or other supporting documents, demonstrating the victim's losses.

'(e) ADDITIONAL DOCUMENTATION AND TESTIMONY—If the court concludes, after reviewing the supporting documentation and considering the defendant's objections, that there is a substantial reason for doubting the authenticity or veracity of the records submitted, the court may require additional documentation or hear testimony on those questions. The privacy of any records filed, or testimony heard, pursuant to this section, shall be maintained to the greatest extent possible, and such records may be filed or testimony heard in camera.

'(f) FINAL DETERMINATION OF LOSSES—If the victim's losses are not ascertainable 10 days before sentencing as provided in subsection (c), the United States Attorney (or the United States Attorney's delegate) shall so inform the court, and the court shall set a date for the final determination of the victim's losses, not to exceed 90 days after sentencing. If the victim subsequently discovers further losses, the victim shall have 90 days after discovery of those losses in which to petition the court for an amended restitution order. Such order may be granted only upon a showing of good cause for the failure to include such losses in the initial claim for restitutionary relief.

'(g) RESTITUTION IN ADDITION TO PUNISHMENT—An award of restitution to the victim of an offense under this chapter is not a substitute for imposition of punishment under this chapter.

'Sec. 2265. Full faith and credit given to protection orders

'(a) FULL FAITH AND CREDIT—Any protection order issued that is consistent with subsection (b) of this section by the court of one State or Indian tribe (the issuing State or Indian tribe) shall be accorded full faith and credit by the court of another State or Indian tribe (the enforcing State or Indian tribe) and enforced as if it were the order of the enforcing State or tribe.

'(b) PROTECTION ORDER—A protection order issued by a State or tribal court is consistent with this subsection if—

'(1) such court has jurisdiction over the parties and matter under the law of such State or Indian tribe; and

'(2) reasonable notice and opportunity to be heard is given to the person against whom the order is sought sufficient to protect that person's right to due process. In the case of ex parte orders, notice and opportunity to be heard must be provided within the time required by State or tribal law, and in any event within a reasonable time after the order is issued, sufficient to protect the respondent's due process rights.

'(c) CROSS OR COUNTER PETITION—A protection order issued by a State or tribal court against one who has petitioned, filed a complaint, or otherwise filed a written pleading for protection against abuse by a spouse or intimate partner is not entitled to full faith and credit if—

'(1) no cross or counter petition, complaint, or other written pleading was filed seeking such a protection order; or

'(2) a cross or counter petition has been filed and the court did not make specific findings that each party was entitled to such an order.

'Sec. 2266. Definitions.

'In this chapter—

'bodily injury' means any act, except one done in self-defense, that results in physical injury or sexual abuse.

'Indian country' has the meaning stated in section 1151.

'protection order' includes any injunction or other order issued for the purpose of preventing violent or threatening acts or harassment against, or contact or communication with or physical proximity to, another person, including temporary and final orders issued by civil and criminal courts (other than support or child custody orders) whether obtained by filing an independent action or as a pendente lite order in another proceeding so long as any civil order was issued in response to a complaint, petition or motion filed by or on behalf of a person seeking protection.

'spouse or intimate partner' includes—

'(A) a spouse, a former spouse, a person who shares a child in common with the abuser, and a person who cohabits or has cohabited with the abuser as a spouse; and

'(B) any other person similarly situated to a spouse who is protected by the domestic or family violence laws of the State in which the injury occurred or where the victim resides.

'State' includes a State of the United States, the District of Columbia, a commonwealth, territory, or possession of the United States.

'travel across State lines' does not include travel across State lines by an individual who is a member of an Indian tribe when such individual remains at all times in the territory of the Indian tribe of which the individual is a member.'.

SEC. 40231. ENCOURAGING ARREST POLICIES.

(3) by inserting after part T the following new part:

'PART U—GRANTS TO ENCOURAGE ARREST POLICIES

'SEC. 2101. GRANTS.

'(a) PURPOSE—The purpose of this part is to encourage States, Indian tribal governments, and units of local government to treat domestic violence as a serious violation of criminal law.

'(b) GRANT AUTHORITY—The Attorney General may make grants to eligible States, Indian tribal governments, or units of local government for the following purposes:

'(1) To implement mandatory arrest or proarrest programs and policies in police departments, including mandatory arrest programs and policies for protection order violations.

'(2) To develop policies and training in police departments to improve tracking of cases involving domestic violence.

'(3) To centralize and coordinate police enforcement, prosecution, or judicial responsibility for domestic violence cases in groups or units of police officers, prosecutors, or judges.

'(4) To coordinate computer tracking systems to ensure communication between police, prosecutors, and both criminal and family courts.

'(5) To strengthen legal advocacy service programs for victims of domestic violence.

'(6) To educate judges in criminal and other courts about domestic violence and to improve judicial handling of such cases.

'SEC. 2105. DEFINITIONS.

'For purposes of this part—

'(1) the term 'domestic violence' includes felony or misdemeanor crimes of violence committed by a current or former spouse of the victim, by a person with whom the victim shares a child in common, by a person who is cohabitating with or has cohabitated with the victim as a spouse, by a person similarly situated to a spouse of the victim under the domestic or family violence laws of the jurisdiction receiving grant monies, or by any other adult person against a victim who is protected from that person's acts under the domestic or family violence laws of the eligible State, Indian tribal government, or unit of local government that receives a grant under this part; and

'(2) the term 'protection order' includes any injunction issued for the purpose of preventing violent or threatening acts of domestic violence, including temporary and final orders issued by civil or criminal courts (other than support or child custody orders or provisions) whether obtained by filing an independent action or as a pendente lite order in another proceeding.'.

The Law of Violence Against Women

SEC. 40241. GRANTS FOR BATTERED WOMEN'S SHELTERS

SEC. 40251. YOUTH EDUCATION AND DOMESTIC VIOLENCE.

The Family Violence Prevention and Services Act (42 U.S.C. 10401 et seq.), as amended by section 40211, is amended by adding at the end the following new section:

'SEC. 317. YOUTH EDUCATION AND DOMESTIC VIOLENCE.

'(a) GENERAL PURPOSE—For purposes of this section, the Secretary may, in consultation with the Secretary of Education, select, implement and evaluate 4 model programs for education of young people about domestic violence and violence among intimate partners.

'(b) NATURE OF PROGRAM—The Secretary shall select, implement and evaluate separate model programs for 4 different audiences: primary schools, middle schools, secondary schools, and institutions of higher education. The model programs shall be selected, implemented, and evaluated in consultation with educational experts, legal and psychological experts on battering, and victim advocate organizations such as battered women's shelters, State coalitions and resource centers.

SEC. 40261. ESTABLISHMENT OF COMMUNITY PROGRAMS ON DOMESTIC VIOLENCE.

The Family Violence Prevention and Services Act (42 U.S.C. 10401 et seq.), as amended by section 40251, is amended by adding at the end the following new section:

'SEC. 318. DEMONSTRATION GRANTS FOR COMMUNITY INITIATIVES. '(a) IN GENERAL—The Secretary shall provide grants to nonprofit private organizations to establish projects in local communities involving many sectors of each community to coordinate intervention and prevention of domestic violence.

'(b) ELIGIBILITY—To be eligible for a grant under this section, an entity—

'(1) shall be a nonprofit organization organized for the purpose of coordinating community projects for the intervention in and prevention of domestic violence; and

'(2) shall include representatives of pertinent sectors of the local community, which may include—

'(A) health care providers;

'(B) the education community;

'(C) the religious community;

'(D) the justice system;

'(E) domestic violence program advocates;

'(F) human service entities such as State child services divisions;

'(G) business and civic leaders; and

'(H) other pertinent sectors.

SEC. 40281. CONFIDENTIALITY OF ABUSED PERSON'S ADDRESS.

(a) REGULATIONS—Not later than 90 days after the date of enactment of this Act, the United States Postal Service shall promulgate regulations to secure the confidentiality of domestic violence shelters and abused persons' addresses.

(b) REQUIREMENTS—The regulations under subsection (a) shall require—

(1) in the case of an individual, the presentation to an appropriate postal official of a valid, outstanding protection order; and

(2) in the case of a domestic violence shelter, the presentation to an appropriate postal authority of proof from a State domestic violence coalition that meets the requirements of section 311 of the Family Violence Prevention and Services Act (42 U.S.C. 10410)) verifying that the organization is a domestic violence shelter.

(c) DISCLOSURE FOR CERTAIN PURPOSES—The regulations under subsection (a) shall not prohibit the disclosure of addresses to State or Federal agencies for legitimate law enforcement or other governmental purposes.

(d) EXISTING COMPILATIONS—Compilations of addresses existing at the time at which order is presented to an appropriate postal official shall be excluded from the scope of the regulations under subsection (a).

SEC. 40292. STATE DATABASES

(a) IN GENERAL—The Attorney General shall study and report to the States and to Congress on how the States may collect centralized databases on the incidence of sexual and domestic violence offenses within a State.

SEC. 40293. NUMBER AND COST OF INJURIES.

(a) STUDY—The Secretary of Health and Human Services, acting through the Centers for Disease Control Injury Control Division, shall conduct a study to obtain a national projection of the incidence of injuries resulting from domestic violence, the cost of injuries to health care facilities, and recommend health care strategies for reducing the incidence and cost of such injuries.

SEC. 40295. RURAL DOMESTIC VIOLENCE AND CHILD ABUSE ENFORCEMENT ASSISTANCE.

(a) GRANTS—The Attorney General may make grants to States, Indian tribal governments, and local governments of rural States, and to other public or private entities of rural States—

(1) to implement, expand, and establish cooperative efforts and projects between law enforcement officers, prosecutors, victim advocacy groups, and other related parties to investigate and prosecute incidents of domestic violence and child abuse;

(2) to provide treatment and counseling to victims of domestic violence and child abuse; and

(3) to work in cooperation with the community to develop education and prevention strategies directed toward such issues.

(b) DEFINITIONS—In this section—

'Indian tribe' means a tribe, band, pueblo, nation, or other organized group or community of Indians, including an Alaska Native village (as defined in or established under the Alaska Native Claims Settlement Act (43 U.S.C. 1601 et seq.), that is recognized as eligible for the special programs and services provided by the United States to Indians because of their status as Indians.

'rural State' has the meaning stated in section 1501(b) of title I of the Omnibus Crime Control and Safe Streets Act of 1968 (42 U.S.C. 3796bb(B)).

APPENDIX 4:
SUBTITLE C—THE CIVIL RIGHTS FOR GENDER-MOTIVATED VIOLENCE ACT—SELECTED PROVISIONS

SECTION 40302. CIVIL RIGHTS.

(a) PURPOSE—Pursuant to the affirmative power of Congress to enact this subtitle under section 5 of the Fourteenth Amendment to the Constitution, as well as under section 8 of Article I of the Constitution, it is the purpose of this subtitle to protect the civil rights of victims of gender motivated violence and to promote public safety, health, and activities affecting interstate commerce by establishing a Federal civil rights cause of action for victims of crimes of violence motivated by gender.

(b) RIGHT TO BE FREE FROM CRIMES OF VIOLENCE—All persons within the United States shall have the right to be free from crimes of violence motivated by gender (as defined in subsection (d)).

(c) CAUSE OF ACTION—A person (including a person who acts under color of any statute, ordinance, regulation, custom, or usage of any State) who commits a crime of violence motivated by gender and thus deprives another of the right declared in subsection (b) shall be liable to the party injured, in an action for the recovery of compensatory and punitive damages, injunctive and declaratory relief, and such other relief as a court may deem appropriate.

(d) DEFINITIONS—For purposes of this section—

   (1) the term 'Crime of Violence Motivated by Gender' means a crime of violence committed because of gender or on the basis of gender, and due, at least in part, to an animus based on the victim's gender; and

   (2) the term 'Crime of Violence' means—

      (A) an act or series of acts that would constitute a felony against the person or that would constitute a felony against property if the conduct presents a serious risk of physical injury to another, and that would come within the meaning of State or Federal offenses described in section 16 of title 18, United States Code, whether or not those acts have actually resulted in criminal charges, prosecution, or conviction and whether or not those acts were committed in the special maritime, territorial, or prison jurisdiction of the United States; and

(B) includes an act or series of acts that would constitute a felony described in subparagraph (A) but for the relationship between the person who takes such action and the individual against whom such action is taken.

(e) Limitation and Procedures—

(1) LIMITATION—Nothing in this section entitles a person to a cause of action under subsection (c) for random acts of violence unrelated to gender or for acts that cannot be demonstrated, by a preponderance of the evidence, to be motivated by gender (within the meaning of subsection (d)).

(2) NO PRIOR CRIMINAL ACTION—Nothing in this section requires a prior criminal complaint, prosecution, or conviction to establish the elements of a cause of action under subsection (c).

(3) CONCURRENT JURISDICTION—The Federal and State courts shall have concurrent jurisdiction over actions brought pursuant to this subtitle.

(4) SUPPLEMENTAL JURISDICTION—Neither section 1367 of title 28, United States Code, nor subsection (c) of this section shall be construed, by reason of a claim arising under such subsection, to confer on the courts of the United States jurisdiction over any State law claim seeking the establishment of a divorce, alimony, equitable distribution of marital property, or child custody decree.

(5) LIMITATION ON REMOVAL—Section 1445 of title 28, United States Code, is amended by adding at the end the following new subsection:

'(d) A civil action in any State court arising under section 40302 of the Violence Against Women Act of 1994 may not be removed to any district court of the United States.'.

SECTION 40304. SENSE OF THE SENATE CONCERNING PROTECTION OF THE PRIVACY OF RAPE VICTIMS.

It is the sense of the Senate that news media, law enforcement officers, and other persons should exercise restraint and respect a rape victim's privacy by not disclosing the victim's identity to the general public or facilitating such disclosure without the consent of the victim.

APPENDIX 5:
SUBTITLE D—THE EQUAL JUSTICE FOR WOMEN IN THE COURTS ACT— SELECTED PROVISIONS

CHAPTER 1—EDUCATION AND TRAINING FOR JUDGES AND COURT PERSONNEL IN STATE COURTS

SECTION 40411. GRANTS AUTHORIZED.

The State Justice Institute may award grants for the purpose of developing, testing, presenting, and disseminating model programs to be used by States (as defined in section 202 of the State Justice Institute Act of 1984 (42 U.S.C. 10701)) in training judges and court personnel in the laws of the States and by Indian tribes in training tribal judges and court personnel in the laws of the tribes on rape, sexual assault, domestic violence, and other crimes of violence motivated by the victim's gender.

SECTION 40412. TRAINING PROVIDED BY GRANTS.

Training provided pursuant to grants made under this subtitle may include current information, existing studies, or current data on—

(1) the nature and incidence of rape and sexual assault by strangers and nonstrangers, marital rape, and incest;

(2) the underreporting of rape, sexual assault, and child sexual abuse;

(3) the physical, psychological, and economic impact of rape and sexual assault on the victim, the costs to society, and the implications for sentencing;

(4) the psychology of sex offenders, their high rate of recidivism, and the implications for sentencing;

(5) the historical evolution of laws and attitudes on rape and sexual assault;

(6) sex stereotyping of female and male victims of rape and sexual assault, racial stereotyping of rape victims and defendants, and the impact of such stereotypes on credibility of witnesses, sentencing, and other aspects of the administration of justice;

(7) application of rape shield laws and other limits on introduction of evidence that may subject victims to improper sex stereotyping and harassment in both rape and nonrape cases, including the need for *sua sponte* judicial intervention in inappropriate cross-examination;

(8) the use of expert witness testimony on rape trauma syndrome, child sexual abuse accommodation syndrome, posttraumatic stress syndrome, and similar issues;

(9) the legitimate reasons why victims of rape, sexual assault, and incest may refuse to testify against a defendant;

(10) the nature and incidence of domestic violence;

(11) the physical, psychological, and economic impact of domestic violence on the victim, the costs to society, and the implications for court procedures and sentencing;

(12) the psychology and self-presentation of batterers and victims and the implications for court proceedings and credibility of witnesses;

(13) sex stereotyping of female and male victims of domestic violence, myths about presence or absence of domestic violence in certain racial, ethnic, religious, or socioeconomic groups, and their impact on the administration of justice;

(14) historical evolution of laws and attitudes on domestic violence;

(15) proper and improper interpretations of the defenses of self-defense and provocation, and the use of expert witness testimony on battered woman syndrome;

(16) the likelihood of retaliation, recidivism, and escalation of violence by batterers, and the potential impact of incarceration and other meaningful sanctions for acts of domestic violence including violations of orders of protection;

(17) economic, psychological, social and institutional reasons for victims' inability to leave the batterer, to report domestic violence or to follow through on complaints, including the influence of lack of support from police, judges, and court personnel, and the legitimate reasons why victims of domestic violence may refuse to testify against a defendant;

(18) the need for orders of protection, and the implications of mutual orders of protection, dual arrest policies, and mediation in domestic violence cases; and

(19) recognition of and response to gender-motivated crimes of violence other than rape, sexual assault and domestic violence, such as mass or serial murder motivated by the gender of the victims.

SECTION 40413. COOPERATION IN DEVELOPING PROGRAMS IN MAKING GRANTS UNDER THIS TITLE.

The State Justice Institute shall ensure that model programs carried out pursuant to grants made under this subtitle are developed with the participation of law enforcement officials, public and private nonprofit victim advocates, legal experts, prosecutors, defense attorneys, and recognized experts on gender bias in the courts.

CHAPTER 2—EDUCATION AND TRAINING FOR JUDGES AND COURT PERSONNEL IN FEDERAL COURTS

SECTION 40421. AUTHORIZATIONS OF CIRCUIT STUDIES; EDUCATION AND TRAINING GRANTS.

(a) STUDIES- In order to gain a better understanding of the nature and the extent of gender bias in the Federal courts, the circuit judicial councils are encouraged to conduct studies of the instances, if any, of gender bias in their respective circuits and to implement recommended reforms.

(b) MATTERS FOR EXAMINATION- The studies under subsection (a) may include an examination of the effects of gender on—

(1) the treatment of litigants, witnesses, attorneys, jurors, and judges in the courts, including before magistrate and bankruptcy judges;

(2) the interpretation and application of the law, both civil and criminal;

(3) treatment of defendants in criminal cases;

(4) treatment of victims of violent crimes in judicial proceedings;

(5) sentencing;

(6) sentencing alternatives and the nature of supervision of probation and parole;

(7) appointments to committees of the Judicial Conference and the courts;

(8) case management and court sponsored alternative dispute resolution programs;

(9) the selection, retention, promotion, and treatment of employees;

(10) appointment of arbitrators, experts, and special masters;

(11) the admissibility of the victim's past sexual history in civil and criminal cases; and

(12) the aspects of the topics listed in section 40412 that pertain to issues within the jurisdiction of the Federal courts.

(c) CLEARINGHOUSE—The Administrative Office of the United States Courts shall act as a clearinghouse to disseminate any reports and materials issued by the gender bias task forces under subsection (a) and to respond to requests for such reports and materials. The gender bias task forces shall provide the Administrative Office of the Courts of the United States with their reports and related material.

APPENDIX 6:
SUBTITLE E—VIOLENCE AGAINST WOMEN
ACT IMPROVEMENTS—
SELECTED PROVISIONS

SECTION 40502. INCREASED PENALTIES FOR SEX OFFENSES AGAINST VICTIMS BELOW THE AGE OF 16.

Section 2245(2) of title 18, United States Code, is amended—

(3) by inserting after subparagraph (C) the following new subparagraph:

'(D) the intentional touching, not through the clothing, of the genitalia of another person who has not attained the age of 16 years with an intent to abuse, humiliate, harass, degradc, or arouse or gratify the sexual desire of any person;'.

SECTION 40503. PAYMENT OF COST OF TESTING FOR SEXUALLY TRANSMITTED DISEASES.

(a) FOR VICTIMS IN SEX OFFENSE CASES—Section 503(c)(7) of the Victims' Rights and Restitution Act of 1990 (42 U.S.C. 10607(c)(7)) is amended by adding at the end the following: 'The Attorney General shall provide for the payment of the cost of up to 2 anonymous and confidential tests of the victim for sexually transmitted diseases, including HIV, gonorrhea, herpes, chlamydia, and syphilis, during the 12 months following sexual assaults that pose a risk of transmission, and the cost of a counseling session by a medically trained professional on the accuracy of such tests and the risk of transmission of sexually transmitted diseases to the victim as the result of the assault. A victim may waive anonymity and confidentiality of any tests paid for under this section.'.

(b) Limited Testing of Defendants—

(1) COURT ORDER—The victim of an offense of the type referred to in subsection (a) may obtain an order in the district court of the United States for the district in which charges are brought against the defendant charged with the offense, after notice to the defendant and an opportunity to be heard, requiring that the defendant be tested for the presence of the etiologic agent for acquired immune deficiency syndrome, and that the results of the test be communicated to the victim and the defendant. Any test result of the defendant given to the victim or the defendant must be accompanied by appropriate counseling.

(2) SHOWING REQUIRED—To obtain an order under paragraph (1), the victim must demonstrate that—

(A) the defendant has been charged with the offense in a State or Federal court, and if the defendant has been arrested without a warrant, a probable cause determination has been made;

(B) the test for the etiologic agent for acquired immune deficiency syndrome is requested by the victim after appropriate counseling; and

(C) the test would provide information necessary for the health of the victim of the alleged offense and the court determines that the alleged conduct of the defendant created a risk of transmission, as determined by the Centers for Disease Control, of the etiologic agent for acquired immune deficiency syndrome to the victim.

(3) FOLLOW-UP TESTING—The court may order follow-up tests and counseling under paragraph (b)(1) if the initial test was negative. Such follow-up tests and counseling shall be performed at the request of the victim on dates that occur six months and twelve months following the initial test.

(4) TERMINATION OF TESTING REQUIREMENTS—An order for follow-up testing under paragraph (3) shall be terminated if the person obtains an acquittal on, or dismissal of, all charges of the type referred to in subsection (a).

(5) CONFIDENTIALITY OF TEST—The results of any test ordered under this subsection shall be disclosed only to the victim or, where the court deems appropriate, to the parent or legal guardian of the victim, and to the person tested. The victim may disclose the test results only to any medical professional, counselor, family member or sexual partner(s) the victim may have had since the attack. Any such individual to whom the test results are disclosed by the victim shall maintain the confidentiality of such information.

(6) DISCLOSURE OF TEST RESULTS—The court shall issue an order to prohibit the disclosure by the victim of the results of any test performed under this subsection to anyone other than those mentioned in paragraph (5). The contents of the court proceedings and test results pursuant to this section shall be sealed. The results of such test performed on the defendant under this section shall not be used as evidence in any criminal trial.

(7) CONTEMPT FOR DISCLOSURE—Any person who discloses the results of a test in violation of this subsection may be held in contempt of court.

(c) PENALTIES FOR INTENTIONAL TRANSMISSION OF HIV—Not later than 6 months after the date of enactment of this Act, the United States Sentencing Commission shall conduct a study and prepare and submit to the committees on the Judiciary of the Senate and the House of Representatives a report concerning recommendations for the revision of sentencing guidelines that relate to offenses in which an HIV infected individual engages in sexual activity if the individual knows that he or she is infected with HIV and intends, through such sexual activity, to expose another to HIV.

SECTION 40504. EXTENSION AND STRENGTHENING OF RESTITUTION.

Section 3663(b) of title 18, United States Code, is amended—

(4) by inserting after paragraph (3) the following new paragraph:

'(4) in any case, reimburse the victim for lost income and necessary child care, transportation, and other expenses related to participation in the investigation or prosecution of the offense or attendance at proceedings related to the offense; and'.

SECTION 40505. ENFORCEMENT OF RESTITUTION ORDERS THROUGH SUSPENSION OF FEDERAL BENEFITS.

Section 3663 of title 18, United States Code, is amended by adding at the end the following new subsection:

'(i)(1) A Federal agency shall immediately suspend all Federal benefits provided by the agency to the defendant, and shall terminate the defendant's eligibility for Federal benefits administered by that agency, upon receipt of a certified copy of a written judicial finding that the defendant is delinquent in making restitution in accordance with any schedule of payments or any requirement of immediate payment imposed under this section.

'(2) Any written finding of delinquency described in paragraph (1) shall be made by a court, after a hearing, upon motion of the victim named in the order to receive the restitution or upon motion of the United States.

'(3) A defendant found to be delinquent may subsequently seek a written finding from the court that the defendant has rectified the delinquency or that the defendant has made and will make good faith efforts to rectify the delinquency. The defendant's eligibility for Federal benefits shall be reinstated upon receipt by the agency of a certified copy of such a finding.

'(4) In this subsection, 'Federal benefit' means a grant, contract, loan, professional license, or commercial license provided by an agency of the United States.'.

SECTION 40506. NATIONAL BASELINE STUDY ON CAMPUS SEXUAL ASSAULT.

(a) STUDY—The Attorney General, in consultation with the Secretary of Education, shall provide for a national baseline study to examine the scope of the problem of campus sexual assaults and the effectiveness of institutional and legal policies in addressing such crimes and protecting victims. The Attorney General may utilize the Bureau of Justice Statistics, the National Institute of Justice, and the Office for Victims of Crime in carrying out this section.

(b) REPORT—Based on the study required by subsection (a) and data collected under the Student Right-To-Know and Campus Security Act (20 U.S.C. 1001 note; Public Law 101-542) and amendments made by that Act, the Attorney General shall prepare a report including an analysis of—

(1) the number of reported allegations and estimated number of unreported allegations of campus sexual assaults, and to whom the allegations are reported (including authorities of the educational institution, sexual assault victim service entities, and local criminal authorities);

(2) the number of campus sexual assault allegations reported to authorities of educational institutions which are reported to criminal authorities;

(3) the number of campus sexual assault allegations that result in criminal prosecution in comparison with the number of non-campus sexual assault allegations that result in criminal prosecution;

(4) Federal and State laws or regulations pertaining specifically to campus sexual assaults;

(5) the adequacy of policies and practices of educational institutions in addressing campus sexual assaults and protecting victims, including consideration of—

(A) the security measures in effect at educational institutions, such as utilization of campus police and security guards, control over access to grounds and buildings, supervision of student activities and student living arrangements, control over the consumption of alcohol by students, lighting, and the availability of escort services;

(B) the articulation and communication to students of the institution's policies concerning sexual assaults;

(C) policies and practices that may prevent or discourage the reporting of campus sexual assaults to local criminal authorities, or that may otherwise obstruct justice or interfere with the prosecution of perpetrators of campus sexual assaults;

(D) the nature and availability of victim services for victims of campus sexual assaults;

(E) the ability of educational institutions' disciplinary processes to address allegations of sexual assault adequately and fairly;

(F) measures that are taken to ensure that victims are free of unwanted contact with alleged assailants, and disciplinary sanctions that are imposed when a sexual assault is determined to have occurred; and

(G) the grounds on which educational institutions are subject to lawsuits based on campus sexual assaults, the resolution of these cases, and measures that can be taken to avoid the likelihood of lawsuits and civil liability;

(6) in conjunction with the report produced by the Department of Education in coordination with institutions of education under the Student Right-To-Know and Campus Security Act (20 U.S.C. 1001 note; Public Law 101-542) and amendments made by that Act, an assessment of the policies and practices of educational institutions that are of greatest effectiveness in addressing campus sexual assaults and protecting victims, including policies and practices relating to the particular issues described in paragraph (5); and

(7) any recommendations the Attorney General may have for reforms to address campus sexual assaults and protect victims more effectively, and any other matters that the Attorney General deems relevant to the subject of the study and report required by this section.

(c) SUBMISSION OF REPORT—The report required by subsection (b) shall be submitted to the Congress no later than September 1, 1996.

(d) DEFINITION—For purposes of this section,

'Campus Sexual Assaults' includes sexual assaults occurring at institutions of postsecondary education and sexual assaults committed against or by students or employees of such institutions.

SECTION 40507. REPORT ON BATTERED WOMEN'S SYNDROME.

(a) REPORT—Not less than 1 year after the date of enactment of this Act, the Attorney General and the Secretary of Health and Human Services shall transmit to the House Committee on Energy and Commerce, the Senate Committee on Labor and Human Resources, and the Committees on the Judiciary of the Senate and the House of Representatives a report on the medical and psychological basis of `battered women's syndrome' and on the extent to which evidence of the syndrome has been considered in criminal trials.

(b) COMPONENTS—The report under subsection (a) shall include—

(1) medical and psychological testimony on the validity of battered women's syndrome as a psychological condition;

(2) a compilation of State, tribal, and Federal court cases in which evidence of battered women's syndrome was offered in criminal trials; and

(3) an assessment by State, tribal, and Federal judges, prosecutors, and defense attorneys of the effects that evidence of battered women's syndrome may have in criminal trials.

SECTION 40508. REPORT ON CONFIDENTIALITY OF ADDRESSES FOR VICTIMS OF DOMESTIC VIOLENCE.

(a) REPORT—The Attorney General shall conduct a study of the means by which abusive spouses may obtain information concerning the addresses or locations of estranged or former spouses, notwithstanding the desire of the victims to have such information withheld to avoid further exposure to abuse. Based on the study, the Attorney General shall transmit a report to Congress including—

(1) the findings of the study concerning the means by which information concerning the addresses or locations of abused spouses may be obtained by abusers; and

(2) analysis of the feasibility of creating effective means of protecting the confidentiality of information concerning the addresses and locations of abused spouses to protect such persons from exposure to further abuse while preserving access to such information for legitimate purposes.

(b) USE OF COMPONENTS—The Attorney General may use the National Institute of Justice and the Office for Victims of Crime in carrying out this section.

SECTION 40509. REPORT ON RECORDKEEPING RELATING TO DOMESTIC VIOLENCE.

Not later than 1 year after the date of enactment of this Act, the Attorney General shall complete a study of, and shall submit to Congress a report and recommendations on, problems of recordkeeping of criminal complaints involving domestic violence. The study and report shall examine—

(1) the efforts that have been made by the Department of Justice, including the Federal Bureau of Investigation, to collect statistics on domestic violence; and

(2) the feasibility of requiring that the relationship between an offender and victim be reported in Federal records of crimes of aggravated assault, rape, and other violent crimes.

APPENDIX 7:
SUBTITLE F—NATIONAL STALKER AND DOMESTIC VIOLENCE REDUCTION— SELECTED PROVISIONS

SECTION 40601. AUTHORIZING ACCESS TO FEDERAL CRIMINAL INFORMATION DATABASES.

(a) ACCESS AND ENTRY—Section 534 of title 28, United States Code, is amended by adding at the end the following:

'(e)(1) Information from national crime information databases consisting of identification records, criminal history records, protection orders, and wanted person records may be disseminated to civil or criminal courts for use in domestic violence or stalking cases. Nothing in this subsection shall be construed to permit access to such records for any other purpose.

'(2) Federal and State criminal justice agencies authorized to enter information into criminal information databases may include—

'(A) arrests, convictions, and arrest warrants for stalking or domestic violence or for violations of protection orders for the protection of parties from stalking or domestic violence; and

'(B) protection orders for the protection of persons from stalking or domestic violence, provided such orders are subject to periodic verification.

'(3) As used in this subsection—

'(A) the term 'National Crime Information Databases' means the National Crime Information Center and its incorporated criminal history databases, including the Interstate Identification Index; and

'(B) the term 'Protection Order' includes an injunction or any other order issued for the purpose of preventing violent or threatening acts or harassment against, or contact or communication with or physical proximity to, another person, including temporary and final orders issued by civil or criminal courts (other than support or child custody orders) whether obtained by filing an independent action or as a pendente lite order in another proceeding so long as any civil order was issued in response to a complaint, petition, or motion filed by or on behalf of a person seeking protection.'.

SECTION 40602. GRANT PROGRAM.

(a) IN GENERAL—The Attorney General is authorized to provide grants to States and units of local government to improve processes for entering data regarding stalking and domestic violence into local, State, and national crime information databases.

(b) ELIGIBILITY—To be eligible to receive a grant under subsection (a), a State or unit of local government shall certify that it has or intends to establish a program that enters into the National Crime Information Center records of—

(1) warrants for the arrest of persons violating protection orders intended to protect victims from stalking or domestic violence;

(2) arrests or convictions of persons violating protection or domestic violence; and

(3) protection orders for the protection of persons from stalking or domestic violence.

SECTION 40606. TECHNICAL ASSISTANCE, TRAINING, AND EVALUATIONS.

The Attorney General may provide technical assistance and training in furtherance of the purposes of this subtitle, and may provide for the evaluation of programs that receive funds under this subtitle, in addition to any evaluation requirements that the Attorney General may prescribe for grantees. The technical assistance, training, and evaluations authorized by this section may be carried out directly by the Attorney General, or through contracts or other arrangements with other entities.

SECTION 40607. TRAINING PROGRAMS FOR JUDGES.

The State Justice Institute, after consultation with nationally recognized nonprofit organizations with expertise in stalking and domestic violence cases, shall conduct training programs for State (as defined in section 202 of the State Justice Institute Authorization Act of 1984 (42 U.S.C. 10701)) and Indian tribal judges to ensure that a judge issuing an order in a stalking or domestic violence case has all available criminal history and other information, whether from State or Federal sources.

SECTION 40608. RECOMMENDATIONS ON INTRASTATE COMMUNICATION.

The State Justice Institute, after consultation with nationally recognized nonprofit associations with expertise in data sharing among criminal justice agencies and familiarity with the issues raised in stalking and domestic violence cases, shall recommend proposals regarding how State courts may increase intrastate communication between civil and criminal courts.

SECTION 40609. INCLUSION IN NATIONAL INCIDENT-BASED REPORTING SYSTEM.

Not later than 2 years after the date of enactment of this Act, the Attorney General, in accordance with the States, shall compile data regarding domestic violence and intimidation (including stalking) as part of the National Incident-Based Reporting System (NIBRS).

SECTION 40610. REPORT TO CONGRESS.

The Attorney General shall submit to the Congress an annual report, beginning one year after the date of the enactment of this Act, that provides information concerning the incidence of stalking and domestic violence, and evaluates the effectiveness of State antistalking efforts and legislation.

SECTION 40611. DEFINITIONS.

As used in this subtitle—

(1) the term 'National Crime Information Databases' refers to the National Crime Information Center and its incorporated criminal history databases, including the Interstate Identification Index; and

(2) the term 'Protection Order' includes an injunction or any other order issued for the purpose of preventing violent or threatening acts or harassment against, or contact or communication with or physical proximity to, another person, including temporary and final orders issued by civil or criminal courts (other than support or child custody orders) whether obtained by filing an independent action or as a pendente lite order in another proceeding so long as any civil order was issued in response to a complaint, petition, or motion filed by or on behalf of a person seeking protection.

APPENDIX 8:
SUBTITLE G—PROTECTIONS FOR BATTERED IMMIGRANT WOMEN AND CHILDREN—SELECTED PROVISIONS

SECTION 40701. ALIEN PETITIONING RIGHTS FOR IMMEDIATE RELATIVE OR SECOND PREFERENCE STATUS.

(a) IN GENERAL—Section 204(a)(1) of the Immigration and Nationality Act (8 U.S.C. 1154(a)(1)) is amended—

(C) by adding at the end the following new clauses:

'(iii) An alien who is the spouse of a citizen of the United States, who is a person of good moral character, who is eligible to be classified as an immediate relative under section 201(b)(2)(A)(i), and who has resided in the United States with the alien's spouse may file a petition with the Attorney General under this subparagraph for classification of the alien (and any child of the alien if such a child has not been classified under clause (iv)) under such section if the alien demonstrates to the Attorney General that—

'(I) the alien is residing in the United States, the marriage between the alien and the spouse was entered into in good faith by the alien, and during the marriage the alien or a child of the alien has been battered by or has been the subject of extreme cruelty perpetrated by the alien's spouse; and

'(II) the alien is a person whose deportation, in the opinion of the Attorney General, would result in extreme hardship to the alien or a child of the alien.

'(iv) An alien who is the child of a citizen of the United States, who is a person of good moral character, who is eligible to be classified as an immediate relative under section 201(b)(2)(A)(i), and who has resided in the United States with the citizen parent may file a petition with the Attorney General under this subparagraph for classification of the alien under such section if the alien demonstrates to the Attorney General that—

'(I) the alien is residing in the United States and during the period of residence with the citizen parent the alien has been battered by or has been the subject of extreme cruelty perpetrated by the alien's citizen parent; and

'(II) the alien is a person whose deportation, in the opinion of the Attorney General, would result in extreme hardship to the alien.';

(2) in subparagraph (B)—

(B) by adding at the end the following new clauses:

'(ii) An alien who is the spouse of an alien lawfully admitted for permanent residence, who is a person of good moral character, who is eligible for classification under section 203(a)(2)(A), and who has resided in the United States with the alien's legal permanent resident spouse may file a petition with the Attorney General under this subparagraph for classification of the alien (and any child of the alien if such a child has not been classified under clause (iii)) under such section if the alien demonstrates to the Attorney General that the conditions described in subclauses (I) and (II) of subparagraph (A)(iii) are met with respect to the alien.

'(iii) An alien who is the child of an alien lawfully admitted for permanent residence, who is a person of good moral character, who is eligible for classification under section 203(a)(2)(A), and who has resided in the United States with the alien's permanent resident alien parent may file a petition with the Attorney General under this subparagraph for classification of the alien under such section if the alien demonstrates to the Attorney General that—

'(I) the alien is residing in the United States and during the period of residence with the permanent resident parent the alien has been battered by or has been the subject of extreme cruelty perpetrated by the alien's permanent resident parent; and

'(II) the alien is a person whose deportation, in the opinion of the Attorney General, would result in extreme hardship to the alien.'; and

(3) by adding at the end the following new subparagraph:

'(H) In acting on petitions filed under clause (iii) or (iv) of subparagraph (A) or clause (ii) or (iii) of subparagraph (B), the Attorney General shall consider any credible evidence relevant to the petition. The determination of what evidence is credible and the weight to be given that evidence shall be within the sole discretion of the Attorney General.'.

(c) SURVIVAL RIGHTS TO PETITION—Section 204 of the Immigration and Nationality Act (8 U.S.C. 1154) is amended by adding at the end the following new subsection:

'(h) The legal termination of a marriage may not be the sole basis for revocation under section 205 of a petition filed under subsection (a)(1)(A)(iii) or a petition filed under subsection (a)(1)(B)(ii) pursuant to conditions described in subsection (a)(1)(A)(iii)(I).'.

SECTION 40702. USE OF CREDIBLE EVIDENCE IN SPOUSAL WAIVER APPLICATIONS.

(a) IN GENERAL—Section 216(c)(4) of the Immigration and Nationality Act (8 U.S.C. 1186a(c)(4)) is amended by inserting after the second sentence the following: 'In acting on applications under this paragraph, the Attorney General shall consider any credible evidence relevant to the application. The determination of what evidence is credible and the weight to be given that evidence shall be within the sole discretion of the Attorney General.'.

SECTION 40703. SUSPENSION OF DEPORTATION.

(a) BATTERED SPOUSE OR CHILD—Section 244(a) of the Immigration and Nationality Act (8 U.S.C. 1254(a)) is amended—

(3) by inserting after paragraph (2) the following:

'(3) is deportable under any law of the United States except section 241(a)(1)(G) and the provisions specified in paragraph (2); has been physically present in the United States for a continuous period of not less than 3 years immediately preceding the date of such application; has been battered or subjected to extreme cruelty in the United States by a spouse or parent who is a United States citizen or lawful permanent resident (or is the parent of a child of a United States citizen or lawful permanent resident and the child has been battered or subjected to extreme cruelty in the United States by such citizen or permanent resident parent); and proves that during all of such time in the United States the alien was and is a person of good moral character; and is a person whose deportation would, in the opinion of the Attorney General, result in extreme hardship to the alien or the alien's parent or child.'.

(b) CONSIDERATION OF EVIDENCE—Section 244 of the Immigration and Nationality Act (8 U.S.C. 1254) is amended by adding at the end the following new subsection:

'(g) In acting on applications under subsection (a)(3), the Attorney General shall consider any credible evidence relevant to the application. The determination of what evidence is credible and the weight to be given that evidence shall be within the sole discretion of the Attorney General.'.

APPENDIX 9:
RATE OF INTIMATE PARTNER VIOLENCE AGAINST FEMALES, BY AGE AND VICTIM/OFFENDER RELATIONSHIP (1993-1999)

AGE OF VICTIM	AVERAGE ANNUAL NUMBER	SPOUSE	EX-SPOUSE	BOYFRIEND/ GIRLFRIEND
Total	902,240	33.4%	13.5%	53.1%
12-15	17,870	2.0	0.0	98.0
16-19	123,760	4.1	2.4	93.5
20-24	185,590	22.2	7.5	70.3
25-34	306,550	38.6	17.3	44.1
35-49	239,370	48.6	20.2	31.3
50 or older	29,110	68.7	13.3	18.0

SOURCE: U.S. Department of Justice, Bureau of Justice Statistics

APPENDIX 10:
INTIMATE PARTNER VIOLENCE AGAINST FEMALES AND RATE OF REPORTING TO POLICE, BY AGE (1993-1999)

AGE OF VICTIM	AVERAGE ANNUAL NUMBER	REPORTED	NOT REPORTED	UNKNOWN
Total	902,240	53.7%	46.1%	0.3%
12-15	17,870	27.9	72.1	0.0
16-19	123,760	45.9	54.1	0.0
20-24	185,590	53.2	46.6	0.2
25-34	306,550	57.3	42.7	0.0
35-49	239,370	56.8	42.5	0.7
50 or older	29,110	41.7	57.3	1.1

SOURCE: U.S. Department of Justice, Bureau of Justice Statistics

APPENDIX 11:
RATE OF INTIMATE PARTNER VIOLENCE AGAINST FEMALES, BY AGE (1999)

VICTIM AGE	NUMBER	RATE PER 1,000	PERCENT
Total	671,110	5.8	100%
12-15	9,900	1.3	1
16-19	119,630	15.4	18
20-24	144,100	15.7	21
25-34	182,070	9.4	27
35-49	194,380	6.0	29
50 or older	21,030	0.5	3

SOURCE: U.S. Department of Justice, Bureau of Justice Statistics

APPENDIX 12:
DIRECTORY OF STATE
NAME CHANGE LAWS

ALASKA

Chapter 09.55. SPECIAL ACTIONS AND PROCEEDINGS

Article 01. CHANGE OF NAME

Sec. 09.55.010. Jurisdiction in action for change of name.

A person may bring an action for change of name in the superior court. A change of name of a person may not be made unless the court finds sufficient reasons for the change and also finds it consistent with the public interest. A change of name upon marriage, dissolution, or divorce meets these requirements.

ARIZONA

Section 2-60112-601. Application; venue; judgment

A. When a person desires to change his name and to adopt another name, he may file an application in the superior court in the county of his residence, setting forth reasons for the change of name and the name he wishes to adopt. The court may enter judgment that the adopted name of the party be substituted for the original name.

B. The parent, guardian *ad litem* or next friend of a minor may file an application for change of the name of the minor in the county of the minor's residence. The court shall consider the best interests of the child in determining whether to enter judgment that the name of the minor be changed. 12-601

12-60212-602. Notice of application; effect of change on rights and obligations

A. If upon the filing of the application for change of name the court deems it proper that notice be given, it may order that notice of the application be given by publication or by service upon any party interested.

B. The change of name shall not operate to release the person from any obligations which he has incurred or is under by the original name, or defeat or destroy any rights of property or action which he had in his original name. 12-602

ARKANSAS

§ 9-2-101. Procedure.

(a) Upon the application of any person within the jurisdiction of the courts, the chancery and circuit courts shall have power, upon good reasons shown, to alter or change the name of the person.

(b) When application is made to the courts under this section, it shall be by petition, in writing, embodying the reasons for the application.

(c)(1) When allowed, the petition shall, by order of the court, be spread upon the record, together with the decree of the court.

(2) An appropriate order, as prescribed in this subsection, may be made by a chancellor or circuit judge in vacation. This order shall have the same force and effect as if made at term time.

§ 9-2-102. Use of new name.

Any person whose name may be so changed by judgment or decree of any of the courts shall afterward be known and designated, sue and be sued, plead and be impleaded, by the name thus conferred, except that records of persons under the jurisdiction and supervision of the Department of Correction shall continue to reflect the name as committed to the department's jurisdiction and supervision by the various circuit courts of the State of Arkansas.

CALIFORNIA

California Code§ 1275 Civ. Proc.

Applications for change of names must be determined by the Superior Courts. (Amended by Stats. 1983, Ch. 486, Sec. 1.)

California Code§ 1276 Civ. Proc.

All applications for change of names shall be made to the superior court of the county where the person whose name is proposed to be changed resides either (a) by petition signed by the person or, if the person is under 18 years of age, by one of the person's parents, if living, or if both parents are dead, then by the guardian of the person and, if there is no guardian, then by some near relative or friend of the person or (b) as provided in Section 7638 of the Family Code. The petition or pleading shall specify the place of birth and residence of the person, his or her present name, the name proposed, and the reason for the change of name, and shall, if neither parent of the person is living, name, as far as known to the person proposing the name change, the near relatives of the person, and their place of residence. In an action for a change of name commenced by the filing of a petition: (a) If the person whose name is proposed to be changed is under 18years of age and the petition is signed by only one parent, the petition shall specify the address, if known, of the other parent if living. (b) If the person whose name is proposed to be changed is 12 years of age or over, has been relinquished to an adoption agency by his or her parent or parents, and has not been legally adopted, the petition shall be signed by the person and the adoption agency to which the person was relinquished. The near relatives of the person and their place of residence shall not be included in the petition unless they are known to the person whose name is proposed to be changed.

(a) Where an action for a change of name is commenced by the filing of a petition, the court shall thereupon make an order reciting the filing of the petition, the name of the person by whom it is filed and the name proposed, and directing all persons interested in the matter to appear before the court at a time and place specified, which shall be not less than four or more than eight weeks from the time of making the order, to show cause why the application for change of name should not be granted. A copy of the order to show cause shall be published pursuant to Section 6064 of the Government Code in a newspaper of general circulation to be designated in the order published in the county. If no newspaper of general circulation is published in the county, a copy of the order to show cause shall be posted by the clerk of the court in three of the most public places in the county in which the court is located, for a like period. Proof shall be made to the satisfaction of the court of this publication or posting, at the time of the hearing of the application. Four weekly publications shall be sufficient publication of the order to show cause. If the order is published in a daily newspaper, publication once a week for four successive weeks shall be sufficient. Where a petition has been filed for a minor and the other parent, if living, does not join in consenting thereto, the petitioner shall cause, not less than 30 days prior to the hearing, to be served notice of the time and place of the hearing or a copy of the order to show cause on the other parent pursuant to Section 413.10, 414.10, 415.10, or 415.40.

California Code§ 1279.5 Civ. Proc.

(a) Except as provided in subdivision (b), (c), (d), or (e), nothing in this title shall be construed to abrogate the common law right of any person to change his or her name.

COLORADO

TITLE 13—COURTS AND COURT PROCEDURE—ARTICLE 15—CHANGE OF NAME

13-15-101—Petition—proceedings.

Every person desiring to change his name may present a petition to that effect, verified by affidavit, to the district or county court in the county of the petitioner's residence. The petition shall set forth the petitioner's full name, the new name desired, and a concise statement of the reason for such desired change. The court shall order such change to be made and spread upon the records of the court in proper form if the court is satisfied that the desired change would be proper and not detrimental to the interests of any other person.

13-15-102—Publication of change.

(1) Public notice of such change of name shall be given at least three times in a newspaper published in the county where such person is residing within twenty days after the order of the court is made, and, if no newspaper is published in that county, such notice shall be published in a newspaper in such county as the court directs.

(2) Public notice of such name change through publication as required in subsection (1) of this section shall not be required if the petitioner has been:

(a) The victim of a crime, the underlying factual basis of which has been found by the court on the record to include an act of domestic violence, as defined in section 18-6-800.3 (1), C.R.S.;

(b) The victim of child abuse, as defined in section 18-6-401, C.R.S.; or

(c) The victim of domestic abuse as that term is defined in section 14-4-101 (2), C.R.S.

CONNECTICUT

Sec. 52-11. Complaints for change of name.

The superior court in each judicial district shall have jurisdiction of complaints praying for a change of name, brought by any person residing in the judicial district, and may change the name of the complainant, who shall thereafter be known by the name prescribed by said court in its decree.

DELAWARE

CHAPTER 59. CHANGE OF NAME

(a) Any person who desires to change his or her name, shall present a petition, duly verified, to the Court of Common Pleas sitting in the county in which the person resides. The petition shall set forth such person's name and the name he or she desires to assume.

(b) Family Court shall have jurisdiction over a change of name as part of divorce proceedings or as part of the establishment of paternity under the Uniform Parentage Act.

(c) The common law right of any person to change his or her name is hereby abrogated as to individuals subject to the supervision of the State of Delaware Department of Correction. Such individuals may only effect a name change by petitioning the Court of Common Pleas as follows:

(1) Individuals subject to the supervision of the Department of Correction shall be prohibited from adopting any names other than their legal names or otherwise effecting name changes, except as provided in this subsection.

(2) When, based upon testimony or sworn affidavits, the court finds that a petition for a name change of an individual subject to the supervision of the Department of Correction is motivated by a sincerely held religious belief, the court may grant such petition. In any case in which an individual subject to the supervision of the Department of Correction petitions the Court of Common Pleas for a change of name, the Court shall provide notice and opportunity to oppose the name change to the Department of Correction and shall permit it to submit any appropriate documentation in support of its opposition.

(3) If an individual is granted a name change pursuant to paragraph 2 of this subsection, he or she must provide all names previously held or adopted, as well as his or her legal name when signing any legal document or providing information to a law enforcement officer.

(4) The granting of any name changes pursuant to this subsection shall not restrict the Department of Correction from maintaining institutional files or otherwise referring to individuals by the names under which they became subject to the Department's supervision.

§ 5902. Requirements for minor's petition.

If the name sought to be changed under this chapter is that of a minor, the petition shall be signed by at least one of the minor's parents, if there is a parent living, or if both parents are dead, by the legal guardian of such minor. When the minor is over the age of 14, the petition shall also be signed by the minor.

§ 5903. Publication of petition prior to filing.

No petition for change of name under this chapter shall be granted unless it affirmatively appears that the petition has been published in a newspaper published in the county in which the proceeding is had, at least once a week for 3 weeks before the petition is filed.

§ 5904. Determination by Court.

Upon presentation of a petition for change of name under this chapter, and it appearing that the requirements of this chapter have been fully complied with, and there appearing no reason for not granting the petition, the prayer of the petition may be granted.

DISTRICT OF COLUMBIA

Title 16 Particular Actions, Proceedings and Matters

Chapter 25 Change of Name

§ 16-2501. Application; persons who may file.

Whoever, being a resident of the District and desiring a change of name, may file an application in the Superior Court setting forth the reasons therefor and also the name desired to be assumed. If the applicant is an infant, the application shall be filed by his parent, guardian, or next friend.

§ 16-2502. Notice; contents.

Prior to a hearing pursuant to this chapter, notice of the filing of the application, containing the substance and prayer thereof, shall be published once a week for three consecutive weeks in a newspaper in general circulation published in the District.

§ 16-2503. Decree.

On proof of the notice prescribed by section 16-2502, and upon a showing that the court deems satisfactory, the court may change the name of the applicant according to the prayer of the application.

FLORIDA

68.07 Change of name.

(1) Chancery courts have jurisdiction to change the name of any person residing in this state on petition of the person filed in the county in which he or she resides.

(2) The petition shall be verified and show:

(a) That petitioner is a bona fide resident of and domiciled in the county where the change of name is sought.

(b) If known, the date and place of birth of petitioner, petitioner's father's name, mother's maiden name, and where petitioner has resided since birth.

(c) If petitioner is married, the name of petitioner's spouse and if petitioner has children, the names and ages of each and where they reside.

(d) If petitioner's name has previously been changed and when and where and by what court.

(e) Petitioner's occupation and where petitioner is employed and has been employed for 5 years next preceding filing of the petition. If petitioner owns and operates a business, the name and place of it shall be stated and petitioner's connection therewith and how long petitioner has been identified with said business. If petitioner is in a profession, the profession shall be stated, where the petitioner has practiced the profession and if a graduate of a school or schools, the name or names thereof, time of graduation, and degrees received.

(f) Whether the petitioner has been generally known or called by any other names and if so, by what names and where.

(g) Whether petitioner has ever been adjudicated a bankrupt and if so, where and when.

(h) Whether petitioner has ever been convicted of a felony and if so, when and where.

(i) Whether any money judgment has ever been entered against petitioner and if so, the name of the judgment creditor, the amount and date thereof, the court by which entered, and whether the judgment has been satisfied.

(j) That the petition is filed for no ulterior or illegal purpose and granting it will not in any manner invade the property rights of others, whether partnership, patent, good will, privacy, trademark, or otherwise.

(k) That the petitioner's civil rights have never been suspended, or if the petitioner's civil rights have been suspended, that full restoration of civil rights has occurred.

(3) The hearing on the petition may be immediately after it is filed.

(4) On filing the final judgment, the clerk shall, if the birth occurred in this state, send a report of the judgment to the Office of Vital Statistics of the Department of Health on a form to be furnished by the department. The form shall contain sufficient information to identify the original birth certificate of the person, the new name, and the file number of the judgment. This report shall be filed by the department with respect to a person born in this state and shall become a part of the vital statistics of this state. With respect to a person born in another state, the clerk shall provide the petitioner with a certified copy of the final judgment.

(5) If the petitioner is a convicted felon, the clerk must, upon the filing of the final judgment, send a report of the judgment to the Florida Department of Law Enforcement on a form to be furnished by that department. The report must contain sufficient information to identify the original criminal record of the petitioner, the new name of the petitioner, and the file number of the judgment. With respect to a person convicted of a felony in another state or of a federal offense, the Florida Department of Law Enforcement must send the report to the respective state's office of law enforcement records or to the office of the Federal Bureau of Investigation.

(6) A husband and wife and minor children may join in one petition for change of name and the petition shall show the facts required of a petitioner as to the husband and wife and the names of the minor children may be changed at the discretion of the court.

(7) When only one parent petitions for a change of name of a minor child, process shall be served on the other parent and proof of such service shall be filed in the cause; provided, however, that where the other parent is a nonresident, constructive notice of the petition may be given pursuant to chapter 49, and proof of publication shall be filed in the cause without the necessity of recordation.

(8) Nothing herein applies to any change of name in proceedings for dissolution of marriage or for adoption of children.

GEORGIA

Georgia Code 19-12-1. Petition for name change; notice of filing; consent of minor's parents or guardian; service on parents or guardian; time of hearing; judgment; clerk's fees.

(a) Any person desirous of changing his name or the name or names of his minor child or children may present a petition to the superior court of the county of his residence, setting forth fully and particularly the reasons why the change is asked, which petition shall be verified by the petitioner.

(b) Within seven days of the filing of the petition, the petitioner shall cause a notice of the filing, signed by him, to be published in the official legal organ of the county once a week for four weeks. The notice shall contain therein the name of the petitioner, the name of the person whose name is to be changed if different from that of the petitioner, the new name desired, the court in which the petition is pending, the date on which the petition was filed, and the right of any interested or affected party to appear and file objections.

(c) If the petition seeks to change the name of a minor child, the written consent of his parent or parents if they are living and have not abandoned the child, or the written consent of the child's guardian if both parents are dead or have abandoned the child, shall be filed with the petition, except that the written consent of a parent shall not be required if the parent has not contributed to the support of the child for a continuous period of five years or more immediately preceding the filing of the petition.

(d) In all cases, before a minor child's name may be changed, the parent or parents of the child shall be served with a copy of the petition. If the parent or parents reside within this state, service of the petition shall be made in person, except that if the location or address of the parent is unknown, service of the petition on the parent shall be made by publication as provided in this Code section. If the parent or parents reside outside this state, service of the petition on the parent or parents residing outside this state shall be made by certified mail if the address is known or by publication as provided in this Code section if the address is not known.

(e) Where a child resides with persons other than his parent or parents, a copy of the petition shall be served upon the person acting as guardian of the child in the same manner as service would be made on a parent.

(f) Upon the expiration of: (1) Thirty days from the filing of the petition if the person whose name to be changed is an adult; (2) Thirty days from the date of service upon the parent, parents, or guardian of a minor whose name is to be changed if the parent, parents, or guardian reside within this state; or (3) Sixty days from the date of service upon the parent, parents, or guardian of a minor whose name is to be changed if either the parent, parents, or guardian reside outside the state and the petition is served by mail, and after proof to the court of publication of the notice as required in this Code section is made, if no objection is filed, the court shall proceed at chambers at such date as the court shall fix to hear and determine all matters raised by the petition and to render final judgment or decree thereon. For such service, the clerk shall receive the fees prescribed in Code Section 15-6-77, relating to fees of clerks of the superior courts for civil cases.

Georgia Code 19-12-2. Hearing on objections to petition.

If written objections are filed by any interested or affected party within the time limits specified in subsection (f) of Code Section 19-12-1, the court shall thereupon proceed to hear the matter at chambers.

Georgia Code 19-12-3. Certificate of change of name; use as evidence; form of certificate.

(a) At any time after the entry of the final order of change of name, upon the request of the petitioner requesting the change of name, the clerk of the court granting the same shall issue to the petitioner a certificate of change of name, under the seal of the court, upon payment to the clerk of the fee provided in paragraph (4) of subsection (g) of Code Section 15-6-77. The certificate shall be received as evidence of the facts contained in the certificate.

(b) The certificate of change of name shall be in substantially the following form:

> This is to certify that _____ (name of petitioner) has obtained final order of change of name in the Superior Court of _____ County, Georgia, on the _____ day of _____, _____, as shown by the records of the court. The name (or names) of _____ (full name prior to entry of the final order of change of name) has (or have) been changed to _____(full name after entry of the final order of change of name). Given under the hand and seal of said court, this the _____ day of _____, _____. (Seal of court) _____ Clerk

Georgia Code 19-12-4. Change of name with fraudulent intent not authorized.

Nothing contained in this chapter shall authorize any person to change his name with a view to deprive another fraudulently of any right under the law.

HAWAII

§574-5 Change of Name Procedure.

(a) It shall be unlawful to change any name adopted or conferred under this chapter, except:

(1) Upon an order of the lieutenant governor;

(2) By a final order, decree, or judgment of the family court issued as follows:

(A) When in an adoption proceeding a change of name of the person to be adopted is requested and the court includes the change of name in the adoption decree;

(B) When in a divorce proceeding either party to the proceeding requests to resume the middle name or names and the last name used by the party prior to the marriage or a middle name or names and last name declared and used during any prior marriage and the court includes the change of names in the divorce decree; or

(C) When in a proceeding for a change of name of a legitimate or legitimated minor initiated by one parent, the family court, upon proof that the parent initiating the name change has made all reasonable efforts to locate and notify the other parent of the name change proceeding but has not been able to locate, notify, or elicit a response from the other parent, and after an appropriate hearing, orders a change of name determined to be in the best interests of the minor; provided that the family court may waive the notice requirement to the non-initiating, non-custodial parent where the court finds that the waiver is necessary for the protection of the minor;

(3) Upon marriage pursuant to section 574-1;

(4) Upon legitimation pursuant to section 338-21; or

(5) By an order or decree of any court of competent jurisdiction within any state of the United States, the District of Columbia, the Commonwealth of Puerto Rico, or any territory or possession of the United States, changing the name of a person born in this State.

(b) The order of change of name by the lieutenant governor shall be founded upon a notarized petition. The petition shall be executed by the person desirous of making the change of name. In the case of a minor, the petition shall be executed:

(1) By the parents;

(2) By the parent who has custody of the minor with the notarized consent of the noncustodial parent; or

(3) By the guardian of the person of the minor.

(c) The filing fee of $100 shall accompany the petition when submitted and shall not be refundable.

(d) A notice of change of name signed by the lieutenant governor shall be published once in a newspaper of general circulation in the State as mentioned in the order for change of name, and the petitioner within sixty days of the signing of the notice of change of name shall deposit at the office of the lieutenant governor an affidavit executed by an officer of the newspaper publishing the notice showing that the notice has been published therein. The affidavit shall have attached to it a clipping showing the notice as published. Failure to deposit the affidavit of publication as required shall void that petition for a change of name by that petitioner.

(e) When the petition is accompanied by an affidavit executed by a prosecuting attorney of this State, the affidavit shall show that for the protection of the person desirous of making a change of name, the following actions shall not be necessary:

(1) Publication in a newspaper of general circulation in the State; and

(2) Recordation in the bureau of conveyances.

IDAHO

TITLE 7 SPECIAL PROCEEDINGS—CHAPTER 8 CHANGE OF NAMES

7-801. JURISDICTION IN DISTRICT COURT.

Application for change of names must be heard and determined by the district courts.

7-802. PETITION FOR CHANGE.

All applications for change of names must be made to the district court of the county where the person whose name is proposed to be changed resides, by petition, signed by such person; and if such person is under the age of eighteen (18) years, by one (1) of the parents, if living; or if both be dead, then by the guardian; and if there be no guardian, then by some near relative or friend. The petition must specify the place of birth and residence of such person, his or her present same, the name proposed, and reason for such change of name, and must, if the father of such person be not living, name, as far as known to the petitioner, the near relatives of such person, and their place of residence.

7-803. PUBLICATION OF PETITION.

A notice of hearing of such petition signed by the clerk and issued under the seal of the court, must be published for four (4) successive weeks in some newspaper printed in the county, if a newspaper be printed therein, but if no newspaper be printed in the county a copy of such notice of hearing must be posted at three [(3)] of the most public places in the county for a like period, and proofs must be made of such publication or posting before the petition can be considered. The notice of hearing may be substantially in the following form:

NOTICE OF HEARING

In the District Court of the .... Judicial District of the State of Idaho in and for .... County.

In the matter of the application of .... for change in name.

(Assertions herein contained refer to assertions in the petition)

A petition by ...., born .... at .... now residing at .... proposing a change in name to .... has been filed in the above entitled court, the reason for the change in name being.......................................

....

the name of the petitioner's father is .... address .... (if living); the

names and addresses of petitioner's near relatives (if father be dead) are:

....

....

....

such petition will be heard at such time as the court may appoint, and objections may be filed by any person who can, in such objections, show to the court a good reason against such a change of name.

WITNESS my hand and seal of said District Court this .... day of .... 20...

.... Attorney for petitioner .... Clerk

.... Residence or post office address .... Deputy Idaho.

7-804. (R) HEARING AND ORDER.

Such application must be heard at such time during term as the court may appoint, and objections may be filed by any person who can, in such objections, show to the court good reason against such change of name. On the hearing the court may examine, upon oath, any of the petitioners, remonstrants or other persons touching the application, and may make an order changing the name or dismissing the application, as to the court may seem right and proper.

ILLINOIS

Illinois Statutes 735 IL CS 5/21-101 Proceedings; parties.

If any person who is a resident of this State and has resided in this State for 6 months desires to change his or her name and to assume another name by which to be afterwards called and known, the person may file a petition in the circuit court of the county wherein he or she resides praying for that relief. If it appears to the court that the conditions herein aftermentioned have been complied with and that there is no reason why the prayer should not be granted, the court, by an order to be entered of record, may direct and provide that the name of that person be changed in accordance with the prayer in the petition. The filing of a petition in accordance with this Section shall be the sole and exclusive means by which any person committed under the laws of this State to a penal institution may change his or her name and assume another name. However, any person convicted of a felony, misdemeanor criminal sexual abuse when the victim of the offense at the time of its commission is under 18 years of age, misdemeanor sexual exploitation of a child, misdemeanor indecent solicitation of a child, or misdemeanor indecent solicitation of an adult in this State or any other state who has not been pardoned may not file a petition for a name change until 2 years have passed since completion and discharge from his or her sentence. A petitioner may include his or her spouse and adult unmarried children, with their consent, and his or her minor children where it appears to the court that it is for their best interest, in the petition and prayer, and the court's order shall then include the spouse and children. Whenever any minor has resided in the family of any person for the space of 3 years and has been recognized and known as an adopted child in the family of that person, the application herein provided for may be made by the person having that minor in his or her family. An order shall be entered as to a minor only if the court finds by clear and convincing evidence that the change is necessary to serve the best interest of the child. In determining the best interest of a minor child under this Section, the court shall consider all relevant factors, including:

(1) The wishes of the child's parents and any person acting as a parent who has physical custody of the child.

(2) The wishes of the child and the reasons for those wishes. The court may interview the child in chambers to ascertain the child's wishes with respect to the change of name. Counsel shall be present at the interview unless otherwise agreed upon by the parties. The court shall cause a court reporter to be present who shall make a complete record of the interview instantaneously to be part of the record in the case.

(3) The interaction and interrelationship of the child with his or her parents or persons acting as parents who have physical custody of the child, step-parents, siblings, step-siblings, or any other person who may significantly affect the child's best interest.

(4) The child's adjustment to his or her home, school, and community.

Illinois Statutes735 IL CS 5/21-102 Petition.

The petition shall set forth the name then held, the name sought to be assumed, the residence of the petitioner, the length of time the petitioner has resided in this State, and the state or country of the petitioner's nativity or supposed nativity. The petition shall be signed by the person petitioning or, in case of minors, by the parent or guardian having the legal custody of the minor. The petition shall be verified by the affidavit of some credible person.

Illinois Statutes735 IL CS 5/21-103 Notice by publication.

(a) Previous notice shall be given of the intended application by publishing a notice thereof in some newspaper published in the municipality in which the person resides if the municipality is in a county with a population under 2,000,000, or if the person does not reside in a municipality in a county with a population under 2,000,000, or if no newspaper is published in the municipality or if the person resides in a county with a population of 2,000,000 or more, then in some newspaper published in the county where the person resides, or if no newspaper is published in that county, then in some convenient newspaper published in this State. The notice shall be inserted for 3consecutive weeks, the first insertion to be at least 6 weeks before the return day upon which the petition is to be filed, and shall be signed by the petitioner or, in case of a minor, the minor's parent or guardian, and shall set forth the return day of court on which the petition is to be filed and the name sought to be assumed.

INDIANA

IC 34-28-2 Chapter 2. Change of Name

IC 34-28-2-1

Sec. 1. Except as provided in section 1.5 of this chapter, the circuit courts in Indiana may change the names of natural persons on application by petition. As added by P.L.1-1998, SEC.24. Amended by P.L.18-1998, SEC.1. IC 34-28-2-1.5

Sec. 1.5. A person may not petition for a change of name under this chapter if the person is confined to a department of correction facility. As added by P.L.18-1998, SEC.2. IC 34-28-2-2

Sec. 2. (a) The petition described in section (1) of this chapter may be filed with the circuit court of the county in which the person resides.

(b) In the case of a parent or guardian who wishes to change the name of a minor child, the petition must be verified, and it must state in detail the reason the change is requested. In addition, except where a parent's consent is not required under IC 31-19-9, the written consent of a parent, or the written consent of the guardian if both parents are dead, must be filed with the petition.

(c) Before a minor child's name may be changed, the parents or guardian of the child must be served with a copy of the petition as required by the Indiana trial rules. As added by P.L.1-1998, SEC.24. IC 34-28-2-3

Sec. 3. (a) Upon filing a petition for a name change, the applicant shall give notice of the petition as follows:

(1) By three (3) weekly publications in a newspaper of general circulation published in the county in which the petition is filed in court.

(2) If no newspaper is published in the county in which the petition is filed, the applicant shall give notice in a newspaper published nearest to that county in an adjoining county.

(3) The last weekly publication shall be published not less than thirty (30) days before the day the petition will be heard as indicated in the notice.

(b) In the case of a petition described in section 2(b) of this chapter, the petitioner must publish the first notice of the petition not more than seven (7) days after the date the petition is filed.

(c) In the case of a petition described in section 2(b) of this chapter, the notice required by this section must include the following:

(1) The name of the petitioner.

(2) The name of the minor child whose name is to be changed.

(3) The new name desired.

(4) The name of the court in which the action is pending.

(5) The date on which the petition was filed.

(6) A statement that any person has the right to appear at the hearing and to file objections.

(d) Except as provided in section 1.5 of this chapter, in the case of a person who has had a felony conviction within ten (10) years before filing a petition for a change of name, at least thirty (30) days before the hearing the petitioner must give notice of the filing of the petition to:

(1) the sheriff of the county in which the petitioner resides;

(2) the prosecuting attorney of the county in which the petitioner resides; and

(3) the Indiana central repository for criminal history information.

(e) The notice given to the Indiana central repository for criminal history information under subsection (d) must include the petitioner's full current name, requested name change, date of birth, address, physical description, and a full set of classifiable fingerprints.

(f) The Indiana central repository for criminal history information shall forward a copy of any criminal records of the petitioner to the court for the court's information.

(g) A copy of the court decree granting or denying such a petition shall be sent to the Indiana state police.

(h) A person who violates subsection (d) commits a Class A misdemeanor.

Sec. 4. (a) Proof of the publication required in this chapter is made by filing a copy of the published notice, verified by the affidavit of a disinterested person, and when proof of publication is made, the court shall, subject to the limitations imposed by subsections (b), (c), and (d), proceed to hear the petition and make an order and decree the court determines is just and reasonable.

(b) In the case of a petition described in section 2(b) of this chapter, the court may not hear the petition and issue a final decree until after thirty (30) days from the later of:

(1) the filing of proof of publication of the notice required under subsection (a); or

(2) the service of the petition upon the parents or guardian of the minor child.

(c) In the case of a petition described in section 2(b) of this chapter, the court shall set a date for a hearing on the petition if:

(1) written objections have been filed; or

(2) either parent or the guardian of the minor child has refused or failed to give written consent as described in section 2(b) of this chapter.

The court shall require that appropriate notice of the hearing be given to the parent or guardian of the minor child or to any person who has filed written objections.

(d) In deciding on a petition to change the name of a minor child, the court shall be guided by the best interest of the child rule under IC 31-17-2-8. However, there is a presumption in favor of a parent of a minor child who:

(1) has been making support payments and fulfilling other duties in accordance with a decree issued under IC 31-15, IC 31-16, or IC 17 (or IC 31-1-11.5 before its repeal); and

(2) objects to the proposed name change of the child.

(e) In the case of a person required to give notice under section 3(d) of this chapter, the petitioner must certify to the court that the petitioner has complied with the notice requirements of that subsection.

Sec. 5. (a) A copy of the decree of the court changing the name of any natural person, certified under the seal of the court by the clerk of the court, is sufficient evidence of the name of the person, and of a change having been made, in any court of Indiana.

(b) In the case of a petition described in section 2(b) of this chapter, the court shall send a copy of the final decree to the state department of health and to the local health department of the county.

(c) In the case of a petition filed by a person at least seventeen (17) years of age, the court shall send a copy of the final decree to the clerk of the circuit court or board of registration of the county where the person resides.

IOWA

674.1 Authorization.

A person who has attained the age of majority and who does not have any civil disabilities may apply to the court to change the person's name by filing a verified petition as provided in this chapter. The verified petition may request a name change for minor children of the petitioner as well as the petitioner or a parent may file a verified petition requesting a name change on behalf of a minor child of the parent.

674.2 Petition to court.

The verified petition shall be addressed to the district court of the county where the applicant resides and shall state and provide for each person seeking a name change:

1. The name at the time the petition is filed of the person whose name is to be changed and the person's county of residence. If the person whose name is to be changed is a minor child, the petition shall state the name of the petitioner and the petitioner's relationship to the minor child.

2. A description including height, weight, color of hair, color of eyes, race, sex, and date and place of birth.

3. Residence at time of petition and any prior residences for the past five years.

4. Reason for change of name, briefly and concisely stated.

5. A legal description of all real property in this state owned by the petitioner.

6. The name the petitioner proposes to take.

7. A certified copy of the birth certificate to be attached to the petition.

674.3 Petition copy.

A copy of the petition shall be filed by the clerk of court with the division for records and statistics of the Iowa department of public health.

674.4 When granted.

A decree of change of name may be granted any time after thirty days of the filing of the petition. Section History: Early form.

674.5 Contents of decree.

The decree shall describe the petitioner, giving the petitioner's name and former name, height, weight, color of hair, color of eyes, race, sex, date and place of birth and the given name of the spouse and any minor children affected by the change. The decree shall also give a legal description of all real property owned by the petitioner.

674.6 Notice—consent.

If the petitioner is married, the petitioner must give legal notice to the spouse, in the manner of an original notice, of the filing of the petition. If the petition includes or is filed on behalf of a minor child fourteen years of age or older, the child's written consent to the change of name of that child is required. If the petition includes or is filed on behalf of a minor child under fourteen, both parents as stated on the birth certificate of the minor child shall file their written consent to the name change. If one of the parents does not consent to the name change, a hearing shall be set on the petition on twenty days' notice to the non-consenting parent pursuant to the rules of civil procedure. At the hearing the court may waive the requirement of consent as to one of the parents if it finds:

1. That the parent has abandoned the child;

2. That the parent has been ordered to contribute to the support of the child or to financially aid in the child's birth and has failed to do so without good cause; or

3. That the parent does not object to the name change after having been given due and proper notice. Section History: Early form [C73, 75, 77, 79, 81, § 674.6; 81 Acts, ch 201, § 3]

674.13 Further change barred.

A person shall not change the person's name more than once under this chapter unless just cause is shown. However, in a decree dissolving a person's marriage, the person's name may be changed back to the name appearing on the person's original birth certificate or to a legal name previously acquired in a former marriage.

KANSAS

CHAPTER 60.—PROCEDURE, CIVIL

ARTICLE 14.—CHANGE OF NAME

60-1401. Jurisdiction and costs. The district court shall have authority to change the name of any person, township, town or city within this state at the cost of the petitioner without affecting any legal right.

60-1402. Change of name of person; notice; order.

(a) Petition. A petition may be filed in the county in which the petitioner resides stating: (1) That the petitioner has been a resident of the state for at least 60 days, (2) the reason for the change of name, and (3) the name desired.

(b) Notice. Service of notice of the hearing may be made either by mail or by publication, in the discretion of the court. If notice is directed by publication, such notice shall be published as provided in subsection (d) of K.S.A. 60-307, and amendments thereto; and if notice of hearing is directed to be given by mail, service of notice may be made by registered or certified mail to parties of interest, as prescribed by the court.

(c) Order. If upon hearing the judge is satisfied as to the truth of the allegations of the petition, and that there is reasonable cause for changing the name of the petitioner the judge shall so order.

60-1403. Municipalities.

A petition for the change of name of any township, town, or city may be filed in the district court of such county, signed by a majority of the legal voters of such body, setting forth the cause why such change is desirable and the name to be substituted. The court, upon being satisfied by proof that the prayer of the petitioners is just and reasonable, that notice as required in the foregoing section has been given, that the petitioners are legal voters of such township, town, or city and that they desire the change, and that such change will not result in an objectionable confusion of names within the state, may order the change prayed for in such petition.

KENTUCKY

401.010 Who may have name changed.

Any person at least eighteen (18) years of age may have his name changed by the District Court of the county in which he resides. If he resides on a United States Army post, military reservation or fort his name may be changed by the District Court of any county adjacent thereto. Effective: January 2, 1978

401.020 Child, who may have name changed.

Both parents, provided both are living, or one (1) parent if one (1) is deceased, or if no parent is living, the guardian, may have the name of a child under the age of eighteen (18) changed by the District Court of the county in which the child resides. However, if one (1) parent refuses or is unavailable to execute the petition, proper notice of filing the petition shall be served in accordance with the Rules of Civil Procedure. If the child resides on a United States Army post, military reservation or fort his name may be changed by the District Court of any county adjacent thereto.

401.030 Facts shown on order book of court.

The original name, age and place of birth, the name to which the change is made, and the names of the infant's father and mother, if known, and of the person on whose motion the change is made shall be entered on the order book of the District Court.

401.040 Certification of order for name change—Index kept by county clerk.

(1) If the District Court orders any person's name to be changed under this chapter, a copy of the order shall be certified by the clerk of that court to the county clerk, for record.

(2) The county clerk shall keep an alphabetical index for each book of records, referring to the page on which each person's name change appears, and giving the name from and to which it is changed.

LOUISIANA

PART IV. CHANGE OF NAME

§4751. Petition for name change; adults; minors

A. The name of a person may be changed as provided in this Section.

B. Whenever any person who has attained the age of majority desires to change his name, he shall present a petition to the district court of the parish of his residence or, in the case of a person incarcerated in a penal institution, to the district court of the parish in which he was sentenced, setting forth the reasons for the desired change.

C. If the person desiring such change is a minor or if the parents or parent or the tutor of the minor desire to change the name of the minor:

(1) The petition shall be signed by the father and mother of the minor or by the survivor in case one of them be dead.

(2) If one parent has been granted custody of the minor by a court of competent jurisdiction, the consent of the other parent is not necessary if the other parent has been served with a copy of the petition and any of the following exists:

(a) The other parent has refused or failed to comply with a court order of support for a period of one year.

(b) The other parent has failed to support the child for a period of three years after judgment awarding custody to the parent signing the petition.

(c) The other parent is not paying support and has refused or failed to visit, communicate, or attempt to communicate with the child without just cause for a period of two years.

(d) The other parent has refused or failed to visit, communicate, or attempt to communicate with the child without just cause for a period of ten years.

(3) In case the minor has no father or mother living, the petition shall be signed by the tutor or tutrix of the minor and in default of any tutor or tutrix, shall be signed by a special tutor appointed by the judge for that purpose.

(4) The petition may be signed by either the mother or the father acting alone if a child has been given a surname which is different from that authorized in R.S. 40:34(B)(1)(a).

D.(1) A person who has been convicted of a felony shall not be entitled to petition for a change of name under the provisions of this Section until his sentence has been satisfied. This Subsection shall apply whether the offender is actually imprisoned or on probation or parole.

(2) Notwithstanding the provisions of Paragraph (1) of this Subsection or any other provision of law to the contrary, a person convicted of any felony enumerated in R.S. 14:2(13) shall not be entitled to petition for a change of name.

MASSACHUSETTS

Chapter 210: Section 12. Petitions for change of name.

Section 12. A petition for the change of name of a person may be heard by the probate court in the county where the petitioner resides. The change of name of a person shall be granted unless such change is inconsistent with public interests.

Chapter 210: Section 13. Notice and certificate; decree; entry; conditions precedent.

Section 13. The court shall, before decreeing a change of name, request a report from the commissioner of probation on the person filing the petition and, except for good cause shown, require public notice of the petition to be given and any person may be heard thereon, and, upon entry of a decree, the name as established thereby shall be the legal name of the petitioner, and the register may issue a certificate, under the seal of the court, of the name as so established.

No decree shall be entered, however, until there has been filed in the court a copy of the birth record of the person whose name is sought to be changed and, in case such person's name has previously been changed by decree of court or at marriage pursuant to section one D of chapter forty-six, either a copy of the record of his birth amended to conform to the previous decree changing his name, a copy of such decree, or a copy of the record of marriage; provided, that the filing of any such copy may be dispensed with if the judge is satisfied that it cannot be obtained.

Chapter 210: Section 14. Annual return of changes.

Section 14. Each register of probate shall annually, in December, make a return to the commissioner of public health and the commissioner of probation of all changes of name made in his court.

MARYLAND

Rule 15-901. Action for change of name.

(a) Applicability.-This Rule applies to actions for change of name other than in connection with an adoption or divorce.

(b) Venue.-An action for change of name shall be brought in the county where the person whose name is sought to be changed resides.

(c) Petition.—(1) Contents.—The action for change of name shall be commenced by filing a petition captioned "In the Matter of . . ." [stating the name of the person whose name is sought to be changed] "for change of name to . . ." [stating the change of name desired]. The petition shall be under oath and shall contain at least the following information; (A) the name, address, and date and place of birth of the person whose name is sought to be; (B) whether the person whose name is sought to be changed has ever been known by any other name and, if so, the name or names and the circumstances under which they were used; (C) the change of name desired; (D) all reasons for the requested change; (E) a certification that the petitioner is not requesting the name change for any illegal or fraudulent purpose; and (F) if the person whose name is sought to be changed is a minor, the names and addresses of that person's parents and any guardian or custodian. (2) Documents to be attached to petition.—The petitioner shall attach to the petition a copy of a birth certificate or other documentary evidence from which the court can find that the current name of the person whose name is sought to be changed is as alleged.

(d) Service of petition.—When required.-If the person whose name is sought to be changed is a minor, a copy of the petition, any attachments, and the notice issued pursuant to section (e) of this Rule shall be served upon that person's parents and any guardian or custodian in the manner provided by Rule 2-121. When proof is made by affidavit that good faith efforts to serve a parent, guardian, or custodian pursuant to Rule 2-121 (a) have not succeeded and that Rule 2-121 (b) is inapplicable or that service pursuant to that Rule is impracticable, the court may order that service may be made by (1) the publication required by subsection (e)(2) of this Rule and (2) mailing a copy of the petition, any attachments, and notice by first class mail to the last known address of the parent, guardian, or custodian to be served.

(e) Notice.—(1) Issued by clerk.—Upon the filing of the petition, the clerk shall sign and issue a notice that (A) includes the caption of the action, (B) describes the substance of the petition and the relief sought, and (C) states the latest date by which an objection to the petition may be filed. (2) Publication.—Unless the court on motion of the petitioner orders otherwise, the notice shall be published one time in a newspaper of general circulation in the county at least fifteen days before the date specified in the notice for filing an objection to the petition. The petitioner shall thereafter file a certificate of publication.

(f) Objection to petition.—Any person may file an objection to the petition. The objection shall be filed within the time specified in the notice and shall be supported by an affidavit which sets forth the reasons for the objection. The affidavit shall be made on personal knowledge, shall set forth facts that would be admissible in evidence, and shall show affirmatively that the affiant is competent to testify to the matters stated in the affidavit. The objection and affidavit shall be served upon the petitioner in accordance with Rule 1-321. The petitioner may file a response within 15 days after being served with the objection and affidavit. A person desiring a hearing shall so request in the objection or response under the heading "Request for Hearing."

(g) Action by court.—After the time for filing objections and responses has expired, the court may hold a hearing or may rule on the petition without a hearing and shall enter an appropriate order, except that the court shall not deny the petition without a hearing if one was requested by the petitioner.

MAINE

§ 1-701. Petition to change name

If a person desires to have that person's name changed, the person may petition the judge of probate in the county where the person resides; or, if the person is a minor, that person's legal custodian may petition in the person's behalf, and the judge, after due notice, may change the name of the person and shall make and preserve a record of the name change. The fee for filing the petition is $25.

MICHIGAN

MICHIGAN COMPILED LAWS

711.1. Change of name; procedure, minors Sec. 1.

(1) The family division of the circuit court, or until January 1, 1998, the probate court, for a county may enter an order to change the name of a person who has been a resident of the county for not less than 1 year and who in accordance with subsection (2) petitions in writing to the court for that purpose showing a sufficient reason for the proposed change and that the change is not sought with any fraudulent intent. If the person who petitions for a name change has a criminal record, the person is presumed to be seeking a name change with a fraudulent intent. The burden of proof is on a petitioner who has a criminal record to rebut the presumption. The court shall set a time and place for hearing and order publication as provided by supreme court rule.

(2) A person who is 22 years of age or older and who petitions to have his or her name changed shall have 2 complete sets of his or her fingerprints taken at a local police agency. The fingerprints, along with a copy of the petition and the required processing fees, shall be forwarded to the department of state police. The department of state police shall compare those fingerprints with its records and shall forward a complete set of fingerprints to the federal bureau of investigation for a comparison with the records available to that agency. The department of state police shall report to the court in which the petition is filed the information contained in the department's records with respect to any pending charges against the petitioner or any record of conviction of the petitioner and shall report to the court similar information obtained from the federal bureau of investigation. If there are no pending charges against the petitioner or any record of conviction

against the petitioner, the department of state police shall destroy its copy of the petitioner's fingerprints. The court shall not act upon the petition for a name change until the department of state police reports the information required by this subsection to the court.

(3) If the court enters an order to change the name of a person who has a criminal record, the court shall forward the order to the central records division of the Michigan state police and to 1 or more of the following: (a) The department of corrections if the person named in the order is in prison or on parole or has been imprisoned or released from parole in the immediately preceding 2 years. (b) The sheriff of the county in which the person named in the order was last convicted if the person was incarcerated in a county jail or released from a county jail within the immediately preceding 2 years. (c) The court that has jurisdiction over the person named in the order if the person named in the order is under the jurisdiction of the family division of the circuit court, or until January 1, 1998, the probate court, or has been discharged from the jurisdiction of that court within the immediately preceding 2 years.

(4) The court may permit a person having the same name, or a similar name to that which the petitioner proposes to assume, to intervene in the proceeding for the purpose of showing fraudulent intent.

(5) Except as provided in subsection (7), if the petitioner is a minor, the petition shall be signed by the mother and father jointly; by the surviving parent if 1 is deceased; if both parents are deceased, by the guardian of the minor; or by 1 of the minor's parents if there is only 1 legal parent available to give consent. If either parent has been declared mentally incompetent, the petition may be signed by the guardian for that parent. The written consent to the change of name of a minor 14 years of age or older, signed by the minor in the presence of the court, shall be filed with the court before any order changing the name of the minor is entered. If the court considers the child to be of sufficient age to express a preference, the court shall consult a minor under 14 years of age as to a change in his or her name, and the court shall consider the minor's wishes.

(6) If the petitioner is married, the court, in its order changing the name of the petitioner, may include the name of the spouse, if the spouse consents, and may include the names of minor children of the petitioner of whom the petitioner has legal custody. The written consent to the change of name of a child 14 years of age or older, signed by the child in the presence of the court, shall be filed with the court before the court includes that child in its order. Except as provided in subsection (7), the name of a minor under 14 years of age may not be changed unless he or she is the natural or adopted child of the peti-

tioner and unless consent is obtained from the mother and father jointly, from the surviving parent if 1 is deceased, or from 1 of the minor's parents if there is only 1 legal parent available to give consent. If the court considers the child to be of sufficient age to express a preference, the court shall consult a minor under 14 years of age as to a change in his or her name, and the court shall consider the minor's wishes.

(7) The name of a minor may be changed pursuant to subsection (5) or (6) with the consent or signature of the custodial parent upon notice to the non custodial parent pursuant to supreme court rule and after a hearing in either of the following circumstances: (a) If both of the following occur: (i) The other parent, having the ability to support or assist in supporting the child, has failed or neglected to provide regular and substantial support for the child or, if a support order has been entered, has failed to substantially comply with the order, for 2 years or more before the filing of the petition. (ii) The other parent, having the ability to visit, contact, or communicate with the child, has regularly and substantially failed or neglected to do so for 2 years or more before the filing of the petition. (b) The other parent has been convicted of a violation of section 136b, 520b, 520c, 520d, 520e, or 520g of the Michigan penal code, Act No. 328 of the Public Acts of 1931, being sections 750.136b, 750.520b to 750.520e, and 750.520g of the Michigan Compiled Laws, and the child or a sibling of the child is a victim of the crime.

MINNESOTA

MINNESOTA STATUTES

259.10 General requirements. Subdivision 1. Procedure.

A person who shall have resided in this state for six months may apply to the district court in the county where the person resides to change the person's name, the names of minor children, if any, and the name of a spouse, if the spouse joins in the application, in the manner herein specified. The person shall state in the application the name and age of the spouse and each of the children, if any, and shall describe all lands in the state in or upon which the person, the children and the spouse if their names are also to be changed by the application, claim any interest or lien, and shall appear personally before the court and prove identity by at least two witnesses. If the person be a minor, the application shall be made by the person's guardian or next of kin. The court shall accept the certificate of dissolution prepared pursuant to section 518.148 as conclusive evidence of the facts recited in the certificate and may not require the person to provide the court a copy of the judgment and decree of dissolution. Every person who, with intent to defraud, shall make a false statement in any such application shall be guilty of a misdemeanor provided, however, that no minor child's name may be changed without both parents having notice of the pending of the application for change of name, whenever practicable, as determined by the court.

Subd. 2. Witness and victim protection name changes; private data. If the court determines that the name change for an individual is made in connection with the individual's participation in a witness and victim protection program, the court shall order that the court records of the name change are not accessible to the public; except that they may be released, upon request, to a law enforcement agency, probation officer, or corrections agent conducting a lawful investigation. The existence of an application for a name change described in this subdivision may not be disclosed except to a law enforcement agency conducting a lawful investigation.

259.11 Order; filing copies.

(a) Upon meeting the requirements of section 259.10, the court shall grant the application unless it finds that there is an intent to defraud or mislead or in the case of the change of a minor child's name, the court finds that such name change is not in the best interests of the child. The court shall set forth in the order the name and age of the applicant's spouse and each child of the applicant, if any, and shall state a description of the lands, if any, in which the applicant and the spouse and children, if any, claim to have an interest. The court administrator shall file such order, and record the same in the judgment book. If lands be described therein, a certified copy of the order shall be filed for record, by the applicant, with the county recorder of each county wherein any of the same are situated. Before doing so the court administrator shall present the same to the county auditor who shall enter the change of name in the auditor's official records and note upon the instrument, over an official signature, the words "change of name recorded." Any such order shall not be filed, nor any certified copy thereof be issued, until the applicant shall have paid to the county recorder and court administrator the fee required by law. No application shall be denied on the basis of the marital status of the applicant.

(b) When a person applies for a name change, the court shall determine whether the person has been convicted of a felony in this or any other state. If so, the court shall, within ten days after the name change application is granted, report the name change to the bureau of criminal apprehension. The person whose name is changed shall also report the change to the bureau of criminal apprehension within ten days. The court granting the name change application must explain this reporting duty in its order. Any person required to report the person's name change to the bureau of criminal apprehension who fails to report the name change as required under this paragraph is guilty of a gross misdemeanor.

MISSISSIPPI

§ 93-17-1. Jurisdiction to alter names and legitimate offspring; legitimation by subsequent marriage.

(1) The chancery court or the chancellor in vacation of the county of the residence of the petitioners shall have jurisdiction upon the petition of any person to alter the names of such person to make legitimate any living offspring of the petitioner not born in wedlock and to decree said offspring to be an heir of the petitioner.

(2) An illegitimate child shall become a legitimate child of the natural father if the natural father marries the natural mother and acknowledges the child.

MISSOURI

Petition where presented—contents—proceedings.

527.270. Hereafter every person desiring to change his or her name may present a petition to that effect, verified by affidavit, to the circuit court in the county of the petitioner's residence, which petition shall set forth the petitioner's full name, the new name desired, and a concise statement of the reason for such desired change; and it shall be the duty of the judge of such court to order such change to be made, and spread upon the records of the court, in proper form, if such judge is satisfied that the desired change would be proper and not detrimental to the interests of any other person.

527.280. The fees for proceedings under sections 527.270 to 527.290 shall be the same as are now or may hereafter be allowed in similar cases in said court, to be paid by the petitioner.

Notice of change to be given, when and how.

527.290. Public notice of such a change of name shall be given at least three times in a newspaper published in the county where such person is residing, within twenty days after the order of court is made, and if no newspaper is published in his or any adjacent county, then such notice shall be given in a newspaper published in the city of St. Louis, or at the seat of government.

MONTANA

CHAPTER 31. CHANGE OF NAME

PART 1. GENERAL PROVISIONS

27-31-101. Petition for change of name of natural person.

All applications for change of names must be made to the district court of the county where the person whose name is proposed to be changed resides, by petition signed by such person and, if such person is under 18 years of age, by one of the parents, if living, or if both be dead, then by the guardian, and if there be no guardian, then by some near relative or friend. The petition must specify the place of birth and residence of such person, his or her present name, the name proposed, and the reason for such change of name and must, if neither parent of such person be living, name as far as known to the petitioner the near relatives of such person and their place of residence.

PART 2. PROCEDURE

27-31-201. Order setting hearing date—notice—safety.

(1) When a petition setting out the matters contained in 27-31-101 or 27-31-102 is filed, the court or judge may appoint a time for hearing the petition. Except as provided in subsections (2) and (3), notice of the time and place of hearing the petition must be published for 4 successive weeks in some newspaper published in the county, if a newspaper is printed in the county. If a newspaper is not printed in the county, a copy of the notice must be posted in at least three public places in the county for 4 successive weeks.

27-31-204. Court order.

The court or judge may make an order changing the name or dismissing the applications, as to the court or judge may seem right and proper.

NEBRASKA

61-101. Change of name; authority of district court.

The district court shall have authority to change the names of persons, towns, villages and cities within this state.

> Annotations: Whether a minor child's surname may be changed depends on, and is determined by, the best interests of the child. Factors to be considered are (1) the misconduct by one of the child's parents, (2) a parent's failure to support the child, (3) parental fail-

ure to maintain contact with the child, (4) the length of time that a surname has been used for or by the child, and (5) whether the child's surname is different from the surname of the child's custodial parent. Additionally, a court may consider the child's reasonable preference for a surname; the effect of the name change on the child's relationship with each parent; community respect associated with the surname; the difficulties, harassment, or embarrassment associated with either the present or proposed surname; and the identification of the child as part of the family unit.

61-102. Change of name; persons; procedure.

(1) Any person desiring to change his or her name may file a petition in the district court of the county in which such person may be a resident, setting forth (a) that the petitioner has been a bona fide citizen of such county for at least one year prior to the filing of the petition, (b) the cause for which the change of petitioner's name is sought, and (c) the name asked for.

(2) Notice of the filing of the petition shall be published in a newspaper in the county, and if no newspaper is printed in the county, then in a newspaper of general circulation therein. The notice shall be published (a) once a week for four consecutive weeks if the petitioner is nineteen years of age or older at the time the action is filed and (b) once a week for two consecutive weeks if the petitioner is under nineteen years of age at the time the action is filed. In an action involving a petitioner under nineteen years of age who has a noncustodial parent, notice of the filing of the petition shall be sent by certified mail within five days after publication to the noncustodial parent at the address provided to the clerk of the district court pursuant to subsection (1) of section 42-364.13 for the noncustodial parent if he or she has provided an address. The clerk of the district court shall provide the petitioner with the address upon request.

(3) It shall be the duty of the district court, upon being duly satisfied by proof in open court of the truth of the allegations set forth in the petition, that there exists proper and reasonable cause for changing the name of the petitioner, and that notice of the filing of the petition has been given as required by this section, to order and direct a change of name of such petitioner and that an order for the purpose be made in the journals of the court.

NEVADA

PROCEEDINGS TO CHANGE NAMES OF PERSONS

NRS 41.270 Verified petition.

Any person desiring to have his name changed may file a verified petition with the clerk of the district court of the district in which he resides. The petition shall be addressed to the court and shall state the applicant's present name, the name which he desires to bear in the future, the reason for desiring the change and whether he has been convicted of a felony.

NRS 41.280 Publication of notice.

Upon the filing of the petition the applicant shall make out and procure a notice, which shall state the fact of the filing of the petition, its object, his present name and the name which he desires to bear in the future. The notice shall be published in some newspaper of general circulation in the county once a week for 3 successive weeks.

NRS 41.290 Order of court; hearing on objections; disposition and rescission of order.

1. If, within 10 days after the last publication of the notice no written objection is filed with the clerk, upon proof of the filing of the petition and publication of notice as required in NRS 41.280, and upon being satisfied by the statements in the petition, or by other evidence, that good reason exists therefor, the court shall make an order changing the name of the applicant as prayed for in the petition. If, within the period an objection is filed, the court shall appoint a day for hearing the proofs, respectively, of the applicant and the objection, upon reasonable notice. Upon that day the court shall hear the proofs, and grant or refuse the prayer of the petitioner, according to whether the proofs show satisfactory reasons for making the change. Before issuing its order, the court shall specifically take into consideration the applicant's criminal record, if any, which is stated in the petition.

2. Upon the making of an order either granting or denying the prayer of the applicant, the order must be recorded as a judgment of the court. If the petition is granted, the name of the applicant must thereupon be as stated in the order and the clerk shall transmit a certified copy of the order to the state registrar of vital statistics.

3. If an order grants a change of name to a person who has a criminal record, the clerk shall transmit a certified copy of the order to the central repository for Nevada records of criminal history for inclusion in that person's record of criminal history.

4. Upon receiving uncontrovertible proof that an applicant in his petition falsely denied having been convicted of a felony, the court shall rescind its order granting the change of name and the clerk shall transmit a certified copy of the order rescinding the previous order to:

(a) The state registrar of vital statistics for inclusion in his records.

(b) The central repository for Nevada records of criminal history for inclusion in his record of criminal history.

NEW HAMPSHIRE

TITLE 56 PROBATE COURTS AND DECEDENTS' ESTATES

CHAPTER 547 JUDGES OF PROBATE AND THEIR JURISDICTION

SECTION 547:3-i Change of Name.

The probate court may grant the petition of any person to change the name of that person or the name of another person. The court shall not require the petitioner to obtain consents to the name change. The court may proceed with or without notice, in accordance with RSA 550:4.

NEW JERSEY

NEW JERSEY PERMANENT STATUTES

TITLE 2A ADMINISTRATION OF CIVIL AND CRIMINAL JUSTICE2A:52-1.

2A:52-1. Action for change of name.

Any person may institute an action in Superior Court, for authority to assume another name. The complaint for a change of name shall be accompanied by a sworn affidavit stating the applicant's name, date of birth, social security number, whether or not the applicant has ever been convicted of a crime, and whether any criminal charges are pending against him and, if such convictions or pending charges exist, shall provide such details in connection therewith sufficient to readily identify the matter referred to. The sworn affidavit shall also recite that the action for a change of name is not being instituted for purposes of avoiding or obstructing criminal prosecution or for avoiding creditors or perpetrating a criminal or civil fraud. If criminal charges are pending, the applicant shall serve a copy of the complaint and affidavit upon any State or county prosecuting authority responsible for the prosecution of any pending charges. A person commits a crime of the fourth degree if he knowingly gives or causes to be given false information under this section. Amended 1981,c.362,s.1, 1993,c.228,s.1.

NEW MEXICO

NEW MEXICO STATUTES 40-8-1.

Change of name; petition and order.

Any resident of this state over the age of fourteen years may, upon petition to the district court of the district in which the petitioner resides and upon filing the notice required with proof of publication, if no sufficient cause is shown to the contrary, have his name changed or established by order of the court. The parent or guardian of any resident of this state under the age of fourteen years may, upon petition to the district court of the district in which the petitioner resides and upon filing the notice required with proof of publication, if no sufficient cause is shown to the contrary, have the name of his child or ward changed or established by order of the court. When residents under the age of fourteen years petition the district court for a name change, the required notice shall include notice to both legal parents. The order shall be entered at length upon the record of the court, and a copy of the order, duly certified, shall be filed in the office of the county clerk of the county in which the person resides. The county clerk shall record the same in a record book to be kept by him for that purpose.

Before making application to the court for changing or establishing a name as above provided, the applicant must cause a notice thereof, stating therein the nature of the application, the time and place, when and where the same will be made, to be published in the county where such application is to be made, and where said applicant resides, said notice to be published at least once each week for two consecutive weeks, in some newspaper printed in said county, and if there be no newspaper published in the county where said applicant resides, then said notice shall be published in a newspaper printed in a county nearest to the residence of said person, and having a circulation in the county where such person resides.

That the hearing and determination of all proceedings instituted under the provisions of this chapter, and the final order of the court therein, shall be had and made at some regular term of the district court sitting within and for the county wherein said petitioner resides.

NEW YORK

NEW YORK STATE CONSOLIDATED LAWS: CIVIL RIGHTS

ARTICLE 6 CHANGE OF NAME

Sec. 60. Petition for change of name.

A petition for leave to assume another name may be made by a resident of the state to the county court of the county or the supreme court in the county in which he resides, or, if he resides in the city of New York, either to the supreme court or to any branch of the civil court of the city of New York, in any county of the city of New York. The petition to change the name of an infant may be made by the infant through his next friend, or by either of his parents, or by his general guardian, or by the guardian of his person.

Sec. 61. Contents.

The petition must be in writing, signed by the petitioner and verified in like manner as a pleading in a court of record, and must specify the grounds of the application, the name, date of birth, place of birth, age and residence of the individual whose name is proposed to be changed and the name which he proposes to assume. The petition must also specify whether or not the petitioner has been convicted of a crime or adjudicated a bankrupt, and whether or not there are any judgments or liens of record against the petitioner or actions or proceedings pending to which the petitioner is a party, and, if so, the petitioner must give descriptive details in connection therewith sufficient to readily identify the matter referred to.

Upon all applications for change of name by persons born in the state of New York, there shall be annexed to such petition either a birth certificate or a certified transcript thereof or a certificate of the commissioner or local board of health that none is available.

Sec. 62. Notice.

If the petition be to change the name of an infant, notice of the time and place when and where the petition will be presented must be served, in like manner as a notice of a motion upon an attorney in an action, upon (a) both parents of the infant, if they be living, unless the petition be made by one of the parents, in which case notice must be served upon the other, if he or she be living, and (b) the general guardian or guardian of the person, if there be one. But if any of the persons, required to be given notice by this section, reside without the state, then the notice required by this section must be sent by registered mail to the last known address of the person to be served. If it appears to the satisfaction of the court that a person required to be given notice by this section cannot be located with due diligence within the state, and that such person has no known address without the state, then the court may dispense with notice or require notice to be given to such persons and in such manner as the court thinks proper.

Sec. 63. Order.

If the court to which the petition is presented is satisfied thereby, or by the affidavit and certificate presented therewith, that the petition is true, and that there is no reasonable objection to the change of name proposed, and if the petition be to change the name of an infant, that the interests of the infant will be substantially promoted by the change, the court shall make an order authorizing the petitioner to assume the name proposed. The order shall further recite the date and place of birth of the applicant and, if the applicant was born in the state of New York, such order shall set forth the number of his birth certificate or that no birth certificate is available. The order shall be directed to be entered and the papers on which it was granted to be filed prior to the publication hereinafter directed in the clerk's office of the county in which the petitioner resides if he be an individual, or in the office of the clerk of the civil court of the city of New York if the order be made by that court. Such order shall also direct the publication, at least once, within twenty days after the making of the order, in a designated newspaper in the county in which the order is directed to be entered, of a notice in substantially the following form:

Notice is hereby given that an order entered by the............ court,............ county, on the...... day

of......., bearing Index Number.........., a copy of which may be examined at the office of the clerk, located at..........., in room number......., grants me the right to assume the name of.............

My present address is....................; the date of my birth is....................; the place of my birth

is....................; my present name

is...........................

Sec. 64-a. Exemption from publication requirements.

If the court shall find that the publication of an applicant's change of name would jeopardize such applicant's personal safety, the provisions of sections sixty-three and sixty-four of this article requiring publication shall be waived and shall be inapplicable. The court shall order the records of such change of name proceeding to be sealed, to be opened only by order of the court for good cause shown or at the request of the applicant.

Sec. 65. Optional change of name upon marriage, divorce or annulment.

1. Any person may, upon marriage, elect to assume a new name according to the provisions of paragraph (b) of subdivision one of section fifteen of the domestic relations law.

2. Any person may, upon divorce or annulment, elect to resume the use of a former surname according to the provisions of section 240a of the domestic relations law.

3. The effect of the name changes accomplished in the manner prescribed in subdivisions one and two of this section shall be as set forth in section sixty-four of this chapter.

4. Nothing in this article shall be construed to abrogate or alter the common law right of every person, whether married or single, to retain his or her name or to assume a new one so long as the new name is used consistently and without intent to defraud.

NORTH CAROLINA

North Carolina General Statutes 101-1. Legislature may regulate change by general but not private law.

The General Assembly shall not have power to pass any private law to alter the name of any person, but shall have power to pass general laws regulating the same.

North Carolina General Statutes 101-2. Procedure for changing name; petition; notice.

A person who wishes, for good cause shown, to change his name must file his application before the clerk of the superior court of the county in which he lives, having first given 10 days' notice of the application by publication at the courthouse door. Applications to change the name of minor children may be filed by their parent or parents or guardian or next friend of such minor children, and such applications may be joined in the application for a change of name filed by their parent or parents: Provided nothing herein shall be construed to permit one parent to make such application on behalf of a minor child without the consent of the other parent of such minor child if both parents be living, except that a minor who has reached the age of 16 years, upon proper application to the clerk may change his or her name, with the consent of the a parent who has custody of the minor and has supported the minor, without the necessity of obtaining the consent of the other parent, when the clerk of court is satisfied that the other parent has abandoned the minor. Provided, further, that a change of parentage or the addition of information relating to parentage on the birth certificate of any person shall be made pursuant to G.S.130A-118. Notwithstanding any other provisions of this section, the consent of a parent who has abandoned a minor child shall not be required if there is filed with the clerk a copy of an order of a court of competent jurisdiction adjudicating that such parent has abandoned such minor child. In the event that a court of competent jurisdiction has not therefore declared the minor child to be an abandoned child then on written notice of not less than 10 days to the parent allege to have abandoned the child, by registered or certified mail directed to such parent's last known address, the clerk of superior court is hereby authorized to determine whether an abandonment has taken place. If said parent denies that an abandonment has taken place, this issue of fact shall be determined as provided in G.S. 1-273, and if abandonment is determined, then the consent of said parent shall not be required. Upon final determination of this issue of fact the proceeding shall be transferred back to the special proceedings docket for further action by the clerk.

North Carolina General Statutes 101-3. Contents of petition.

The applicant shall state in the application his true name, county of birth, date of birth, the full name of parents as shown on birth certificate, the name he desires to adopt, his reasons for desiring such change, and whether his name has ever before been changed by law, and, if so, the facts with respect thereto.

North Carolina General Statutes 101-4. Proof of good character to accompany petition.

The applicant shall also file with said petition proof of his good character, which proof must be made by at least two citizens of the county who know his standing: Provided, however, proof of good character shall not be required when the application is for the change of name of a child under 16 years of age.

North Carolina General Statutes 101-5. Clerk to order change; certificate and record.

If the clerk thinks that good and sufficient reason exists for the change of name, it shall be his duty to issue an order changing the name of the applicant from his true name to the name sought to be adopted. Such order shall contain the true name, the county of birth, the date of birth, the full name of parents as shown on birth certificate, and the name sought to be adopted. He shall issue to the applicant a certificate under his hand and seal of office, stating the change made in the applicant's name, and shall also record said application and order on the docket of special proceedings in his court. He shall forward the order to the State Registrar of Vital Statistics on a form provided by him. If the applicant was born in North Carolina, the State Registrar shall note the change of name of the individual or individuals specified in the order on the birth certificate of that individual or those individuals and shall notify the register of deeds in the county of birth. If the applicant was born in another state of the United States, the State Registrar shall forward the notice of change of name to the registration office of the state of birth.

North Carolina General Statutes 101-6. Effect of change; only one change, except as provided. (a) When the order is made and the applicant's name changed, he is entitled to all the privileges and protection under his new name as he would have been under the old name. No person shall be allowed to change his name under this Chapter but once, except that he shall be permitted to resume his former name upon compliance with the requirements and procedure set forth in this Chapter for change of name, and except as provided in subsection (b) of this section. (b) For good cause shown, and upon compliance with the requirements and procedure set forth in this Chapter for change of name the name of a minor child may be changed not more than two times under this Chapter.(1891, c. 145; Rev., ss. 2147, 2149; C.S., s. 2975; 1945, c. 37,s. 2; 1991, c. 333, s. 1.)

North Carolina General Statutes 101-8. Resumption of name by widow or widower.

A person at any time after the person is widowed may, upon application to the clerk of court of the county in which the person resides setting forth the person's intention to do so, resume the use of her maiden name or the name of a prior deceased husband or of a previously divorced husband in the case of a widow, or his pre-marriage surname in the case of a widower. The application shall set forth the full name of the last spouse of the applicant, shall include a copy of the spouse's death certificate, and shall be signed by the applicant in the applicant's full name. The clerks of court of the several counties of this State shall record and index such applications in the manner required by the Administrative Office of the Courts.

NORTH DAKOTA

N.D.Code, Title 32 Judicial Remedies, Chapter 32-28 Change of Names of Persons and Places, §32-28-01

1. Any person desiring to change that person's name may file a petition in the district court of the county in which the person is a resident, setting forth:

   a. That the petitioner has been a bona fide resident of the county for at least six months before the filing of the petition.

   b. The reason for which the change of the petitioner's name is sought.

   c. The name requested.

2. The judge of the district court, upon being duly satisfied by affidavit or proof in open court of the truth of the allegations set forth in the petition, that there exists proper and reasonable cause for changing the name of the petitioner, and that thirty days' previous notice of the intended application has been given in the official newspaper of the county in which the petitioner resides, shall order a change of the name of the petitioner. The court may waive publication of the notice when the proposed change relates only to a first or given name as distinguished from a surname or upon evidence satisfactory to the court that the petitioner has been the victim of domestic violence as defined in section 14-07.1-01.

OHIO

SECTION 2717.01 GENERAL ASSEMBLY: 116.

Bill Number: Amended Sub. S.B. 248 Effective Date: 12-17-86

(A) A person desiring a change of name may file an application in the probate court of the county in which the person resides. The application shall set forth that the applicant has been a bona fide resident of that county for at least one year prior to the filing of the application, the cause for which the change of name is sought, and the requested new name.

Notice of the application shall be given once by publication in a newspaper of general circulation in the county at least thirty days before the hearing on the application. The notice shall set forth the court in which the application was filed, the case number, and the date and time of the hearing. Upon proof that proper notice was given and that the facts set forth in the application show reasonable and proper cause for changing the name of the applicant, the court may order the change of name.

(B) An application for change of name may be made on behalf of a minor by either of the minor's parents, a legal guardian, or a guardian *ad litem*. When application is made on behalf of a minor, in addition to the notice and proof required pursuant to division (A) of this section, the consent of both living, legal parents of the minor shall be filed, or notice of the hearing shall be given to the parent or parents not consenting by certified mail, return receipt requested. If there is no known father of the minor, the notice shall be given to the person who the mother of the minor alleges to be the father. If no father is so alleged, or if either parent or the address if either parent is unknown, notice pursuant to division (A) of this section shall be sufficient as to the father or parent. Any additional notice required by this division may be waived in writing by any person entitled to the notice.

OKLAHOMA

TITLE 12. CIVIL PROCEDURE

Chapter 33 §1631. Right to Petition for Change of Name.

Any natural person, who has been domiciled in this state or who has been residing upon any military reservation located in said state, for more than thirty (30) days, and has been an actual resident of the county or such military reservation situated in said county, or county in which the military reservation is situated, for more than thirty (30) days, next preceding the filing of the action, may petition for a change of name in a civil action in the district court. If the person be a minor, the action may be brought by guardian or next friend as in other actions.

Chapter 33 §1632. Required Context of Petition.

The petition shall be verified and shall state: (a) The name and address of the petitioner; (b) The facts as to domicile and residence; (c) The date and place of birth; (d) The birth certificate number, and place where the birth is registered, if registered; (e) The name desired by petitioner; (f) A clear and concise statement of the reasons for the desired change; (g) A positive statement that the change is not sought for any illegal or fraudulent purpose, or to delay or hinder creditors.

Chapter 33 §1633. Notice—Protest—Hearing Date—Continuance.

Notice of filing of such petition shall be given, in the manner provided for publication notice in civil cases, by publishing the same one time at least ten (10) days prior to the date set for hearing in some newspaper authorized by law to publish legal notices printed in the county where the petition is filed if there be any printed in such county, and if there be none, then in some such newspaper printed in this state of general circulation in that county. The notice shall contain the style and number of the case, the time, date and place where the same is to be heard, and that any person may file a written protest in the case prior to the date set for the hearing. The hearing date may be any day after completion of the publication. The court or judge, for cause, may continue the matter to a later date.

OREGON

CHANGE OF NAME 33.410 Jurisdiction; grounds.

Application for change of name of a person may be heard and determined by the probate court or, if the circuit court is not the probate court, the circuit court if its jurisdiction has been extended to include this section pursuant to ORS 3.275 of the county in which the person resides. The change of name shall be granted by the court unless the court finds that the change is not consistent with the public interest. [Amended by 1967 c.534 s.11; 1975 c.733 s.1]

33.420 Notice of application and decree; certificate; minor children.

(1) Before decreeing a change of name, except as provided in ORS 109.360, the court shall require public notice of the application to be given, that all persons may show cause why the same should not be granted. The court shall also require public notice to be given of the change after the entry of the decree.

(2) Before decreeing a change of name in the case of a minor child the court shall require that, in addition to the notice required under subsection (1) of this section, written notice be given to the parents of the child, both custodial and noncustodial, and to any legal guardian of the child. [Amended by 1983 c.369 s.6; 1997 c.872 s.22]

33.430 Name of child on birth certificate, how changed; court conference with child.

(1) In the case of a change, by court order, of the name of the parents of any minor child, if the child's birth certificate is on file in this state, the State Registrar of the Center for Health Statistics, upon receipt of a certified copy of the court order changing the name, together with the information required to locate the original birth certificate of the child, shall prepare a new birth certificate for the child in the new name of the parents of the child. The name of the parents as so changed shall be set forth in the new certificate, in place of their original name.

(2) The evidence upon which the new certificate was made, and the original certificate, shall be sealed and filed by the State Registrar of the Center for Health Statistics, and may be opened only upon demand

of the person whose name was changed, if of legal age, or by an order of a court of competent jurisdiction.

(3) When a change of name by parents will affect the name of their child or children under subsection (1) of this section, the court, on its own motion or on request of a child of the parents, may take testimony from or confer with the child or children and may exclude from the conference the parents and other persons if the court finds that such action would be in the best interests of the child or children. However, the court shall permit an attorney for the parents to attend the conference, and the conference shall be reported. If the court finds that a change of name would not be in the best interests of the child, the court may provide in the order changing the name of the parents that such change of name shall not affect the child, and a new birth certificate shall not be prepared for the child.

33.440 Application by minor child; court conference.

When a minor child applies for a change of name under ORS 33.410, the court may, upon its own motion, confer with the child and may exclude from the conference the parents and other persons if the court finds that such action would be in the best interests of the child. However, the court shall permit an attorney for the child to attend the conference, and the conference shall be reported.

PENNSYLVANIA

§ 6. Change of name of individual.

(a) Petition for change of name.-Any person desiring to change his or her name shall file a petition in the court of common pleas of the county in which he or she shall reside, setting forth such desire and intention and the reason therefor, together with the residence of petitioner, and his or her residence or residences for and during five years prior thereto. Where the petitioner is a married person, the other spouse may join as a party petitioner, in which event, upon compliance with the provisions of this section, said spouse shall also be entitled to the benefits hereof. The court shall, thereupon, enter an order directing that notice be given of the filing of said petition and of the day set for the hearing thereon, which hearing shall be not less than one month or more than three months after the filing of said petition, and said notice shall be:

(1) Published in two newspapers of general circulation in said county or county contiguous thereto, one of which publications may be in the official paper for the publication of legal notices in said county.

(2) Given to any nonpetitioning parent of a child whose name may be affected by the proceedings.

(b) Court hearing and decree.-At the hearing of said petition, any person having lawful objection to the change of name may appear and be heard. If the court be satisfied after said hearing that there is no lawful objection to the granting of the prayer of said petition, a decree may be entered by said court changing the name as prayed for, if at said hearing the petitioner or petitioners shall present to the court proof of publication of said notice as required by the order, together with official searches of the proper offices of the county wherein petitioner or petitioners reside and of any other county wherein petitioner or petitioners may have resided within five years of the filing of his or her petition for change of name, or a certificate in lieu thereof given by a corporation authorized by law to make such searches, showing that there are no judgments or decrees of record or any other matter of like character against said petitioner or petitioners.

RHODE ISLAND

TITLE 33 PROBATE PRACTICE AND PROCEDURE.

CHAPTER 33-22 PRACTICE IN PROBATE COURTS

§ 33-22-28 Name change.

In every petition for change of name in the probate court, the judge shall grant or deny the petition without consideration of presence or absence of spousal consent.

§ 15-7-15 Decree of change of name.

If, in a petition for the adoption of a child, a change of the child's name is requested, the court, upon decreeing the adoption, may also decree the change of name and grant a certificate thereof.

SOUTH CAROLINA

TITLE 15—CIVIL REMEDIES AND PROCEDURES

CHAPTER 49. CHANGE OF NAME

SECTION 15-49-10. Application for change of name.

(A) A person who desires to change his name may petition, in writing, a family court judge in the appropriate circuit, setting forth the reason for the change, his age, his place of residence and birth, and the name by which he desires to be known.

(B) A parent who desires to change the name of his minor child may petition, in writing, a family court judge in the appropriate circuit. The other parent, if there is not one then the child, must be named as a party in the action unless waived by the court. The court shall appoint a guardian *ad litem* to represent the child. The court shall grant the petition if it finds that it is in the best interest of the child.

SOUTH DAKOTA

CHAPTER 21-37. CHANGE OF NAME

§ 21-37-1. Circuit court power to change names—Pending proceedings and existing rights unaffected.

The circuit court shall have authority to change the names of persons, municipalities, and the name of any recorded plat or map of land situated within the limits of any municipality, as provided in this chapter. The change of names shall in no manner affect or alter any pending action or legal proceeding, nor any right, title, or interest whatsoever.

§ 21-37-3. Petition for change of name of person—Contents.

A petition for change of name of a person must be filed in the office of the clerk of courts of the county of petitioner's said residence, entitled in the circuit court for said county and stating that the petitioner has been a bona fide resident citizen of such county for at least six months prior to filing the petition; the cause for which change of petitioner's name is sought; and the name asked for.

§ 21-37-5. Hearing and order changing name of person.

At the time and place specified in the notice and upon proof in open court to the satisfaction of the judge thereof that notice of the hearing has been given as required in § 21-37-4 and that the allegations of the petition are true, and that there exists proper and reasonable cause for changing the name of the petitioner, the court or judge shall make an order directing a change of the name of the petitioner and directing that such order be entered by the clerk.

TENNESSEE

39.08—Name Change:

a. Adult: The verified petition must comply with the statute and shall state the full legal name of the Petitioner, all prior names by which the Petitioner has been known, the place of residence of the petitioner(s), the birth date, age, social security number of the individual whose name is to be changed, and the State where the original birth certificate was issued. Copes of the original birth certificate, social security card and official photo identification shall be submitted with the petition. The individual whose name is to be changed must appear in Court at the hearing.

b. Minor The verified petition to change the name of a minor must comply with the statute and be sworn to and signed by both parents and include copies of the original birth certificates of the child and both parents, social security card and official photo identification of both parents, photograph of the minor and social security card of the minor, if any. Both parents and the minor must appear in Court. If both parents do not join in the Petition or if the identity or location of a parent is unknown, the petition must be specific as to all pertinent facts including all efforts to identify or locate the parent who did not join in the Petition. If the father is not identified on the birth certificate, legitimation proceedings must be completed prior to filing of a petition to change the name of the minor child. Service of process is required for any parent or guardian who does not join in the petition. The verified petition must establish by clear and convincing evidence that the proposed name change is in the best interest of the minor, otherwise the petition shall not be granted.-

TEXAS FAMILY CODE—SUBTITLE C. CHANGE OF NAME

Sec. 45.102. REQUIREMENTS OF PETITION.

(a) A petition to change the name of an adult must be verified and include:

(1) the present name and place of residence of the petitioner;

(2) the full name requested for the petitioner;

(3) the reason the change in name is requested;

(4) whether the petitioner has been the subject of a final felony conviction; and

(5) whether the petitioner is subject to the registration requirements of Chapter 62, Code of Criminal Procedure.

(6) a legible and complete set of the petitioner's fingerprints on a fingerprint card format acceptable to the Department of Public Safety and the Federal Bureau of Investigation.

(b) The petition must include each of the following or a reasonable explanation why the required information is not included:

(1) the petitioner's:

(A) full name;

(B) sex;

(C) race;

(D) date of birth;

(E) driver's license number for any driver's license issued in the 10 years preceding the date of the petition;

(F) social security number; and

(G) assigned FBI number, state identification number, if known, or any other reference number in a criminal history record system that identifies the petitioner;

(2) any offense above the grade of Class C misdemeanor for which the petitioner has been charged; and

(3) the case number and the court if a warrant was issued or a charging instrument was filed or presented for an offense listed in Subsection (b)(2).

Sec. 45.002. REQUIREMENTS OF PETITION.

(a) A petition to change the name of a child must be verified and include:

(1) the present name and place of residence of the child;

(2) the reason a change of name is requested;

(3) the full name requested for the child;

(4) whether the child is subject to the continuing exclusive jurisdiction of a court under Chapter 155; and

(5) whether the child is subject to the registration requirements of Chapter 62, Code of Criminal Procedure.

(b) If the child is 10 years of age or older, the child's written consent to the change of name must be attached to the petition.

Sec. 45.003. CITATION.

(a) The following persons are entitled to citation in a suit under this subchapter:

(1) a parent of the child whose parental rights have not been terminated;

(2) any managing conservator of the child; and

(3) any guardian of the child.

(b) Citation must be issued and served in the same manner as under Chapter 102.

ORDER.

(a) The court may order the name of a child changed if:

(1) the change is in the best interest of the child; and

(2) for a child subject to the registration requirements of Chapter 62, Code of Criminal Procedure:

(A) the change is in the interest of the public; and

(B) the person petitioning on behalf of the child provides the court with proof that the child has notified the appropriate local law enforcement authority of the proposed name change.

(b) If the child is subject to the continuing jurisdiction of a court under Chapter 155, the court shall send a copy of the order to the central record file as provided in Chapter 108.

(c) In this section, "local law enforcement authority" has the meaning assigned by Article 62.01, Code of Criminal Procedure.

UTAH

42-1-1. By petition to district court—Contents.

Any natural person, desiring to change his name, may file a petition therefor in the district court of the county where he resides, setting forth:

(1) The cause for which the change of name is sought.

(2) The name proposed.

(3) That he has been a bona fide resident of the county for the year immediately prior to the filing of the petition.

42-1-2. Notice of hearing—Order of change.

The court shall order what, if any, notice shall be given of the hearing, and after the giving of such notice, if any, may order the change of name as requested, upon proof in open court of the allegations of the petition and that there exists proper cause for granting the same.

42-1-3. Effect of proceedings.

Such proceedings shall in no manner affect any legal action or proceeding then pending, or any right, title or interest whatsoever.

VERMONT

§ 811. Procedure; form

A person of age and sound mind may change his or her name by making, signing, sealing and acknowledging before the judge of the probate court of the district in which the person resides, an instrument in the following form:

STATE OF VERMONT }

_____ District.}

Be it remembered, that I, A. B. of _____ in the county of _____, will be hereafter known and called _____.

In witness whereof I hereunto set my hand and seal this _____ day of _____, 19 _____.

§ 812. Minor.

A minor may change his name by some person who, under chapter 111 of Title 14, may act for him, making, signing, sealing and acknowledging before the judge of the probate court of the district in which such minor resides, an instrument in substantially the form provided in section 811 of this title. Such instrument shall be signed by the person so acting for such minor. However, the name of the minor, if over fourteen years of age, shall not be changed without his consent given in court.

§ 815. Advertisement of change of name.

The court wherein an instrument changing the name is filed under this chapter shall cause notice thereof to be published for three weeks successively in a newspaper published in the county or in an adjoining county. However, such notice shall not be published when the change of name is in connection with the adoption of a minor under the age of eighteen years. The expense of a change of name and publication shall be borne by the person whose name is changed.

certificate and all copies thereof in accordance with the provisions of Title 18, chapter 101. Such amended certificates shall have the words "Court Amended" stamped, written or typed at the top and shall show that the change of name was made pursuant to this chapter.

VIRGINIA

Virginia Code§ 8.01-217. How name of person may be changed.

Any person desiring to change his own name, or that of his child or ward, may apply therefor to the circuit court of the county or city in which the person whose name is to be changed resides, or if no place of abode exists, such person may apply to any circuit court which shall consider such application if it finds that good cause exists therefor under the circumstances alleged. Applications of probationers and incarcerated persons may be accepted if the court finds that good cause exists for such application. An incarcerated person may apply to the circuit court of the county or city in which such person is incarcerated. In case of a minor who has no living parent or guardian, the application may be made by his next friend. In case of a minor who has both parents living, the parent who does not join in the application shall be served with reasonable notice of the application and, should such parent object to the change of name, a hearing shall be held to determine whether the change of name is in the best interest of the minor. If, after application is made on behalf of a minor and an ex parte hearing is held thereon, the court finds by clear and convincing evidence that such notice would present a serious threat to the health and safety of the applicant, the court may waive such notice. Every application shall be under oath and shall include the place of residence of the applicant, the names of both parents, including the maiden name of his mother, the date and place of birth of the applicant, the applicant's felony conviction record, if any, whether the applicant is presently incarcerated or a probationer with any court, and if the applicant has previously changed his name, his former name or names. On any such application and hearing, if such be demanded, the court, shall, unless the evidence shows that the change of name is sought for a fraudulent purpose or would otherwise infringe upon the rights of others or, in case of a minor, that the change of name is not in the best interest of the minor, order a change of name and the clerk of the court shall spread the order upon the current deed book in his office, index it in both the old and new names, and transmit a certified copy to the State Registrar of Vital Records and the Central Criminal Records Exchange. Transmittal of a copy to the State Registrar of Vital Records and the Central Criminal Records Exchange shall not be required of a person who changed his or her former name by reason of marriage and who makes application to resume a former name pursuant to § 20-121.4. If the applicant shall show cause to believe that in the event his change of name should become a public record, a serious threat to the health or safety of the applicant or his immediate family would exist, the chief judge of the circuit court may waive the requirement that the application be under oath or the court may order the record sealed and direct the clerk not to spread and index any orders entered in the cause, and shall not transmit a certified copy to the State Registrar of Vital Records or the Central Criminal Records Exchange. Upon receipt of such order by the State Registrar of Vital Records, for a person born in this Commonwealth, together with a proper request and payment of required fees, the Registrar shall issue certifications of the amended birth record which do not reveal the former name or names of the applicant unless so ordered by a court of competent jurisdiction. Such certifications shall not be marked "amended" and show the effective date as provided in § 32.1-272. Such order shall set forth the date and place of birth of the person whose name is changed, the full names of his parents, including the maiden name of the mother and, if such person has previously changed his name, his former name or names.

WASHINGTON

(1) Any person desiring a change of his or her name or that of his or her child or ward, may apply therefor to the district court of the judicial district in which he or she resides, by petition setting forth the reasons for such change; thereupon such court in its discretion may order a change of the name and thenceforth the new name shall be in place of the former.

(2) An offender under the jurisdiction of the department of corrections who applies to change his or her name under subsection (1) of this section shall submit a copy of the application to the department of corrections not fewer than five days before the entry of an order granting the name change. No offender under the jurisdiction of the department of corrections at the time of application shall be granted an order changing his or her name if the court finds that doing so will interfere with legitimate penological interests, except that no order shall be denied when the name change is requested for religious or legitimate cultural reasons or in recognition of marriage or dissolution of marriage. An offender under the jurisdiction of the department of corrections who receives an order changing his or her name shall submit a copy of the order to the department of corrections within five days of the entry of the order. Violation of this subsection is a misdemeanor.

(3) A sex offender subject to registration under RCW 9A.44.130 who applies to change his or her name under subsection (1) of this section shall follow the procedures set forth in *RCW 9A.44.130(6).

(4) The district court shall collect the fees authorized by RCW 36.18.010 for filing and recording a name change order, and transmit the fee and the order to the county auditor. The court may collect a reasonable fee to cover the cost of transmitting the order to the county auditor.

(5) Name change petitions may be filed and shall be heard in superior court when the person desiring a change of his or her name or that of his or her child or ward is a victim of domestic violence as defined in

RCW 26.50.010(1) and the person seeks to have the name change file sealed due to reasonable fear for his or her safety or that of his or her child or ward. Upon granting the name change, the superior court shall seal the file if the court finds that the safety of the person seeking the name change or his or her child or ward warrants sealing the file. In all cases filed under this subsection, whether or not the name change petition is granted, there shall be no public access to any court record of the name change filing, proceeding, or order, unless the name change is granted but the file is not sealed. Wa. Rev. Code § 4.24.130 (2000).

WEST VIRGINIA

WEST VIRGINIA ARTICLE 5. CHANGE OF NAME.

§48-5-1. Petition to circuit court for change of name; contents thereof; notice of application.

Any person desiring a change of his own name, or that of his child or ward, may apply therefor to the circuit court or any other court of record having jurisdiction of the county in which he resides, or the judge thereof in vacation, by petition setting forth that he has been a bona fide resident of such county for at least one year prior to the filing of the petition, the cause for which the change of name is sought, and the new name desired; and previous to the filing of such petition such person shall cause to be published a notice of the time and place that such application will be made, which notice shall be published as a Class I legal advertisement in compliance with the provisions of article three, chapter fifty-nine of this code, and the publication area for such publication shall be the county.

§48-5-2. Objections to change of name.

Any person who is likely to be injured by the change of name of any person so petitioning, or who knows of any reason why the name of any such petitioner should not be changed, may appear at the time and place named in the notice, and shall be heard in opposition to such change.

§48-5-3. When court may order change of name.

Upon the filing of such petition, and upon proof of the publication of such notice and of the matters set forth in the petition, and being satisfied that no injury will be done to any person by reason of such change, that reasonable and proper cause exists for changing the name of petitioner, and that such change is not desired because of any fraudulent or evil intent on the part of the petitioner, the court or judge thereof in vacation may order a change of name as applied for except as provided by the provisions of this section. The court may not grant any change of name for any person convicted of any felony during the time that the person is incarcerated. The court may not grant any change of name for any person required to register with the state police pursuant to the provisions of article eight-f, chapter sixty-one of this code during the period that such person is required to register. The court may not grant a change of name for persons convicted of first degree murder in violation of section one, article two, chapter sixty-one of this code for a period of ten years after the person is discharged from imprisonment or is discharged from parole, whichever occurs later. The court may not grant a change of name of any person convicted of violating any provision of section fourteen-a, article two, chapter sixty-one of this code for a period of ten years after the person is discharged from imprisonment or is discharged from parole, whichever occurs later.

§48-5-4. Recordation of order changing name.

When such order is made the petitioner shall forthwith cause a certified copy thereof to be filed in the office of the clerk of the county court of the county where petitioner resides, and such clerk shall record the same in a book to be kept for the purpose and index the same under both the old and the new names. For such recording and indexing the clerk shall be allowed the same fee as for a deed.

§48-5-5. When new name to be used.

When such change has been ordered and a certified copy of the order filed in the office of the county clerk, the new name shall thenceforth be used in place of the former name.

§48-5-6. Unlawful change of name.

Any person residing in this state who shall change his name, or assume another name, unlawfully, shall be guilty of a misdemeanor, and, upon conviction thereof, shall be fined not exceeding one hundred dollars, and upon a repetition thereof shall be confined in jail not exceeding sixty days.

§48-5-7. Unlawful change of name by certain felons and registrants.

(a) It is unlawful for any person convicted of first degree murder in violation of section one, article two, chapter sixty-one of this code, and for any person convicted of violating any provision of section fourteen-a, article two, chapter sixty-one of this code, for which a sentence of life imprisonment is imposed, to apply for a change of name for a period of ten years after the person is discharged from imprisonment or is discharged from parole, whichever occurs later.

(b) It is unlawful for any person required to register with the state police pursuant to the provisions of article twelve, chapter fifteen of this code to apply for a change of name during the period that the person is required to register.

(c) It is unlawful for any person convicted of a felony to apply for a change of name during the period that such person is incarcerated.

(d) A person who violates the provisions of subsections (a), (b) or (c) of this section is guilty of a misdemeanor and, upon conviction thereof, shall be fined not less than two hundred fifty dollars nor more than ten thousand dollars or imprisoned in the county or regional jail for not more than one year, or both fined and incarcerated.

WISCONSIN

786.36 Changing names, court procedure.

Any resident of this state, whether a minor or adult, may upon petition to the circuit court of the county where he or she resides and upon filing a copy of the notice, with proof of publication, as required by s. 786.37, if no sufficient cause is shown to the contrary, have his or her name changed or established by order of the court. If the person whose name is to be changed is a minor under the age of 14 years, the petition may be made by: both parents, if living, or the survivor of them; the guardian or person having legal custody of the minor if both parents are dead or if the parental rights have been terminated by judicial proceedings; or the mother, if the minor is a nonmarital child who is not adopted or whose parents do not subsequently intermarry under s. 767.60, except that the father must also make the petition unless his rights have been legally terminated. The order shall be entered at length upon the records of the court and a certified copy of the record shall be recorded in the office of the register of deeds of the county, who shall make an entry in a book to be kept by the register. The fee for recording a certified copy is the fee specified under s. 59.43 (2) (ag). If the person whose name is changed or established was born or married in this state, the clerk of the court shall send to the state registrar of vital statistics, on a form designed by the state registrar of vital statistics, an abstract of the record, duly certified, accompanied by the fee prescribed in s. 69.22, which fee the clerk of court shall charge to and collect from the petitioner. The state registrar of vital statistics shall then correct the birth record, marriage record or both, and direct the register of deeds and local registrar to make similar corrections on their records. No person engaged in the practice of any profession for which a license is required by the state may change his or her given name or his or her surname to any other given name or any other surname than that under which the person was originally licensed in the profession in this or any other state, in any instance in which the state board or commission for the particular profession, after a hearing, finds that practicing under the changed name operates to unfairly compete with another practitioner or misleads the public as to identity or otherwise results in detriment to the profession or the public. This prohibition against a change of name by a person engaged in the practice of any profession does not apply to any person legally qualified to teach in the public schools in this state, nor to a change of name resulting from marriage or divorce, nor to members of any profession for which there exists no state board or commission authorized to issue licenses or pass upon the qualifications of applicants or hear complaints respecting conduct of members of the profession. Any change of name other than as authorized by law is void.

WYOMING

CHAPTER 25 CHANGE OF NAME

1-25-101. Verified petition to be presented; information to be shown in petition; order of court making change; record to be made.

Every person desiring to change his name may petition the district court of the county of the petitioner's residence for the desired change. The petition shall be verified by affidavit setting forth the petitioner's full name, the name desired, a concise statement of the reason for the desired change, the place of his birth, his place of residence and the length of time he has been an actual bona fide resident of the county in which the petition is filed. If the court is satisfied that the desired change is proper and not detrimental to the interests of any other person, it shall order the change to be made, and record the proceedings in the records of the court.

1-25-102. Residence requirement.

A person petitioning for a change of name shall have been a bona fide resident of the county in which the petition is filed for at least two (2) years immediately preceding filing the petition.

1-25-103. Notice to be given by publication.

Public notice of the petition for a change of name shall be given in the same manner as service by publication upon nonresidents in civil actions.

1-25-104. Change of name in adoption proceedings.

In all cases of the adoption of children in the manner provided by law, the court before which such adoption proceeding is held, may change the name of any child so adopted and make an order to that effect, which shall be recorded in the records of the proceeding of adoption. Each child who has heretofore, in Wyoming, been adopted according to law, may have his or her name changed to that of the parents who have adopted him or her, upon the parents, who have adopted such child, on behalf of such child, filing a petition therefor.

APPENDIX 13:
DIRECTORY OF NATIONAL DOMESTIC VIOLENCE ORGANIZATIONS

ORGANIZATION	ADDRESS	TELEPHONE	FAX	WEBSITE
Battered Women's Justice Project	202 East Superior Street Duluth, MN 55802	218-722-2781	n/a	http://www.duluth-model.org/
Faith Trust Institute	2400 N. 45th Street, #10 Seattle, WA 98103	206-634-1903	206-634-0115	http://www.faithtrustinstitute.org/
Family Violence Prevention Fund	383 Rhode Island Street Suite 304 San Francisco, CA 94103	415-252-8900	415-252-8991	n/a
Health Resource Center on Domestic Violence	383 Rhode Island Street Suite 304 San Francisco, CA 94103	800-313-1310	415-252-8991	http://www.endabuse.org/
National Battered Women's Law Project	275 7th Avenue Suite 1206 New York, NY 10001	212-741-9480	212-741-6438	n/a

ORGANIZATION	ADDRESS	TELEPHONE	FAX	WEBSITE
National Coalition Against Domestic Violence	1633 Q Street NW Suite 210 Washington, DC 20009	202-745-1211	202-745-0088	http://www.ncadv.org/
National Clearinghouse for the Defense of Battered Women	125 South 9th Street Suite 302, Philadelphia, PA 19107	800-903-0111	215-351-0779	
National Clearinghouse on Marital and Date Rape	2325 Oak Street Berkeley, CA 94708	510-524-1582	n/a	http://members.aol.com/ncmdr/
National Network to End Domestic Violence	660 Pennsylvania Avenue SE, Suite 303 Washington, DC 20003	202-543-5566	202-543-5626	http://www.nnedv.org/
National Resource Center on Domestic Violence	6400 Flank Drive Suite 1300 Harrisburg, PA 17112	800-537-2238	717-545-9456	http://www.pcadv.org/
Resource Center on Domestic Violence, Child Protection, and Custody	P.O. Box 8970 Reno, NV 89507	800-527-3223	775-784-6628	http://www.ncjfcj.org/
Victim Services Domestic Violence Shelter Tour	2 Lafayette Street 3rd Floor New York, NY 10007	212-577-7700	212-385-0331	http://www.safehorizon.org/
YWCA Battered Women Task Force	225 SW 12th Street Topeka, KS 66612	785-354-7927	n/a	n/a

SOURCE: Feminist Majority Foundation

APPENDIX 14:
DIRECTORY OF STATE DOMESTIC VIOLENCE COALITIONS

STATE	COALITION	ADDRESS	TELEPHONE	FAX	EMAIL	WEBSITE
ALABAMA	Alabama Coalition Against Domestic Violence	P.O. Box 4762 Montgomery, AL 36101	1-334-832-4842	334-832-4803	info@acadv.org	http://www.acadv.org/
ALASKA	Alaska Network on Domestic Violence and Sexual Assault	130 Seward Street Room 209 Juneau, AK 99801	907-586-3650	907-463-4493	n/a	http://www.andvsa.org/
ARIZONA	Arizona Coalition Against Domestic Violence	301 E. Bethany Home Rd. Phoenix, AZ 85013	602-279-2900	602-279-2980	acadv@azcadv.org	http://www.azcadv.org/

STATE	COALITION	ADDRESS	TELEPHONE	FAX	EMAIL	WEBSITE
ARKANSAS	Arkansas Coalition Against Domestic Violence	1401 West Capitol Avenue Suite 170 Little Rock, AR 72201	501-812-0571	501-812-0578	n/a	http://www.dom esticpeace.com/
CALIFORNIA	California Partnership to End Domestic Violence	P.O. Box 1798 Sacramento CA 95812	916-444-7163	916-444-7165	info@cpedv.org	http://www.thec oalition.org/
COLORADO	Colorado Coalition Against Domestic Violence	P.O. Box 18902 Denver CO 80218	303-831-9632	303-832-7067	n/a.	http://www.ccad v.org/
CONNECTICUT	Connecticut Coalition Against Domestic Violence	135 Broad Street Hartford, CT 06105	860-524-5890	860-249-1408	info@ctcadv.org	http://www.ctca dv.org/
DELAWARE	Delaware Coalition Against Domestic Violence	100 W. 10th Street Suite 703 Wilmington, DE 19801	302-658-2958	302-658-5049	dcadv@dcadv.or g	http://www.dcad v.org/

STATE	COALITION	ADDRESS	TELEPHONE	FAX	EMAIL	WEBSITE
DISTRICT OF COLUMBIA	D.C. Coalition Against Domestic Violence	500 Indiana Avenue NW Superior Court Room 4235 Washington, DC 20001	202-879-7851	202-387-5684	info@dccadv.org	http://www.dcca dv.org/
FLORIDA	Florida Coalition Against Domestic Violence	425 Office Plaza Drive Tallahassee FL 32301	850-425-2749	850-425-3091	n/a	http://www.fcad v.org/
GEORGIA	Georgia Coalition Against Domestic Violence	114 New Street Suite B Decatur, GA 30030	404-209-0280	404-766-3800	n/a	http://www.gcad v.org/
HAWAII	Hawaii State Coalition Against Domestic Violence	716 Umi Street Unit 210 Honolulu HI 96819	808-832-9316	808-841-6028	n/a	http://www.hsca dv.org/
IDAHO	Idaho Coalition Against Sexual and Domestic Violence	815 Park Blvd. Suite 140 Boise, ID 83712	208-384-0419	208-331-0687	jmatsushita@id vsa.org	http://www.idvs a.org/

STATE	COALITION	ADDRESS	TELEPHONE	FAX	EMAIL	WEBSITE
ILLINOIS	Illinois Coalition Against Domestic Violence	801 South 11th Street Springfield IL 62703	217-789-2830	217-789-1939	ilcadv@ilcadv.org	http://www.ilcadv.org/
INDIANA	Indiana Coalition Against Domestic Violence	1915 W. 18th Street Indianapolis, IN 46202	317-917-3685	317-917-3695	icadv@violenceresource.org	http://www.violenceresource.org/
IOWA	Iowa Coalition Against Domestic Violence	515 28th Street Des Moines, IA 50312	515-244-8028	515-244-7417	icadv@aol.com	http://www.icadv.org/
KANSAS	Kansas Coalition Against Sexual and Domestic Violence	634 SW Harrison Street Topeka, KS 66603	785-232-9784	785-266-1874	coalition@kcsdv.org	http://www.kcsdv.org/
KENTUCKY	Kentucky Domestic Violence Association	P.O. Box 356 Frankfort KY 40602	502-209-5382	502-226-5382	n/a	http://www.kdva.org/
LOUISIANA	Louisiana Coalition Against Domestic Violence	P.O. Box 77308 Baton Rouge LA 70879	225-752-1296	225-751-8927	leighlcadv@aol.com	http://www.lcadv.org/

STATE	COALITION	ADDRESS	TELEPHONE	FAX	EMAIL	WEBSITE
MAINE	Maine Coalition for Family Crisis Services	170 Park Street Bangor, ME 04401	207-941-1194	207-941-2327	info@mcedv.org	http://www.mce dv.org/
MARYLAND	Maryland Network Against Domestic Violence	6911 Laurel Bowie Road Suite 309 Bowie MD 20715	301-352-4574	301-809-0422	info@mndadv.or g	http://www.mna dv.org/
MASSACHUSET TS	Massachusetts Coalition Against Sexual Assault and Domestic Violence	14 Beacon Street Suite 507 Boston, MA 02108	617-248-0922	617-248-0902	info@janedoe.or g	http://www.jane doe.org/
MICHIGAN	Michigan Coalition Against Domestic and Sexual Violence	3893 Okemos Road Suite B2 Okemos MI 48864	517-347-7000	517-347-1377	general@mcads v.org	http://www.mca dsv.org/
MINNESOTA	Minnesota Coalition for Battered Women	450 North Syndicate Street Suite 122 St. Paul, MN 55104	612-646-6177	612-646-1527	mcbw@mcbw.or g	http://www.mcb w.org/

STATE	COALITION	ADDRESS	TELEPHONE	FAX	EMAIL	WEBSITE
MISSISSIPPI	Mississippi State Coalition Against Domestic Violence	P.O. Box 4703 Jackson, MS 39296	601-981-9196	601-981-2501	n/a	http://www.mca dv.org/
MISSOURI	Missouri Coalition Against Domestic Violence	718 East Capitol Avenue Jefferson City, MO 65101	573-634-4161	573-636-3728	n/a	http://www.moc adv.org/
MONTANA	Montana Coalition Against Domestic and Sexual Violence	P.O. Box 818 Helena, MT 59624	406-443-7794	406-443-7818	mcadsv@mt.net	http://www.mca dsv.com/
NEBRASKA	Nebraska Domestic Violence and Sexual Assault Coalition	825 M Street Suite 404 Lincoln, NE 68508	402-476-6256	402-476-6806	help@ndvsac.or g	http://www.ndvs ac.org/
NEVADA	Nevada Network Against Domestic Violence	220 S. Rock Blvd. Suite 7 Reno, NV 89502	775-828-1115	775-828-9991	administrator@ nnadv.org	http://www.nnad v.org/

STATE	COALITION	ADDRESS	TELEPHONE	FAX	EMAIL	WEBSITE
NEW HAMPSHIRE	New Hampshire Coalition Against Domestic and Sexual Violence	P.O. Box 353 Concord, NH 03302	603-224-8893	603-228-6096	n/a	http://www.nhca dsv.org/
NEW JERSEY	New Jersey Coalition for Battered Women	1670 Whitehorse/Ham ilton Square Road Trenton, NJ 08690	609-584-8107	609-584-9750	info@njcbw.org	http://www.njcb w.org/
NEW MEXICO	New Mexico State Coalition Against Domestic Violence	200 Oak Street NE #4 Albuquerque, NM 87106	505-246-9240	505-246-9434	n/a	http://www.nmc adv.org/
NEW YORK	New York State Coalition Against Domestic Violence	350 New Scotland Avenue Albany, NY 12208	518-482-5465	518-482-3807	nyscadv@nysca dv.org	http://www.nysc adv.org/
NORTH CAROLINA	North Carolina Coalition Against Domestic Violence	123 West Main Street Suite 700 Durham NC 27701	919-956-9124	919-682-1449	n/a	http://www.ncca dv.org/

STATE	COALITION	ADDRESS	TELEPHONE	FAX	EMAIL	WEBSITE
NORTH DAKOTA	North Dakota Council on Abused Women's Services	418 East Rosser Avenue Suite 320 Bismarck, ND 58501	701-255-6240	701-255-1904	n/a	http://www.ndcaws.org/
OHIO	Ohio Domestic Violence Network	4807 Evanswood Drive Suite 201 Columbus, OH 43229	614-781-9651	614-781-9652	info@odvn.org	http://www.odvn.org/
OKLAHOMA	Oklahoma Coalition Against Domestic Violence and Sexual Assault	3815 N. Santa Fe Avenue Suite 124 Oklahoma City, OK 73118	405-524-0700	405-524-0711	n/a	http://www.ocadvsa.org/
OREGON	Oregon Coalition Against Domestic and Sexual Violence	380 Southeast Spokane Street Suite 100 Portland, OR 97202	503-230-1951	503-230-1973	n/a	http://www.ocadsv.com/
PENNSYLVANIA	Pennsylvania Coalition Against Domestic Violence	6400 Flank Drive Suite 1300 Harrisburg PA 17112	717-545-6400	717-545-9456	n/a	http://www.pcadv.org/

STATE	COALITION	ADDRESS	TELEPHONE	FAX	EMAIL	WEBSITE
RHODE ISLAND	Rhode Island Coalition Against Domestic Violence	422 Post Road Suite 202 Warwick, RI 02888	401-467-9940	401-467-9943	ricadv@ricadv.org	http://www.ricadv.org/
SOUTH CAROLINA	South Carolina Coalition Against Domestic Violence & Sexual Assault	P.O. Box 7776 Columbia, SC 29202	803-256-2900	803-256-1030	n/a	http://www.sccadvasa.org/
SOUTH DAKOTA	South Dakota Coalition Against Domestic Violence and Sexual Assault	P.O. Box 141 Pierre, SD 57501	605-945-0869	605-945-0870	chris@sdcadvsa.org	http://www.southdakotacoalition.org/
TENNESSEE	Tennessee Task Force Against Domestic Violence	P.O. Box 120972 Nashville TN 37212	615-386-9406	615-383-2967	tcadsv@tcadsv.org	http://www.tcadsv.org/
TEXAS	Texas Council on Family Violence	P.O. Box 161810 Austin, TX 78716	512-794-1133	512-794-1199	n/a	http://www.ndvh.org/

STATE	COALITION	ADDRESS	TELEPHONE	FAX	EMAIL	WEBSITE
UTAH	Utah Domestic Violence Advisory Council	120 North 200 West Salt Lake City UT 84103	801-538-4100	801-538-3993	n/a	http://www.udvc .org/
VERMONT	Vermont Network Against Domestic Violence and Sexual Assault	P.O. Box 405 Montpelier, VT 05601	802-223-1302	802-223-6943	vtnetwork@vtne twork.org	http://www.vtnet work.org/
VIRGINIA	Virginia Sexual and Domestic Violence Action Alliance	508 Dale Avenue Charlottesville, VA 22903	434-979-9002	434-979-9003	info@vsdvallian ce.org	http://www.vsdv alliance.org/
WASHINGTON	Washington State Coalition Against Domestic Violence	101 N. Capitol Way Suite 103 Olympia, WA 98501	360-586-1022	360-586-1024	wscadv@wscadv .org	http://www.wsca dv.org/
WEST VIRGINIA	West Virginia Coalition Against Domestic Violence	4710 Chimney Drive Suite A Charleston, WV 25302	304-965-3552	304-965-3572	n/a	http://www.wvca dv.org/

STATE	COALITION	ADDRESS	TELEPHONE	FAX	EMAIL	WEBSITE
WISCONSIN	Wisconsin Domestic Violence Center	307 S. Paterson Street #1 Madison, WI 53703	608-255-0539	608-255-3560	wcadv@wcadv.org	http://www.wcadv.org/
WYOMING	Wyoming Coalition Against Domestic Violence and Sexual Assault	409 South 4th Street P.O. Box 236 Laramie, WY 82073	307-755-5481	307-755-5482	n/a	http://www.wyomingdvsa.org/

SOURCE:, U.S. Department of Justice

APPENDIX 15:
DIRECTORY OF TRIBAL DOMESTIC
VIOLENCE COALITIONS

COALITION	ADDRESS	TELEPHONE	FAX
Alaska Native Women's Coalition	Post Office Box 86 Allakaket AK 99720	907-968-2476	907-968-2233
American Indians Against Abuse	Post Office Box 1617 Hayward, WI 54843	715-634-9980	715-634-9982
Arizona Native American Coalition Against Family Violence	Route 2 Box 730B Laveen, AZ 85339	520-562-3904	520-562-3927
Coalition to Stop Violence Against Native Women	2401 12th Street NW Suite 201N Albuquerque, NM 87104	505-243-9199	505-243-9966
Community Resource Alliance	928 8th Street Southeast Detroit Lakes, MN 56501	218-844-5762	218-844-5763
Great Basin Native Women's Coalition Against Domestic Violence	Post Office Box 245 Owyhee, NV 89832	775-757-2013	775-757-202

COALITION	ADDRESS	TELEPHONE	FAX
Indian Country Coalition Against Domestic Violence and Sexual Assault	4000 North Mississippi Avenue Portland, OR 97227	503-288-8177	503-288-1260
Kene Me-wu Family Healing Center, Inc	Post Office Box 605 Sonora, CA 95370	209-984-8602	n/a
Minnesota Indian Women's Sexual Assault Coalition	1619 Dayton Avenue Suite 303 St. Paul, MN 55104	651-646-4800	651-646-4798
Niwhongwh xw E:na:wh Stop the Violence Coalition	Post Office Box 309 Hoopa, CA 95546	530-625-1662	530-625-1677
Oklahoma Native American Domestic Violence Coalition	3701 Southeast 15th Street Del City, OK 73115	405-619-9707	405-619-9715
Sicangu Coalition Against Sexual Violence	Post Office Box 227 Mission, SD 57555	605-856-2317	605-856-2994
Southwest Indigenous Women's Coalition	Post Office Box 1279 Chinle, AZ 86503	928-674-8314	928-674-8218
Strong Hearted Women's Coalition	Post Office Box 1279 Chinle, AZ 86503	760-742-3579	760-855-1466
We, Asdzani Coalition	Post Office Box 547 Crownpoint, NM 87313	505-786-5622	505-786-5285
Yupik Women's Coalition	Post Office Box 207 Emmonak, AK 99581	907-949-1443	907-949-1718

SOURCE: U.S. Department of Justice

APPENDIX 16:
TABLE OF U.S. FORCIBLE RAPE
STATISTICS BY VOLUME AND RATE
(1990-2005)

YEAR	VOLUME	RATE PER 100,000 PERSONS
1990	102,555	41.1
1991	106,593	42.3
1992	109,062	42.8
1993	106,014	41.1
1994	102,216	39.3
1995	97,470	37.1
1996	96,252	36.3
1997	96,153	35.9
1998	93,144	34.5
1999	89,411	32.8
2000	90,178	32.0
2001	90,863	31.8
2002	95,235	33.1
2003	93,883	32.3
2004	95,089	32.4
2005	93,934	31.7

SOURCE: Federal Bureau of Investigation

APPENDIX 17:
DIRECTORY OF STATE SEXUAL ASSAULT COALITIONS

STATE	COALITION	ADDRESS	TELEPHONE	FAX	EMAIL	WEBSITE
ALABAMA	Alabama Coalition Against Rape	207 Montgomery Street Montgomery, AL 36104	334-264-0123	334-264-0123	acar@acar.org	http://www.acar.org/
ALASKA	Alaska Network on Domestic Violence and Sexual Assault	130 Seward Street Room 209 Juneau, AK 99801	907-586-3650	907-463-4493	n/a	http://www.andvsa.org/
ARIZONA	Arizona Sexual Assault Network	333 West Indian School Road. Phoenix, AZ 85013	602-277-0119	602-266-1958	info@azsan.org	http://www.azsan.org/

STATE	COALITION	ADDRESS	TELEPHONE	FAX	EMAIL	WEBSITE
ARKANSAS	Arkansas Coalition Against Sexual Assault	215 North East Avenue Fayetteville, AR 72701	479-527-0900	479-527-0902	n/a	http://www.acasa.ws/
CALIFORNIA	California Coalition Against Sexual Assault	1215 K Street Suite 1100 Sacramento, CA 95814	916-446-2520	916-446-8166	info@calcasa.org	http://www.calcasa.org/
COLORADO	Colorado Coalition Against Sexual Assault	Post Office Boxes 300398 Denver, CO 80203	303-861-7033	303-832-7067	info@ccasa.org	http://www.ccasa.org/
CONNECTICUT	Connecticut Sexual Assault Crisis Services, Inc.	96 Pitkin Street East Hartford, CT 06108	860-282-9881	860-291-9335	info@connsacs.org	http://www.connsacs.org/
DELAWARE	Contact Delaware, Inc.	Post Office Box 9525 Wilmington, DE 19809	302-761-9800	302-761-4280	n/a	http://www.contactdelaware.org/
DISTRICT OF COLUMBIA	District of Columbia Rape Crisis Center	Post Office Box 34125 Washington, DC 20043	202-232-0789	202-387-3812	drcc@drcc.org	http://www.drcc.org/

STATE	COALITION	ADDRESS	TELEPHONE	FAX	EMAIL	WEBSITE
FLORIDA	Florida Council Against Sexual Violence	1311 North Paul Russell Road Suite A204 Tallahassee, FL 32301	850-297-2000	850-297-2002	information@fcasv.org	http://www.fcasv.org/
GEORGIA	Georgia Network to End Sexual Assault	131 Ponce de Leon Avenue Suite 122 Atlanta, GA 30308	404-815-5261	404-815-5265	gnesa@mindspring.com	http://www.gnesa.org/
HAWAII	Hawaii Coalition for the Prevention of Sexual Assault	Post Office Box 10596 Honolulu, HI 96816	808-733-9038	808-733-9032	n/a	n/a
IDAHO	Idaho Coalition Against Sexual and Domestic Violence	815 Park Blvd. Suite 140 Boise, ID 83712	208-384-0419	208-331-0687	jmatsushita@idvsa.org	http://www.idvsa.org/
ILLINOIS	Illinois Coalition Against Sexual Assault	100 North 16th Street Springfield, IL 62703	217-753-4117	217-753-8229	sblack@icasa.org	http://www.icasa.org/
INDIANA	Indiana Coalition Against Sexual Assault	55 Monument Circle Suite 1224 Indianapolis, IN 46204	317-423-0233	317-423-0237	incasa@incasa.org	http://www.incasa.org/

STATE	COALITION	ADDRESS	TELEPHONE	FAX	EMAIL	WEBSITE
IOWA	Iowa Coalition Against Sexual Assault	515 28th Street Suite 107 Des Moines, IA 50312	515-244-7424	515-244-7417	invo@iowacasa.org	http://www.iowacasa.org/
KANSAS	Kansas Coalition Against Sexual and Domestic Violence	634 SW Harrison Street Topeka, KS 66603	785-232-9784	785-266-1874	coalition@kcsdv.org	http://www.kcsdv.org/
KENTUCKY	Kentucky Association of Sexual Assault Programs	P.O. Box 4028 Frankfort, KY 40604	502-226-2704	502-226-2725	n/a	http://www.kasap.org/
LOUISIANA	Louisiana Foundation Against Sexual Assault	1250 SW Railroad Avenue Suite 170 Hammond, LA 70403	985-345-5995	985-345-5592	resource@lafasa.org	http://www.lafasa.org/
MAINE	Maine Coalition Against Sexual Assault	83 Western Avenue Suite 2 Augusta, ME 04330	207-626-0034	207-626-5503	info@mecasa.org	http://www.mecasa.org/

STATE	COALITION	ADDRESS	TELEPHONE	FAX	EMAIL	WEBSITE
MARYLAND	Maryland Coalition Against Sexual Assault	1517 Governor Ritchie Highway Suite 207 Arnold, MD 21012	410-974-4507	410-757-4770	info@mcasa.org	http://www.mca sa.org/
MASSACHUSETTS	Massachusetts Coalition Against Sexual Assault and Domestic Violence	14 Beacon Street Suite 507 Boston, MA 02108	617-248-0922	617-248-0902	info@janedoe.or g	http://www.jane doe.org
MICHIGAN	Michigan Coalition Against Domestic and Sexual Violence	3893 Okemos Road Suite B2 Okemos, MI 48864	517-347-7000	517-347-1377	general@mcads v.org	http://www.mca dsv.org/
MINNESOTA	Minnesota Coalition Against Sexual Assault	161 St. Anthony Avenue Suite 1001 St. Paul, MN 55103	651-209-9993	651-209-0899	n/a	http://www.mnc asa.org/
MISSISSIPPI	Mississippi Coalition Against Sexual Assault	P.O. Box 4172 Jackson, MS 39296	601-948-0555	601-948-0525	clong@mscasa. org	http://www.msc asa.org/

STATE	COALITION	ADDRESS	TELEPHONE	FAX	EMAIL	WEBSITE
MISSOURI	Missouri Coalition Against Sexual Assault	1000-D Northeast Drive Post Office Box 104866 Jefferson City, MO 65110	573-636-8776	573-636-6613	n/a	http://www.moc asa.org/
MONTANA	Montana Coalition Against Domestic and Sexual Violence	P.O. Box 818 Helena, MT 59624	406-443-7794	406-443-7818	mcadsv@mt.net	http://www.mca dsv.com/
NEBRASKA	Nebraska Domestic Violence and Sexual Assault Coalition	825 M Street Suite 404 Lincoln, NE 68508	402-476-6256	402-476-6806	help@ndvsac.or g	http://www.ndvs ac.org/
NEVADA	Nevada Coalition Against Sexual Violence	Post Office Box 530103 Henderson, NV 89053	702-940-2033	702-940-2032	staff@ncasv.org	http://www.ncas v.org/
NEW HAMPSHIRE	New Hampshire Coalition Against Domestic and Sexual Violence	P.O. Box 353 Concord, NH 03302	603-224-8893	603-228-6096	n/a	http://www.nhca dsv.org/

STATE	COALITION	ADDRESS	TELEPHONE	FAX	EMAIL	WEBSITE
NEW JERSEY	New Jersey Coalition Against Sexual Assault	2333 Whitehorse Mercerville Road Suite B Trenton, NJ 08619	609-631-4450	609-631-4453	n/a	http://www.njcasa.org/
NEW MEXICO	New Mexico Coalition of Sexual Assault Programs	3909 Juan Tabo Northeast Suite 6 Albuquerque, NM 87111	505-883-8020	505-883-7530	nmcsaas@swcp.com	http://www.swcp.com/mncsaas/index.html/
NEW YORK	New York State Coalition Against Sexual Assault	63 Colvin Avenue Albany, NY 12206	518-482-4222	518-482-4248	info@nyscasa.org	http://www.nyscasa.org/
NORTH CAROLINA	North Carolina Coalition Against Sexual Assault	183 Wind Chime Court Suite 100 Raleigh, NC 27615	919-870-8881	919-870-8828	n/a	http://www.nccasa.org/
NORTH DAKOTA	North Dakota Coalition Against Sexual Assault	418 East Rosser Avenue Suite 320 Bismarck, ND 58501	701-255-6240	701-255-1904	n/a	http://www.ndcaws.org/

STATE	COALITION	ADDRESS	TELEPHONE	FAX	EMAIL	WEBSITE
OHIO	Ohio Coalition on Sexual Assault	933 High Street Suite 120-B Worthington, OH 43085	614-781-1902	614-781-1922	ohiocoalition@aol.com	http://www.ocosa.org/
OKLAHOMA	Oklahoma Coalition Against Domestic Violence and Sexual Assault	3815 N. Santa Fe Avenue Suite 124 Oklahoma City, OK 73118	405-524-0700	405-524-0711	n/a	http://www.ocadvsa.org/
OREGON	Oregon Coalition Against Domestic and Sexual Violence	380 Southeast Spokane Street Suite 100 Portland, OR 97202	503-230-1951	503-230-1973	n/a	http://www.ocadsv.com/
PENNSYLVANIA	Pennsylvania Coalition Against Rape	125 North Enola Drive Enola, PA 17025	717-718-9740	717-718-9781	stop@pcar.org	http://www.pcar.org/
RHODE ISLAND	Day One: The Sexual Assault and Trauma Resource Center	100 Medway Street Providence, RI 02906	401-421-4100	401-454-5565	invo@dayoneri.org	http://www.dayoneri.org/

STATE	COALITION	ADDRESS	TELEPHONE	FAX	EMAIL	WEBSITE
SOUTH CAROLINA	South Carolina Coalition Against Domestic Violence & Sexual Assault	P.O. Box 7776 Columbia, SC 29202	803-256-2900	803-256-1030	n/a	http://www.scca dvasa.org/
SOUTH DAKOTA	South Dakota Coalition Against Domestic Violence and Sexual Assault	P.O. Box 141 Pierre, SD 57501	605-945-0869	605-945-0870	chris@sdcadvsa .org	http://www.sout hdakotacoalitio n.org/
TENNESSEE	Tennessee Coalition Against Domestic and Sexual Violence	P.O. Box 120972 Nashville, TN 37212	615-386-9406	615-383-2967	tcadsv@tcadsv. org	http://www.tcad sv.org/
TEXAS	Texas Association Against Sexual Assault	6200 La Calma Drive Suite 110 Austin, TX 78752	512-474-7190	512-474-6490	n/a	http://www.taas a.org/
UTAH	Utah Coalition Against Sexual Assault	284 West 400 North Salt Lake City, UT 84103	801-746-0404	801-746-2929	info@ucasa.org	http://www.ucas a.org/

STATE	COALITION	ADDRESS	TELEPHONE	FAX	EMAIL	WEBSITE
VERMONT	Vermont Network Against Domestic Violence and Sexual Assault	P.O. Box 405 Montpelier, VT 05601	802-223-1302	802-223-6943	vtnetwork@vtnetwork.org	http://www.vtnetwork.org/
VIRGINIA	Virginia Sexual and Domestic Violence Action Alliance	508 Dale Avenue Charlottesville, VA 22903	434-979-9002	434-979-9003	info@vsdvalliance.org	http://www.vsdvalliance.org/
WASHINGTON	Washington Coalition of Sexual Assault Programs	2415 Pacific Avenue Southeast Olympia, WA 98501	360-754-7583	360-786-8707	wcsap@wcsap.org	http://www.wcsap.org/
WEST VIRGINIA	West Virginia Foundation for Rape Information and Services	112 Braddock Street Fairmont, WV 26554	304-366-9500	304-366-9501	fris@labs.net	http://www.fris.org/
WISCONSIN	Wisconsin Coalition Against Sexual Assault	600 Williamson Street Suite N-2 Madison, WI 53703	608-257-1516	608-257-2150	wcasa@wcasa.org	http://www.wcasa.org/

STATE	COALITION	ADDRESS	TELEPHONE	FAX	EMAIL	WEBSITE
WYOMING	Wyoming Coalition Against Domestic Violence and Sexual Assault	409 South 4th Street P.O. Box 236 Laramie, WY 82073	307-755-5481	307-755-5482	n/a	http://www.wyomingdvsa.org/

SOURCE: U.S. Department of Justice

APPENDIX 18:
SELECTED PROVISIONS OF THE SEX OFFENDER REGISTRATION AND NOTIFICATION ACT [PUBLIC LAW 109-248]

SEC. 101. SHORT TITLE.

This title may be cited as the "Sex Offender Registration and Notification Act".

SEC. 112. REGISTRY REQUIREMENTS FOR JURISDICTIONS.

(a) Jurisdiction To Maintain a Registry.—Each jurisdiction shall maintain a jurisdiction-wide sex offender registry conforming to the requirements of this title.

(b) Guidelines and Regulations.—The Attorney General shall issue guidelines and regulations to interpret and implement this title.

SEC. 113. REGISTRY REQUIREMENTS FOR SEX OFFENDERS.

(a) In General.—A sex offender shall register, and keep the registration current, in each jurisdiction where the offender resides, where the offender is an employee, and where the offender is a student. For initial registration purposes only, a sex offender shall also register in the jurisdiction in which convicted if such jurisdiction is different from the jurisdiction of residence.

(b) Initial Registration.—The sex offender shall initially register—

(1) before completing a sentence of imprisonment with respect to the offense giving rise to the registration requirement; or

(2) not later than 3 business days after being sentenced for that offense, if the sex offender is not sentenced to a term of imprisonment.

(c) Keeping the Registration Current.—A sex offender shall, not later than 3 business days after each change of name, residence, employment, or student status, appear in person in at least 1 jurisdiction involved pursuant to subsection (a) and inform that jurisdiction of all changes in the information required for that offender in the sex offender registry. That jurisdiction shall immediately provide that information to all other jurisdictions in which the offender is required to register.

(d) Initial Registration of Sex Offenders Unable To Comply With Subsection (b).—The Attorney General shall have the authority to specify the applicability of the requirements of this title to sex offenders convicted before the enactment of this Act or its implementation in a particular jurisdiction, and to prescribe rules for the registration of any such sex offenders and for other categories of sex offenders who are unable to comply with subsection (b).

(e) State Penalty for Failure To Comply.—Each jurisdiction, other than a Federally recognized Indian tribe, shall provide a criminal penalty that includes a maximum term of imprisonment that is greater than 1 year for the failure of a sex offender to comply with the requirements of this title.

SEC. 114. INFORMATION REQUIRED IN REGISTRATION.

(a) Provided by the Offender.—The sex offender shall provide the following information to the appropriate official for inclusion in the sex offender registry:

(1) The name of the sex offender (including any alias used by the individual).

(2) The Social Security number of the sex offender.

(3) The address of each residence at which the sex offender resides or will reside.

(4) The name and address of any place where the sex offender is an employee or will be an employee.

(5) The name and address of any place where the sex offender is a student or will be a student.

(6) The license plate number and a description of any vehicle owned or operated by the sex offender.

(7) Any other information required by the Attorney General.

(b) Provided by the Jurisdiction.—The jurisdiction in which the sex offender registers shall ensure that the following information is included in the registry for that sex offender:

(1) A physical description of the sex offender.

(2) The text of the provision of law defining the criminal offense for which the sex offender is registered.

(3) The criminal history of the sex offender, including the date of all arrests and convictions; the status of parole, probation, or supervised release; registration status; and the existence of any outstanding arrest warrants for the sex offender.

(4) A current photograph of the sex offender.

(5) A set of fingerprints and palm prints of the sex offender.

(6) A DNA sample of the sex offender.

(7) A photocopy of a valid driver's license or identification card issued to the sex offender by a jurisdiction.

(8) Any other information required by the Attorney General.

SEC. 115. DURATION OF REGISTRATION REQUIREMENT.

(a) Full Registration Period.—A sex offender shall keep the registration current for the full registration period (excluding any time the sex offender is in custody or civilly committed) unless the offender is allowed a reduction under subsection (b). The full registration period is—

(1) 15 years, if the offender is a tier I sex offender;

(2) 25 years, if the offender is a tier II sex offender; and

(3) the life of the offender, if the offender is a tier III sex offender.

(b) Reduced Period for Clean Record.—

(1) Clean record.—The full registration period shall be reduced as described in paragraph (3) for a sex offender who maintains a clean record for the period described in paragraph (2) by—

(A) not being convicted of any offense for which imprisonment for more than 1 year may be imposed;

(B) not being convicted of any sex offense;

(C) successfully completing any periods of supervised release, probation, and parole; and

(D) successfully completing of an appropriate sex offender treatment program certified by a jurisdiction or by the Attorney General.

(2) Period.—In the case of—

(A) a tier I sex offender, the period during which the clean record shall be maintained is 10 years; and

(B) a tier III sex offender adjudicated delinquent for the offense which required registration in a sex registry under this title, the period during which the clean record shall be maintained is 25 years.

(3) Reduction.— In the case of—

(A) a tier I sex offender, the reduction is 5 years;

(B) a tier III sex offender adjudicated delinquent, the reduction is from life to that period for which the clean record under paragraph (2) is maintained.

SEC. 116. PERIODIC IN PERSON VERIFICATION.

A sex offender shall appear in person, allow the jurisdiction to take a current photograph, and verify the information in each registry in which that offender is required to be registered not less frequently than—

(1) each year, if the offender is a tier I sex offender;

(2) every 6 months, if the offender is a tier II sex offender; and

(3) every 3 months, if the offender is a tier III sex offender.

SEC. 117. DUTY TO NOTIFY SEX OFFENDERS OF REGISTRATION REQUIREMENTS AND TO REGISTER.

(a) In General.— An appropriate official shall, shortly before release the sex offender from custody, or, if the sex offender is not in custody, immediately after the sentencing of the sex offender, for the offense giving rise to the duty to register—

(1) inform the sex offender of the duties of a sex offender under this title and explain those duties;

(2) require the sex offender to read and sign a form stating that the duty to register has been explained and that the sex offender understands the registration requirement; and

(3) ensure that the sex offender is registered.

(b) Notification of Sex Offenders Who Cannot Comply With Subsection (a).—The Attorney General shall prescribe rules for the notification of sex offenders who cannot be registered in accordance with subsection (a).

SEC. 118. PUBLIC ACCESS TO SEX OFFENDER INFORMATION THROUGH THE INTERNET.

(a) In General.—Except as provided in this section, each jurisdiction shall make available on the Internet, in a manner that is readily accessible to all jurisdictions and to the public, all information about each sex offender in the registry. The jurisdiction shall maintain the Internet site in a manner that will permit the public to obtain relevant information for each sex offender by a single query for any given zip code or geographic radius set by the user. The jurisdiction shall also include in the design of its Internet site all field search capabilities needed for full participation in the Dru Sjodin National Sex Offender Public Website and shall participate in that website as provided by the Attorney General.

(b) Mandatory Exemptions.—A jurisdiction shall exempt from disclosure—

(1) the identity of any victim of a sex offense;

(2) the Social Security number of the sex offender;

(3) any reference to arrests of the sex offender that did not result in conviction; and

(4) any other information exempted from disclosure by the Attorney General.

(c) Optional Exemptions.—A jurisdiction may exempt from disclosure—

(1) any information about a tier I sex offender convicted of an offense other than a specified offense against a minor;

(2) the name of an employer of the sex offender;

(3) the name of an educational institution where the sex offender is a student; and

(4) any other information exempted from disclosure by the Attorney General.

(d) Links.—The site shall include, to the extent practicable, links to sex offender safety and education resources.

(e) Correction of Errors.—The site shall include instructions on how to seek correction of information that an individual contends is erroneous.

(f) Warning.—The site shall include a warning that information on the site should not be used to unlawfully injure, harass, or commit a crime against any individual named in the registry or residing or working at any reported address. The warning shall note that any such action could result in civil or criminal penalties.

SEC. 119. NATIONAL SEX OFFENDER REGISTRY.

(a) Internet.—The Attorney General shall maintain a national database at the Federal Bureau of Investigation for each sex offender and any other person required to register in a jurisdiction's sex offender registry. The database shall be known as the National Sex Offender Registry.

(b) Electronic Forwarding.—The Attorney General shall ensure (through the National Sex Offender Registry or otherwise) that updated information about a sex offender is immediately transmitted by electronic forwarding to all relevant jurisdictions.

SEC. 120. DRU SJODIN NATIONAL SEX OFFENDER PUBLIC WEBSITE.

(a) Establishment.—There is established the Dru Sjodin National Sex Offender Public Website (hereinafter in this section referred to as the "Website"), which the Attorney General shall maintain.

(b) Information To Be Provided.—The Website shall include relevant information for each sex offender and other person listed on a jurisdiction's Internet site. The Website shall allow the public to obtain relevant information for each sex offender by a single query for any given zip code or geographical radius set by the user in a form and with such limitations as may be established by the Attorney General and shall have such other field search capabilities as the Attorney General may provide.

SEC. 121. MEGAN NICOLE KANKA AND ALEXANDRA NICOLE ZAPP COMMUNITY NOTIFICATION PROGRAM.

(a) Establishment of Program.—There is established the Megan Nicole Kanka and Alexandra Nicole Zapp Community Notification Program (hereinafter in this section referred to as the "Program").

(b) Program Notification.—Except as provided in subsection (c), immediately after a sex offender registers or updates a registration, an appropriate official in the jurisdiction shall provide the information in the registry (other than information exempted from disclosure by the Attorney General) about that offender to the following:

(1) The Attorney General, who shall include that information in the National Sex Offender Registry or other appropriate databases.

(2) Appropriate law enforcement agencies (including probation agencies, if appropriate), and each school and public housing agency, in each area in which the individual resides, is an employee or is a student.

(3) Each jurisdiction where the sex offender resides, is an employee, or is a student, and each jurisdiction from or to which a change of residence, employment, or student status occurs.

(4) Any agency responsible for conducting employment-related background checks under section 3 of the National Child Protection Act of 1993 (42 U.S.C. 5119a).

(5) Social service entities responsible for protecting minors in the child welfare system.

(6) Volunteer organizations in which contact with minors or other vulnerable individuals might occur.

(7) Any organization, company, or individual who requests such notification pursuant to procedures established by the jurisdiction.

(c) Frequency.—Notwithstanding subsection (b), an organization or individual described in subsection (b)(6) or (b)(7) may opt to receive the notification described in that subsection no less frequently than once every five business days.

SEC. 122. ACTIONS TO BE TAKEN WHEN SEX OFFENDER FAILS TO COMPLY.

An appropriate official shall notify the Attorney General and appropriate law enforcement agencies of any failure by a sex offender to comply with the requirements of a registry and revise the jurisdiction's registry to reflect the nature of that failure. The appropriate official, the Attorney General, and each such law enforcement agency shall take any appropriate action to ensure compliance.

SEC. 128. REGISTRATION OF SEX OFFENDERS ENTERING THE UNITED STATES.

The Attorney General, in consultation with the Secretary of State and the Secretary of Homeland Security, shall establish and maintain a system for informing the relevant jurisdictions about persons entering the United States who are required to register under this title. The Secretary of State and the Secretary of Homeland Security shall provide such information and carry out such functions as the Attorney General may direct in the operation of the system.

SEC. 146. OFFICE OF SEX OFFENDER SENTENCING, MONITORING, APPREHENDING, REGISTERING, AND TRACKING.

(a) Establishment.—There is established within the Department of Justice, under the general authority of the Attorney General, an Office of Sex Offender Sentencing, Monitoring, Apprehending, Registering, and Tracking (hereinafter in this section referred to as the "SMART Office").

(b) Director.—The SMART Office shall be headed by a Director who shall be appointed by the President. The Director shall report to the Attorney General through the Assistant Attorney General for the Office of Justice Programs and shall have final authority for all grants, cooperative agreements, and contracts awarded by the SMART Office. The Director shall not engage in any employment other than that of serving as the Director, nor shall the Director hold any office in, or act in any capacity for, any organization, agency, or institution with which the Office makes any contract or other arrangement.

(c) Duties and Functions.—The SMART Office is authorized to—

(1) administer the standards for the sex offender registration and notification program set forth in this Act;

(2) administer grant programs relating to sex offender registration and notification authorized by this Act and other grant programs authorized by this Act as directed by the Attorney General;

(3) cooperate with and provide technical assistance to States, units of local government, tribal governments, and other public and private entities involved in activities related to sex offender registration or notification or to other measures for the protection of children or other members of the public from sexual abuse or exploitation; and

(4) perform such other functions as the Attorney General may delegate.

APPENDIX 19:

TABLE OF STATE LAWS GOVERNING PROTECTION ORDERS FOR TEEN DATING VIOLENCE

STATE	DATING RELATIONSHIPS COVERED UNDER STATUTE	TEENS CAN FILE WITHOUT ADULT	NAME OF PROTECTION ORDER	PROTECTION ORDER ALTERNATIVES
ALABAMA	no	no	protection from abuse order	temporary restraining order
ALASKA	yes	no	protective order	n/a
ARIZONA	no	no	order of protection	injunction against harassment
ARKANSAS	no	no	order of protection	only criminal charges
CALIFORNIA	yes	yes	domestic violence restraining order	n/a
COLORADO	no	no	restraining order	n/a

STATE	DATING RELATIONSHIPS COVERED UNDER STATUTE	TEENS CAN FILE WITHOUT ADULT	NAME OF PROTECTION ORDER	PROTECTION ORDER ALTERNATIVES
CONNECTICUT	yes	yes	restraining order	n/a
DELAWARE	no	no	order of protection from abuse	n/a
DISTRICT OF COLUMBIA	yes	yes	civil protection order	n/a
FLORIDA	yes	no	injunction for protection from domestic violence	injunction against repeat violence
GEORGIA	no	no	family violence protection order	Georgia Stalking Act
HAWAII	yes	no	restraining order	n/a
IDAHO	yes	yes	protection order	n//a
ILLINOIS	yes	yes	order of protection	n/a
INDIANA	yes	no	order for protection	n/a
IOWA	yes	no	protective order	n/a
KANSAS	yes	no	domestic violence protection order	n/a
KENTUCKY	no	no	domestic violence order	n/a
LOUISIANA	yes	yes	restraining order	peace bond
MAINE	no	no	protection from abuse order	protection from harassment order
MARYLAND	no	no	domestic violence protection order	peace order

STATE	DATING RELATIONSHIPS COVERED UNDER STATUTE	TEENS CAN FILE WITHOUT ADULT	NAME OF PROTECTION ORDER	PROTECTION ORDER ALTERNATIVES
MASSACHUSETTS	yes	yes	abuse prevention order	n/a
MICHIGAN	yes	no	personal protection order	n/a
MINNESOTA	yes	no	order for protection	order against harassment
MISSISSIPPI	yes	no	restraining order	n/a
MISSOURI	Yes	no	order of protection	n/a
MONTANA	yes	no	order of protection	n/a
NEBRASKA	no	no	domestic violence protection order	harassment order
NEVADA	yes	no	order of protection	n/a
NEW HAMPSHIRE	yes	yes	protective order	n/a
NEW JERSEY	yes	yes	restraining order	n/a
NEW MEXICO	yes	no	protection order	n/a
NEW YORK	no	yes	order of protection	n/a
NORTH CAROLINA	yes	no	domestic violence protection order	n//a
NORTH DAKOTA	yes	no	domestic violence protection order	n/a
OHIO	no	no	protection order	n/a
OKLAHOMA	yes	yes	protection order	n/a

STATE	DATING RELATIONSHIPS COVERED UNDER STATUTE	TEENS CAN FILE WITHOUT ADULT	NAME OF PROTECTION ORDER	PROTECTION ORDER ALTERNATIVES
OREGON	no	no	restraining order	n/a
PENNSYLVANIA	no	yes	protection from abuse order	n/a
RHODE ISLAND	yes	no	restraining order	n/a
SOUTH CAROLINA	no	no	order of protection	n/a
SOUTH DAKOTA	no	yes	protection order	protection under stalking statute
TENNESSEE	yes	no	protection order	civil restraining order
TEXAS	yes	yes	protective order	n/a
UTAH	no	yes	protection order	civil stalking injunction
VERMONT	yes	yes	relief from abuse order	n/a
VIRGINIA	no	no	protective order	protection under stalking statute
WASHINGTON	yes	yes	domestic violence order of protection	restraining order, civil anti-harassment order
WEST VIRGINIA	yes	no	protective order	n/a
WISCONSIN	yes	yes	domestic abuse restraining order	n/a
WYOMING	yes	yes	order of protection	n/a

SOURCE: The National Center for Victims of Crime

The Law of Violence Against Women

APPENDIX 20:
SELECTED PROVISIONS OF THE
TRAFFICKING VICTIMS PROTECTION ACT
OF 2000

SEC. 101. SHORT TITLE.

This division may be cited as the "Trafficking Victims Protection Act of 2000".

SEC. 102. PURPOSES AND FINDINGS.

(a) PURPOSES.—The purposes of this division are to combat trafficking in persons, a contemporary manifestation of slavery whose victims are predominantly women and children, to ensure just and effective punishment of traffickers, and to protect their victims.

SEC. 105. INTERAGENCY TASK FORCE TO MONITOR AND COMBAT TRAFFICKING.

(a) ESTABLISHMENT.—The President shall establish an Inter-agency Task Force to Monitor and Combat Trafficking.

(b) APPOINTMENT.—The President shall appoint the members of the Task Force, which shall include the Secretary of State, the Administrator of the United States Agency for International Development, the Attorney General, the Secretary of Labor, the Secretary of Health and Human Services, the Director of Central Intelligence, and such other officials as may be designated by the President.

(c) CHAIRMAN.—The Task Force shall be chaired by the Secretary of State.

(d) ACTIVITIES OF THE TASK FORCE.—The Task Force shall carry out the following activities:

(1) Coordinate the implementation of this division.

2) Measure and evaluate progress of the United States and other countries in the areas of trafficking prevention, protection, and assistance to victims of trafficking, and prosecution and enforcement against traffickers, including the role of public corruption in facilitating trafficking. The Task Force shall have primary responsibility for assisting the Secretary of State in the preparation of the reports described in section 110.

(3) Expand interagency procedures to collect and organize data, including significant research and resource information on domestic and international trafficking. Any data collection procedures established under this subsection shall respect the confidentiality of victims of trafficking.

(4) Engage in efforts to facilitate cooperation among countries of origin, transit, and destination. Such efforts shall aim to strengthen local and regional capacities to prevent trafficking, prosecute traffickers and assist trafficking victims, and shall include initiatives to enhance cooperative efforts between destination countries and countries of origin and assist in the appropriate reintegration of stateless victims of trafficking.

(5) Examine the role of the international "sex tourism" industry in the trafficking of persons and in the sexual exploitation of women and children around the world.

(6) Engage in consultation and advocacy with governmental and nongovernmental organizations, among other entities, to advance the purposes of this division.

(e) SUPPORT FOR THE TASK FORCE.—The Secretary of State is authorized to establish within the Department of State an Office to Monitor and Combat Trafficking, which shall provide assistance to the Task Force. Any such Office shall be headed by a Director. The Director shall have the primary responsibility for assisting the Secretary of State in carrying out the purposes of this division and may have additional responsibilities as determined by the Secretary. The Director shall consult with nongovernmental organizations and multilateral organizations, and with trafficking victims or other affected persons. The Director shall have the authority to take evidence in public hearings or by other means. The agencies represented on the Task Force are authorized to provide staff to the Office on a nonreimbursable basis.

SEC. 106. PREVENTION OF TRAFFICKING.

(a) ECONOMIC ALTERNATIVES TO PREVENT AND DETER TRAFFICKING.—

The President shall establish and carry out international initiatives to enhance economic opportunity for potential victims of trafficking as a method to deter trafficking. Such initiatives may include—

(1) microcredit lending programs, training in business development, skills training, and job counseling;

(2) programs to promote women's participation in economic decisionmaking;

(3) programs to keep children, especially girls, in elementary and secondary schools, and to educate persons who have been victims of trafficking;

(4) development of educational curricula regarding the dangers of trafficking; and

(5) grants to nongovernmental organizations to accelerate and advance the political, economic, social, and educational roles and capacities of women in their countries.

(b) PUBLIC AWARENESS AND INFORMATION.—The President, acting through the Secretary of Labor, the Secretary of Health and Human Services, the Attorney General, and the Secretary of State, shall establish and carry out programs to increase public awareness, particularly among potential victims of trafficking, of the dangers of trafficking and the protections that are available for victims of trafficking.

(c) CONSULTATION REQUIREMENT.—The President shall consult with appropriate nongovernmental organizations with respect to the establishment and conduct of initiatives described in subsections (a) and (b).

SEC. 107. PROTECTION AND ASSISTANCE FOR VICTIMS OF TRAFFICKING.

(a) ASSISTANCE FOR VICTIMS IN OTHER COUNTRIES.—

(1) IN GENERAL.—The victims of trafficking, including stateless victims.

(b) VICTIMS IN THE UNITED STATES.—

(1) ASSISTANCE.—

(A) ELIGIBILITY FOR BENEFITS AND SERVICES.—Notwithstanding Title IV of the Personal Responsibility and Work Opportunity

Reconciliation Act of 1996, an alien who is a victim of a severe form of trafficking in persons shall be eligible for benefits and services under any Federal or State program or activity funded or administered by any official or agency described in subparagraph (B) to the same extent as an alien who is admitted to the United States as a refugee under section 207 of the Immigration and Nationality Act.

(B) REQUIREMENT TO EXPAND BENEFITS AND SERVICES.—

Subject to subparagraph (C) and, in the case of nonentitlement programs, to the availability of appropriations, the Secretary of Health and Human Services, the Secretary of Labor, the Board of Directors of the Legal Services Corporation, and the heads of other Federal agencies shall expand benefits and services to victims of severe forms of trafficking in persons in the United States, without regard to the immigration status of such victims.

(C) DEFINITION OF VICTIM OF A SEVERE FORM OF TRAFFICKING

IN PERSONS.—For the purposes of this paragraph, the term "victim of a severe form of trafficking in persons" means only a person—

(i) who has been subjected to an act or practice described in section 103(8) as in effect on the date of the enactment of this Act; and

(ii)(I) who has not attained 18 years of age; or

(II) who is the subject of a certification under subparagraph (E).

(D) ANNUAL REPORT.—Not later than December 31 of each year, the Secretary of Health and Human Services, in consultation with the Secretary of Labor, the Board of Directors of the Legal Services Corporation, and the heads of other appropriate Federal agencies shall submit a report, which includes information on the number of persons who received benefits or other services under this paragraph in connection with programs or activities funded or administered by such agencies or officials during the preceding fiscal year, to the Committee on Ways and Means, the Committee on International Relations, and the Committee on the Judiciary of the House of Representatives and the Committee on Finance, the Committee on Foreign Relations, and the Committee on the Judiciary of the Senate.

(E) CERTIFICATION.—

(i) IN GENERAL.—Subject to clause (ii), the certification referred to in subparagraph (C) is a certification by the Secretary of Health and Human Services, after consultation with the Attorney General, that the person referred to in subparagraph (C)(ii)(II)—

(I) is willing to assist in every reasonable way in the investigation and prosecution of severe forms of trafficking in persons; and

(II)(aa) has made a bona fide application for a visa under section 101(a)(15)(T) of the Immigration and Nationality Act, as added by subsection(e), that has not been denied; or

(bb) is a person whose continued presence in the United States the Attorney General is ensuring in order to effectuate prosecution of traffickers in persons.

(ii) PERIOD OF EFFECTIVENESS.—A certification referred to in subparagraph (C), with respect to a person described in clause (i)(II)(bb), shall be effective only for so long as the Attorney General determines that the continued presence of such person is necessary to effectuate prosecution of traffickers in persons.

(iii) INVESTIGATION AND PROSECUTION DEFINED.—

For the purpose of a certification under this subparagraph, the term "investigation and prosecution" includes—

(I) identification of a person or persons who have committed severe forms of trafficking in persons;

(II) location and apprehension of such persons; and

(III) testimony at proceedings against such persons.

(2) GRANTS.—

(A) IN GENERAL.—Subject to the availability of appropriations, the Attorney General may make grants to States, Indian tribes, units of local government, and nonprofit, nongovernmental victims' service organizations to develop, expand, or strengthen victim service programs for victims of trafficking.

(B) ALLOCATION OF GRANT FUNDS.—Of amounts made available for grants under this paragraph, there shall be set aside—

(i) three percent for research, evaluation, and statistics;

(ii) two percent for training and technical assistance; and

(iii) one percent for management and administration.

(C) LIMITATION ON FEDERAL SHARE.—The Federal share of a grant made under this paragraph may not exceed 75 percent of the total costs of the projects described in the application submitted.

(c) TRAFFICKING VICTIM REGULATIONS.—Not later than 180 days after the date of the enactment of this Act, the Attorney General and the Secretary of State shall promulgate regulations for law enforcement personnel, immigration officials, and Department of State officials to implement the following:

(1) PROTECTIONS WHILE IN CUSTODY.—Victims of severe forms of trafficking, while in the custody of the Federal Government and to the extent practicable, shall—

(A) not be detained in facilities inappropriate to their status as crime victims;

(B) receive necessary medical care and other assistance; and

(C) be provided protection if a victim's safety is at risk or if there is danger of additional harm by recapture of the victim by a trafficker, including—

(i) taking measures to protect trafficked persons and their family members from intimidation and threats of reprisals and reprisals from traffickers and their associates; and

(ii) ensuring that the names and identifying information of trafficked persons and their family members are not disclosed to the public.

(2) ACCESS TO INFORMATION.—Victims of severe forms of trafficking shall have access to information about their rights and translation services.

(3) AUTHORITY TO PERMIT CONTINUED PRESENCE IN THE UNITED STATES.—Federal law enforcement officials may permit an alien individual's continued presence in the United States, if after an assessment, it is determined that such individual is a victim of a severe form of trafficking and a potential witness to such trafficking, in order to effectuate prosecution of those responsible, and such officials in investigating and prosecuting traffickers shall protect the safety of trafficking victims, including taking measures to protect trafficked persons and their family members from intimidation, threats of reprisals, and reprisals from traffickers and their associates.

(4) TRAINING OF GOVERNMENT PERSONNEL.—Appropriate personnel of the Department of State and the Department of Justice shall be trained in identifying victims of severe forms of trafficking and providing for the protection of such victims.

(d) CONSTRUCTION.—Nothing in subsection (c) shall be construed as creating any private cause of action against the United States or its officers or employees.

(e) PROTECTION FROM REMOVAL FOR CERTAIN CRIME VICTIMS.—

(1) IN GENERAL.—Section 101(a)(15) of the Immigration and Nationality Act (8 U.S.C. 1101(a)(15)) is amended—

(A) by striking "or" at the end of subparagraph (R);

(B) by striking the period at the end of subparagraph (S) and inserting "; or"; and

(C) by adding at the end the following new subparagraph:

"(T)(i) subject to section 214(n), an alien who the Attorney General determines—

"(I) is or has been a victim of a severe form of trafficking in persons, as defined in section 103 of the Trafficking Victims Protection Act of 2000,

"(II) is physically present in the United States, American Samoa, or the Commonwealth of the Northern Mariana Islands, or at a port of entry thereto, on account of such trafficking,

"(III)(aa) has complied with any reasonable request for assistance in the investigation or prosecution of acts of trafficking, or

"(bb) has not attained 15 years of age, and

"(IV) the alien would suffer extreme hardship involving unusual and severe harm upon removal; and

"(ii) if the Attorney General considers it necessary to avoid extreme hardship—

"(I) in the case of an alien described in clause (i) who is under 21 years of age, the spouse, children, and parents of such alien; and

"(II) in the case of an alien described in clause (i) who is 21 years of age or older, the spouse and children of such alien, if accompanying, or following to join, the alien described in clause (i).".

(2) CONDITIONS OF NONIMMIGRANT STATUS.—Section 214 of the Immigration and Nationality Act (8 U.S.C. 1184) is amended—

(A) by redesignating the subsection (l) added by section 625(a) of the Illegal Immigration Reform and Immigrant Responsibility Act of 1996 (Public Law 104-208; 110 Stat. 3009-1820) as subsection (m); and

(B) by adding at the end the following:

"(n)(1) No alien shall be eligible for admission to the United States under section 101(a)(15)(T) if there is substantial reason to believe that the alien has committed an act of a severe form of trafficking in persons (as defined in section 103 of the Trafficking Victims Protection Act of 2000).

"(2) The total number of aliens who may be issued visas or otherwise provided nonimmigrant status during any fiscal year under section 101(a)(15)(T) may not exceed 5,000.

"(3) The numerical limitation of paragraph (2) shall only apply to principal aliens and not to the spouses, sons, daughters, or parents of such aliens.".

(3) WAIVER OF GROUNDS FOR INELIGIBILITY FOR ADMISSION.—

Section 212(d) of the Immigration and Nationality Act (8 U.S.C. 1182(d)) is amended by adding at the end the following:

"(13)(A) The Attorney General shall determine whether a ground for inadmissibility exists with respect to a nonimmigrant described in section 101(a)(15)(T).

"(B) In addition to any other waiver that may be available under this section, in the case of a nonimmigrant described in section 101(a)(15)(T), if the Attorney General considers it to be in the national interest to do so, the Attorney General, in the Attorney General's discretion, may waive the application of—

"(i) paragraphs (1) and (4) of subsection (a); and

"(ii) any other provision of such subsection (excluding paragraphs (3), (10)(C), and (10(E)) if the activities rendering the alien inadmissible under the provision were caused by, or were incident to, the victimization described in section 101(a)(15)(T)(i)(I).".

(4) DUTIES OF THE ATTORNEY GENERAL WITH RESPECT TO "T" VISA NONIMMIGRANTS.—Section 101 of the Immigration and Nationality Act (8 U.S.C. 1101) is amended by adding at the end the following new subsection:

"(i) With respect to each nonimmigrant alien described in sub-section (a)(15)(T)(i)—

"(1) the Attorney General and other Government officials, where appropriate, shall provide the alien with a referral to a nongovernmental organization that would advise the alien regarding the alien's options while in the United States and the resources available to the alien; and

"(2) the Attorney General shall, during the period the alien is in lawful temporary resident status under that subsection, grant the alien authorization to engage in employment in the United States and provide the alien with an 'employment authorized' endorsement or other appropriate work permit.".

(5) STATUTORY CONSTRUCTION.—Nothing in this section, or in the amendments made by this section, shall be construed as prohibiting the Attorney General from instituting removal proceedings under section 240 of the Immigration and Nationality Act (8 U.S.C. 1229a) against an alien admitted as a nonimmigrant under section 101(a)(15)(T)(i) of that Act, as added by subsection (e), for conduct committed after the alien's admission into the United States, or for conduct or a condition that was not disclosed to the Attorney General prior to the alien's admission as a nonimmigrant under such section 101(a)(15)(T)(i).

(f) ADJUSTMENT TO PERMANENT RESIDENT STATUS.—Section 245 of such Act (8 U.S.C 1255) is amended by adding at the end the following new subsection:

"(l)(1) If, in the opinion of the Attorney General, a non-immigrant admitted into the United States under section 101(a)(15)(T)(i)—

"(A) has been physically present in the United States for a continuous period of at least 3 years since the date of admission as a nonimmigrant under section 101(a)(15)(T)(i),

"(B) has, throughout such period, been a person of good moral character, and

"(C)(i) has, during such period, complied with any reasonable request for assistance in the investigation or prosecution of acts of trafficking, or

"(ii) the alien would suffer extreme hardship involving unusual and severe harm upon removal from the United States, the Attorney General may adjust the status of the alien (and any person admitted under that section as the spouse, parent, or child of the alien) to that of an alien lawfully admitted for permanent residence.

"(2) Paragraph (1) shall not apply to an alien admitted under section 101(a)(15)(T) who is inadmissible to the United States by reason of a ground that has not been waived under section 212, except that, if the Attorney General considers it to be in the national interest to do so, the Attorney General, in the Attorney General's discretion, may waive the application of—

"(A) paragraphs (1) and (4) of section 212(a); and

"(B) any other provision of such section (excluding paragraphs (3), (10)(C), and (10(E)), if the activities rendering the alien inadmissible under the provision were caused by, or were incident to, the victimization described in section 101(a)(15)(T)(i)(I).

"(2) An alien shall be considered to have failed to maintain continuous physical presence in the United States under paragraph (1)(A) if the alien has departed from the United States for any period in excess of 90 days or for any periods in the aggregate exceeding 180 days.

"(3)(A) The total number of aliens whose status may be adjusted under paragraph (1) during any fiscal year may not exceed 5,000.

"(B) The numerical limitation of subparagraph (A) shall only apply to principal aliens and not to the spouses, sons, daughters, or parents of such aliens.

"(4) Upon the approval of adjustment of status under paragraph (1), the Attorney General shall record the alien's lawful admission for permanent residence as of the date of such approval.".

(g) ANNUAL REPORTS.—On or before October 31 of each year, the Attorney General shall submit a report to the appropriate congressional committees setting forth, with respect to the preceding fiscal year, the number, if any, of otherwise eligible applicants who did not receive visas under section 101(a)(15)(T) of the Immigration and Nationality Act, as added by subsection (e), or who were unable to adjust their status under section 245(l) of such Act, solely on account of the unavailability of visas due to a limitation imposed by section 214(n)(1) or 245(l)(4)(A) of such Act.

SEC. 108. MINIMUM STANDARDS FOR THE ELIMINATION OF TRAFFICKING.

(a) MINIMUM STANDARDS.—For purposes of this division, the minimum standards for the elimination of trafficking applicable to the government of a country of origin, transit, or destination for a significant number of victims of severe forms of trafficking are the following:

(1) The government of the country should prohibit severe forms of trafficking in persons and punish acts of such trafficking.

(2) For the knowing commission of any act of sex trafficking involving force, fraud, coercion, or in which the victim of sex trafficking is a child incapable of giving meaningful consent, or of trafficking which includes rape or kidnapping or which causes a death, the government of the country should prescribe punishment commensurate with that for grave crimes, such as forcible sexual assault.

(3) For the knowing commission of any act of a severe form of trafficking in persons, the government of the country should prescribe punishment that is sufficiently stringent to deter and that adequately reflects the heinous nature of the offense.

(4) The government of the country should make serious and sustained efforts to eliminate severe forms of trafficking in persons.

(b) CRITERIA.—In determinations under subsection (a)(4), the following factors should be considered as indicia of serious and sustained efforts to eliminate severe forms of trafficking in persons:

(1) Whether the government of the country vigorously investigates and prosecutes acts of severe forms of trafficking in persons that take place wholly or partly within the territory of the country.

(2) Whether the government of the country protects victims of severe forms of trafficking in persons and encourages their assistance in the investigation and prosecution of such trafficking, including provisions for legal alternatives to their removal to countries in which they would face retribution or hardship, and ensures that victims are not inappropriately incarcerated, fined, or otherwise penalized solely for unlawful acts as a direct result of being trafficked.

(3) Whether the government of the country has adopted measures to prevent severe forms of trafficking in persons, such as measures to inform and educate the public, including potential victims, about the causes and consequences of severe forms of trafficking in persons.

(4) Whether the government of the country cooperates with other governments in the investigation and prosecution of severe forms of trafficking in persons.

(5) Whether the government of the country extradites persons charged with acts of severe forms of trafficking in persons on substantially the same terms and to substantially the same extent as persons charged with other serious crimes (or, to the extent such extradition would be inconsistent with the laws of such country or with international agreements to which the country is a party, whether the government is taking all appropriate measures to modify or replace such laws and treaties so as to permit such extradition).

(6) Whether the government of the country monitors immigration and emigration patterns for evidence of severe forms of trafficking in persons and whether law enforcement agencies of the country respond to any such evidence in a manner that is consistent with the vigorous investigation and prosecution of acts of such trafficking, as well as with the protection of human rights of victims and the internationally recognized human right to leave any country, including one's own, and to return to one's own country.

(7) Whether the government of the country vigorously investigates and prosecutes public officials who participate in or facilitate severe forms of trafficking in persons, and takes all appropriate measures against officials who condone such trafficking.

SEC. 111. ACTIONS AGAINST SIGNIFICANT TRAFFICKERS IN PERSONS.

(a) AUTHORITY TO SANCTION SIGNIFICANT TRAFFICKERS IN PERSONS.—

(1) IN GENERAL.—The President may exercise the authorities set forth in section 203 of the International Emergency Economic Powers Act (50 U.S.C. 1701) without regard to section 202 of that Act (50 U.S.C. 1701) in the case of any of the following persons:

(A) Any foreign person that plays a significant role in a severe form of trafficking in persons, directly or indirectly in the United States.

(B) Foreign persons that materially assist in, or provide financial or technological support for or to, or provide goods or services in support of, activities of a significant foreign trafficker in persons identified pursuant to subparagraph (A).

(C) Foreign persons that are owned, controlled, or directed by, or acting for or on behalf of, a significant foreign trafficker identified pursuant to subparagraph (A).

(2) PENALTIES.—The penalties set forth in section 206 of the International Emergency Economic Powers Act (50 U.S.C. 1705) apply to violations of any license, order, or regulation issued under this section.

SEC. 112. STRENGTHENING PROSECUTION AND PUNISHMENT OF TRAFFICKERS.

(a) TITLE 18 AMENDMENTS.—Chapter 77 of title 18, United States Code, is amended—

(1) in each of sections 1581(a), 1583, and 1584—

(A) by striking "10 years" and inserting "20 years"; and

(B) by adding at the end the following: "If death results from the violation of this section, or if the violation includes kidnapping or an attempt to kidnap, aggravated sexual abuse or the attempt to commit aggravated sexual abuse, or an attempt to kill, the defendant shall be fined under this title or imprisoned for any term of years or life, or both.";

(2) by inserting at the end the following:

"§1589. Forced labor

"Whoever knowingly provides or obtains the labor or services of a person—

"(1) by threats of serious harm to, or physical restraint against, that person or another person;

"(2) by means of any scheme, plan, or pattern intended to cause the person to believe that, if the person did not perform such labor or services, that person or another person would suffer serious harm or physical restraint; or

"(3) by means of the abuse or threatened abuse of law or the legal process, shall be fined under this title or imprisoned not more than 20 years, or both. If death results from the violation of this section, or if the violation includes kidnapping or an attempt to kidnap, aggravated sexual abuse or the attempt to commit aggravated sexual abuse, or an attempt to kill, the defendant shall be fined under this title or imprisoned for any term of years or life, or both.

"§1590. Trafficking with respect to peonage, slavery, involuntary servitude, or forced labor

"Whoever knowingly recruits, harbors, transports, provides, or obtains by any means, any person for labor or services in violation of this chapter shall be fined under this title or imprisoned not more than 20 years, or both. If death results from the violation of this section, or if the violation includes kidnapping or an attempt to kidnap, aggravated sexual abuse, or the attempt to commit aggravated sexual abuse, or an attempt to kill, the defendant shall be fined under this title or imprisoned for any term of years or life, or both.

"§1591. Sex trafficking of children or by force, fraud or coercion

"(a) Whoever knowingly—

"(1) in or affecting interstate commerce, recruits, entices, harbors, transports, provides, or obtains by any means a person; or

"(2) benefits, financially or by receiving anything of value, from participation in a venture which has engaged in an act described in violation of paragraph (1), knowing that force, fraud, or coercion described in subsection (c)(2) will be used to cause the person to engage in a commercial sex act, or that the person has not attained the age of 18 years and will be caused to engage in a commercial sex act, shall be punished as provided in subsection (b).

"(b) The punishment for an offense under subsection (a) is—

"(1) if the offense was effected by force, fraud, or coercion or if the person transported had not attained the age of 14 years at the time of such offense, by a fine under this title or imprisonment for any term of years or for life, or both; or

"(2) if the offense was not so effected, and the person transported had attained the age of 14 years but had not attained the age of 18 years at the time of such offense, by a fine under this title or imprisonment for not more than 20 years, or both.

"(c) In this section: ·

"(1) The term 'commercial sex act' means any sex act, on account of which anything of value is given to or received by any person.

"(2) The term 'coercion' means—

"(A) threats of serious harm to or physical restraint against any person;

"(B) any scheme, plan, or pattern intended to cause a person to believe that failure to perform an act would result in serious harm to or physical restraint against any person; or

"(C) the abuse or threatened abuse of law or the legal process.

"(3) The term 'venture' means any group of two or more individuals associated in fact, whether or not a legal entity.

"§1592. Unlawful conduct with respect to documents in furtherance of trafficking, peonage, slavery, involuntary servitude, or forced labor

"(a) Whoever knowingly destroys, conceals, removes, confiscates, or possesses any actual or purported passport or other immigration document, or any other actual or purported government identification document, of another person—

"(1) in the course of a violation of section 1581, 1583, 1584, 1589, 1590, 1591, or 1594(a);

"(2) with intent to violate section 1581, 1583, 1584, 1589, 1590, or 1591; or

"(3) to prevent or restrict or to attempt to prevent or restrict, without lawful authority, the person's liberty to move or travel, in order to maintain the labor or services of that person, when the person is or has been a victim of a severe form of trafficking in persons, as defined in section 103 of the Trafficking Victims Protection Act of 2000, shall be fined under this title or imprisoned for not more than 5 years, or both.

"(b) Subsection (a) does not apply to the conduct of a person who is or has been a victim of a severe form of trafficking in persons, as defined in section 103 of the Trafficking Victims Protection Act of 2000, if that conduct is caused by, or incident to, that trafficking.

"§1593. Mandatory restitution

"(a) Notwithstanding section 3663 or 3663A, and in addition to any other civil or criminal penalties authorized by law, the court shall order restitution for any offense under this chapter.

"(b)(1) The order of restitution under this section shall direct the defendant to pay the victim (through the appropriate court mechanism) the full amount of the victim's losses, as determined by the court under paragraph (3) of this subsection.

"(2) An order of restitution under this section shall be issued and enforced in accordance with section 3664 in the same manner as an order under section 3663A.

"(3) As used in this subsection, the term 'full amount of the victim's losses' has the same meaning as provided in section 2259(b)(3) and shall in addition include the greater of the gross income or value to the defendant of the victim's services or labor or the value of the victim's labor as guaranteed under the minimum wage and overtime guarantees of the Fair Labor Standards Act (29 U.S.C. 201 et seq.).

"(c) As used in this section, the term 'victim' means the individual harmed as a result of a crime under this chapter, including, in the case of a victim who is under 18 years of age, incompetent, incapacitated, or deceased, the legal guardian of the victim or a representative of the victim's estate, or another family member, or any other person appointed as suitable by the court, but in no event shall the defendant be named such representative or guardian.

"§1594. General provisions

"(a) Whoever attempts to violate section 1581, 1583, 1584, 1589, 1590, or 1591 shall be punishable in the same manner as a completed violation of that section.

"(b) The court, in imposing sentence on any person convicted of a violation of this chapter, shall order, in addition to any other sentence imposed and irrespective of any provision of State law, that such person shall forfeit to the United States—

"(1) such person's interest in any property, real or personal, that was used or intended to be used to commit or to facilitate the commission of such violation; and

"(2) any property, real or personal, constituting or derived from, any proceeds that such person obtained, directly or indirectly, as a result of such violation.

"(c)(1) The following shall be subject to forfeiture to the United States and no property right shall exist in them:

"(A) Any property, real or personal, used or intended to be used to commit or to facilitate the commission of any violation of this chapter.

"(B) Any property, real or personal, which constitutes or is derived from proceeds traceable to any violation of this chapter.

"(2) The provisions of chapter 46 of this title relating to civil forfeitures shall extend to any seizure or civil forfeiture under this subsection.

"(d) WITNESS PROTECTION.—Any violation of this chapter shall be considered an organized criminal activity or other serious offense for the purposes of application of chapter 224 (relating to witness protection)."; and

(3) by amending the table of sections at the beginning of chapter 77 by adding at the end the following new items:

"1589. Forced labor.

"1590. Trafficking with respect to peonage, slavery, involuntary servitude, or forced labor.

"1591. Sex trafficking of children or by force, fraud, or coercion.

"1592. Unlawful conduct with respect to documents in furtherance of trafficking, peonage, slavery, involuntary servitude, or forced labor.

"1593. Mandatory restitution.

"1594. General provisions.".

(b) AMENDMENT TO THE SENTENCING GUIDELINES.—

(1) Pursuant to its authority under section 994 of title 28, United States Code, and in accordance with this section, the United States Sentencing Commission shall review and, if appropriate, amend the sentencing guidelines and policy statements applicable to persons convicted of offenses involving the trafficking of persons including component or related crimes of peonage, involuntary servitude, slave trade offenses, and possession, transfer or sale of false immigration documents in furtherance of trafficking, and the Fair Labor Standards Act and the Migrant and Seasonal Agricultural Worker Protection Act.

(2) In carrying out this subsection, the Sentencing Commission shall—

(A) take all appropriate measures to ensure that these sentencing guidelines and policy statements applicable to the offenses described in paragraph (1) of this subsection are sufficiently stringent to deter and adequately reflect the heinous nature of such offenses;

(B) consider conforming the sentencing guidelines applicable to offenses involving trafficking in persons to the guidelines applicable to peonage, involuntary servitude, and slave trade offenses; and

(C) consider providing sentencing enhancements for those convicted of the offenses described in paragraph (1) of this subsection that—

(i) involve a large number of victims;

(ii) involve a pattern of continued and flagrant violations;

(iii) involve the use or threatened use of a dangerous weapon; or

(iv) result in the death or bodily injury of any person.

(3) The Commission may promulgate the guidelines or amendments under this subsection in accordance with the procedures set forth in section 21(a) of the Sentencing Act of 1987, as though the authority under that Act had not expired.

GLOSSARY

Abduction—The criminal or tortious act of taking and carrying away by force.

Accusation—An indictment, presentment, information or any other form in which a charge of a crime or offense can be made against an individual.

Accusatory Instrument—The initial pleading which forms the procedural basis for a criminal charge, such as an indictment.

Accuse—To directly and formally institute legal proceedings against a person, charging that he or she has committed an offense.

Acquit—A verdict of "not guilty" which determines that the person is absolved of the charge and prevents a retrial pursuant to the doctrine of double jeopardy.

Acquittal—One who is acquitted receives an acquittal, which is a release without further prosecution.

Adjourn—To briefly postpone or delay a court proceeding.

Adjudication—The determination of a controversy and pronouncement of judgment.

Admissible Evidence—Evidence which may be received by a trial court to assist the trier of fact, either the judge or jury, in deciding a dispute.

Admission—In criminal law, the voluntary acknowledgment that certain facts are true.

American Bar Association (ABA)—A national organization of lawyers and law students.

American Civil Liberties Union (ACLU)—A nationwide organization dedicated to the enforcement and preservation of rights and civil liberties guaranteed by the federal and state constitutions.

Appearance—To come into court, personally or through an attorney, after being summoned.

Arraign—In a criminal proceeding, to accuse one of committing a wrong.

Arraignment—The initial step in the criminal process when the defendant is formally charged with the wrongful conduct.

Arrest—To deprive a person of his liberty by legal authority.

Battery—The unlawful application of force to the person of another.

Bench Warrant—An order of the court empowering the police or other legal authority to seize a person.

Bodily Injury—Generally refers to any act, except one done in self-defense, that results in physical injury or sexual abuse.

Burden of Proof—The duty of a party to substantiate an allegation or issue to convince the trier of fact as to the truth of their claim.

Capital Crime—A crime for which the death penalty may, but need not necessarily, be imposed.

Capital Punishment—The penalty of death.

Child Abuse—Any form of cruelty to a child's physical, moral or mental well-being.

Child Custody—The care, control and maintenance of a child which may be awarded by a court to one of the parents of the child.

Child Protective Agency—A state agency responsible for the investigation of child abuse and neglect reports.

Child Support—The legal obligation of parents to contribute to the economic maintenance of their children.

Child Welfare—A generic term which embraces the totality of measures necessary for a child's well being; physical, moral and mental.

Circumstantial Evidence—Indirect evidence by which a principal fact may be inferred.

Coercion—Refers to (a) threats of serious harm to or physical restraint against any person; (b) any scheme, plan, or pattern intended to cause a person to believe that failure to perform an act would result in serious harm to or physical restraint against any person; or (c) the abuse or threatened abuse of the legal process.

Commercial Sex Act—Any sex act on account of which anything of value is given to or received by any person.

Court—The branch of government responsible for the resolution of disputes arising under the laws of the government.

Cross-Examination—The questioning of a witness by someone other than the one who called the witness to the stand concerning matters about which the witness testified during direct examination.

Cruelty—The intentional and malicious infliction of physical or mental suffering on one's spouse.

Culpable—Referring to conduct, it is that which is deserving of moral blame.

Debt Bondage—The status or condition of a debtor arising from a pledge by the debtor of his or her personal services or of those of a person under his or her control as a security for debt, if the value of those services as reasonably assessed is not applied toward the liquidation of the debt or the length and nature of those services are not respectively limited and defined.

District Attorney—An officer of a governmental body with the duty to prosecute those accused of crimes.

Domestic Violence—Generally refers to felony or misdemeanor crimes of violence committed by a current or former spouse of the victim, by a person with whom the victim shares a child in common, by a person who is cohabitating with or has cohabitated with the victim as a spouse, or by a person similarly situated to a spouse.

Duress—Refers to the action of one person which compels another to do something he or she would not otherwise do.

Felony—A crime of a graver or more serious nature than those designated as misdemeanors.

Fine—A financial penalty imposed upon a defendant.

Hearing—A proceeding to determine an issue of fact based on the evidence presented.

Homicide—The killing of a human being by another human being.

Illegal—Against the law.

Imprisonment—The confinement of an individual, usually as punishment for a crime.

Injury—Any damage done to another's person, rights, reputation or property.

Involuntary Servitude—A condition of servitude induced by means of (a) any scheme, plan, or pattern intended to cause a person to believe that, if the person did not enter into or continue in such condition, that person or another person would suffer serious harm or physical restraint; or (b) the abuse or threatened abuse of the legal process.

Jail—Place of confinement where a person in custody of the government awaits trial or serves a sentence after conviction.

Judge—The individual who presides over a court, and whose function it is to determine controversies.

Jury—A group of individuals summoned to decide the facts in issue in a lawsuit.

Jury Trial—A trial during which the evidence is presented to a jury so that they can determine the issues of fact, and render a verdict based upon the law as it applies to their findings of fact.

Law Enforcement—Generally refers to public agencies charged with policing functions, including any of their component bureaus.

Legal Aid—A national organization established to provide legal services to those who are unable to afford private representation.

Malice—A state of mind that accompanies the intentional commission of a wrongful act.

Manslaughter—The unlawful taking of another's life without malice aforethought.

Mens Rea—A guilty mind.

Misdemeanor—Criminal offenses which are less serious than felonies and carry lesser penalties.

National Domestic Violence Hotline—A national, toll-free telephone hotline operated for the purpose of providing information and assistance to victims of domestic violence.

Not Guilty—The plea of a defendant in a criminal action denying the offense with which he or she is charged.

Offense—Any misdemeanor or felony violation of the law for which a penalty is prescribed.

Parole—The conditional release from imprisonment whereby the victed individual serves the remainder of his or her sentence outside prison as long as he or she is in compliance with the terms and conditions of parole.

Penal Institution—A place of confinement for convicted criminals.

Prosecutor—The individual who prepares a criminal case against an individual accused of a crime.

Protection Order—Generally refers to any injunction issued for the purpose of preventing violent or threatening acts of domestic violence or harassment, including temporary and final orders issued by civil or criminal courts.

Public Defender—A lawyer hired by the government to represent an indigent person accused of a crime.

Rape—The unlawful sexual intercourse with a person without his or her consent.

Restitution—The act of making an aggrieved party whole by compensating him or her for any loss or damage sustained.

Self-Defense—The right to protect oneself, one's family, and one's property from an aggressor.

Sentence—The punishment given a convicted criminal by the court.

Severe Forms of Trafficking in Persons—Refers to (a) sex trafficking in which a commercial sex act is induced by force, fraud, or coercion, or in which the person induced to perform such act has not attained 18 years of age; or (b) the recruitment, harboring, transportation, provision, or obtaining of a person for labor or services, through the use of force, fraud, or coercion for the purpose of subjection to involuntary servitude, peonage, debt bondage, or slavery.

Sex Trafficking—The recruitment, harboring, transportation, provision, or obtaining of a person for the purpose of a commercial sex act.

Testify—The offering of a statement in a judicial proceeding, under oath and subject to the penalty of perjury.

Testimony—The sworn statement made by a witness in a judicial proceeding.

Verdict—The definitive answer given by the jury to the court concerning the matters of fact committed to the jury for their deliberation and determination.

ım Services—Generally refers to organizations that assist domes-
violence or sexual assault victims, such as rape crisis centers and
attered women's shelters.

Warrant—An official order directing that a certain act be undertaken,
such as an arrest.

BIBLIOGRAPHY AND ADDITIONAL READING

Black's Law Dictionary, Fifth Edition. St. Paul, MN: West Publishing Company, 1979.

Family Violence Prevention Fund (Date Visited: May 2007) <http://www.endabuse.org/>.

Feminist.Com (Date Visited: May 2007) http://www.feminist.com/>.

Feminist Majority Foundation (Date Visited: May 2007) <http://www.feminist.org/911/>.

Evaluation Guidebook: Projects Funded by S.T.O.P. Formula Grants under the Violence Against Women Act (Date Visited: May 2007) <http://www.urban.org/crime/evalguide.html>.

Federal Bureau of Investigation (Date Visited: May 2007) <http://www.fbi.gov/>.

Justice Information Center (Date Visited: May 2007) <http://www.ncjrs.org/>.

Namechangelaw.com (Date Visited: May 2007) <http://www.namechangelaw.com/>.

The National Center for Victims of Crime (Date Visited: May 2007) <http://www.ncvc.org/>.

The National Center for Women and Policing (Date Visited: May 2007) <http://www.womenandpolicing.org/>.

The National Domestic Violence Hotline (Date Visited: May 2007) <http://www.ndvh.org/>.

Office of Justice Programs (Date Visited: May 2007) <http://www.ojp.gov/>.

pe, Abuse and Incest National Network (Date Visited: May 2007) <http://www.rainn.org/>.

U.S. Citizenship and Immigration Services (Date Visited: May 2007) <http://uscis.gov/>.

The U.S. Department of Health and Human Services (Date Visited: May 2007) <http://www.acf.hhs.gov/trafficking/>.

The U.S. Department of Justice (Date Visited: May 2007) <http://www.usdoj.gov/>.

U.S. Legal Forms (Date Visited: May 2007) <http://www.uslegalforms.com/>.

World Health Organization (WHO) (Date Visited: May 2007) <http://www.who.int/gender/violence/sexual_violence/en/>